BAUDELAIRE · LAUTRÉAMONT · RIMBAUD

MALLARMÉ · VALÉRY · SAINT-JOHN PERSE · PROUST · GIDE

Climate of Violence

THE FRENCH LITERARY TRADITION
FROM BAUDELAIRE TO THE PRESENT

CLAUDEL · APOLLINAIRE · JACOB · MAURIAC · SARTRE

IONESCO · GENET · LE CLÉZIO

by Wallace Fowlie

THE MACMILLAN COMPANY, NEW YORK

COLLIER-MACMILLAN LTD., LONDON

Library of Congress Catalog Card Number: 67-22399

FIRST PRINTING

The Macmillan Company, New York
Collier-Macmillan Canada Ltd., Toronto, Ontario

Printed in the United States of America

The author wishes to acknowledge the following publishers for permission to quote copyrighted material:

Harcourt, Brace & World, Inc., for quotations from T. S. Eliot, *Collected Poems 1909-1962* (1963).

The Bollingen Foundation for quotations from St.-John Perse, *Seamarks* (1958), translated by Wallace Fowlie

Editions Gallimard for quotations from Valéry, St.-John Perse, Max Jacob, and Apollinaire.

Contents

Introduction

To ATTEMPT A consideration of one hundred years of French literary expression, within the space of a single book, is tantamount to absurdity, if the critic hopes to incorporate all the themes and all the major works. I have tried deliberately to limit myself to the origins and expression of violence in specific authors and specific literary and artistic movements, with the hope that the absurdity might be lessened and with the conviction that this chosen theme is the most significant of those characterizing modern French literature.

These studies begin, then, with *Les Fleurs du Mal* of 1857, and end with reference to *Le Déluge*, a novel by Jean-Marie Le Clézio, published in 1966. They begin with the violence of Baudelaire's Paris and end with the violence of Nice as experienced by a new writer today. The first world evoked is the *bohême dorée* of a literary group in the Second Empire and the last world is the solitariness of today's writer in a large city on the Mediterranean.

Since everything started with Baudelaire, it is difficult indeed to separate one of his themes, such as violence, from the others. The cruelty of the city, felt by Baudelaire's swan, reoccurs in Eliot's "Unreal City." The Anglo-American poet has named Baudelaire the truly modern poet.

Lautréamont's epic is the obvious treatise on violence, the work replete with scenes that are shocking. It is the adolescent work where violence fulfills its function of destroying life. Each stanza of the six cantos relates some aspect of violence and turpitude. The hostility of human relationships and the hostility of nature are itemized here in a lengthy repertory.

The violence of Rimbaud, as deep-seated and as adolescent as that of Lautréamont, is expressed in more original, more artistic form. It is in the power of the poet's images as much as it is in the semiautobiographical writing of *Une Saison en Enfer*. At the genesis of this violence is the ennui of a provincial town, as Paris, in its bigness and cruelty, is at the genesis of Baudelaire's spleen. The affiliation is direct: Rimbaud is the provincial heir of Baudelaire. He went from Charleville to Paris in order to conquer it with his poems, but he impressed almost no one, and he turned inwardly to the violence of his nature which then had more reason than ever for expressing itself.

But such direct violence as we find in Baudelaire, Lautréamont, and Rimbaud, can be transcended in the poet's art. This is the subject of the second part of this book where Mallarmé, whose personal dramas were not unlike Baudelaire's, perfected a technique of writing that was a distillation. Each poem was a victory over some dream, some harassment, some anguish. The symbols of his major poems are means of transcending experience, often very violent, and which, when explored as poems, lead back to an understanding of violence. I have chosen here to speak first of Mallarmé's relation with impressionist painters whose art also is a transcendence of violence. And then, to speak of Mallarmé's use of symbol which is his search for reality and which comprehends and explains violence.

For Narcissus, one of the chief poetic figures of Paul Valéry, the world is a mirror that gives back to the poet his own image. Narcissus is the container of violence who dreams of peace that lies beyond violence. All men are Narcissus when they create their dreams, as all men are Orpheus when they create their poems. And Narcissus is the poet when he acknowledges that he is duped by his dreams, and that his repressed violences are more real than his dreams.

The contemporary poet, Saint-John Perse, after celebrating the violence of exile in his poem *Exil*, has attempted in *Amers* to explore the patterns of alliances as they occur in the poet's mind and imagination. This search is exalted, and it may appear violent in the sense that it is inhuman and abstract. The cosmos is always about us, and always severe in contrast with the trivial and passing violences of men. *Seamarks* are signs of reconciliation and help. A fresh contact with the elements, with the sea, for example, will enable us to measure the meaning and the ultimate insignificance of eruptions in nature and in man's nature.

Allied with the symbolist movement, especially in their early years, and orientated toward literature by the examples of Baudelaire and the symbolists, Proust, Gide, and Claudel each evolved as writers concerned with forms of exterior and inner turmoil, with the upheavals of modern society and the new explorations of man's subconscious worlds.

For Proust, man's nature is a receptacle of the past, a kind of prisoner (*la prisonnière*) who may be liberated only at certain privileged moments of illumination. The action of society is the violence in Proust. It is that network of forces that tend to create a being foreign to the real self. In Proust's hierarchy, the artist is the type of man able to reach the real self and reveal himself in his work as the citizen of an unknown country, precisely that country forgotten by most men because of the impinging dramas of society.

The violence of society is seen by Gide to be the violence of morality, those moral strictures that tend to imprison a man and prevent his growth. Like Nietzsche, Gide believed that the hour had come for man to become truly himself. But with more subtlety than the German philosopher, Gide asked at the same time: What is a man and what does he want exactly? Gide denounced that kind of violence deriving from habit and conformity, in order to proclaim, in such a prophetic work as *Les Nourritures Terrestres*, the kind of absolute that is found in fervor, and the kind of eternity that is found in the present.

In the work of Claudel, violence is explained as a mystical experience. In the night of man's soul—Claudel speaks as often as Baudelaire does, of boredom and solitude and anguish—there is a divine Presence. Claudel's discoveries, in his understanding of poetry and of man, were made in the midst of violence, or of what he looked upon as the violence of Rimbaud, and of those writers he called the Molochs of the nineteenth century: Taine and Renan.

For fifty years, from Baudelaire to the beginning of the twentieth century, symbolism was the new mode of the French writer. And then, at the turn of the century, in keeping with the inevitable changes of time and taste, a still newer mode was launched in Paris by a group of poets and painters. Their leaders were Picasso, Apollinaire, and Max Jacob. By the end of the first decade, cubism had replaced impressionism in painting, and the poets, especially Apollinaire and Jacob, had restored the more familiar and common objects of daily life which had been scorned by the symbolist poets. There is less revolutionary violence in Apollinaire and Jacob than there had been in Baudelaire and Rimbaud, but there is a form of violence in their way of looking at crowds in the cities and galaxies in the heavens.

Apollinaire's *Alcools* of 1913 occupies in the twentieth century a place almost comparable to *Les Fleurs du Mal* in the nineteenth. It represents a technique which the surrealists will develop, whereby the slightest events are captured by the poet's art. The dramas of man's inner life and the visible conflicts of the outside world are often called violent in the writings of Sade. They are also called violent by Baudelaire, who probably read Sade. By Apollinaire, who read Sade more extensively than Baudelaire, this violence was treated as a commonplace. The imagination was the faculty in the poet that joined the two worlds of the mind and nature. The new violence for Apollinaire and Jacob was the violence of hope.

> *Comme la vie est lente*
> *Et comme l'Espérance est violente*
> (*La chanson du mal aimé*)

At the mid-century mark, three literary expressions appeared almost as answers to the violence of man's nature: the theatre of the absurd, existentialism, and Christian thought as manifested, for example, in the continuing work of Mauriac.

The plays of Beckett and Genet have been called antitheatre because they fail to express the traditional logic, the traditional explanations of theatrical dialogue. Conventional masks are dropped in this kind of theatre, and the spectator comes face to face with the despair of beings who seem inhuman because they appear foreign to themselves. After the "death of God," ominously announced by Nietzsche, a fundamental absurdity, apparent in *Godot*, for example, almost brings about a collapse of human reason.

Prior to the advent of antitheatre, existentialist literature had presented characters and themes similar to those found in the new plays of the 1950's. The characters of Sartre and Camus are not unlike those of Beckett and Ionesco. The tramp (*clochard*) and such unattached figures as Meursault and Roquentin, are amnesiacs suffering from nostalgia and anxiety. They are so stripped of conventional reactions and masks that they seem to be man's conscience.

The theatre is still, in the new French plays, the site where man's violence is liberated, and where the public is purged, at least momentarily, of its own dreams of violence. For the Christian, the work of purification is long, is, in fact, endless because it begins over again each day. Reality may appear absurd for Sartre, as it proliferates day after day, but for a Claudel, it is a daily source of wonderment, a miracle he celebrates in his words of a poet. The absurdity of the concrete object Sartre's character touched, his metaphysical experience of contingency, provoked nausea. And for a Bernanos or a Mauriac, that same experience of contingency can provoke both anguish and jubilation which the Christian writer will interpret as rising up from the proximity of the sacred.

WALLACE FOWLIE

January, 1967

PART I
Violence

1. Baudelaire's Paris

CHARLES BAUDELAIRE WAS BORN in Paris, in 1821, the year of Napoleon's death. At the age of twenty-one, independent of his mother and stepfather, thanks to a small inheritance, he lived the life of a dandy, of the youthful artist intoxicated with ambition and power. He took his place beside a few other fervent spirits for whom the writing of poetry was a sacred mission: Banville, Gautier, Nerval. A strange voyage of nine months (June, 1841–February, 1842) had taken Baudelaire away from Paris, but on his return he saw it more clearly, he saw more lucidly the many ways in which Paris was changing:

> *La forme d'une ville*
> *Change plus vite, hélas! que le coeur d'un mortel.*

It was a world of parvenus and enriched bourgeois. Stores now had tall glass windows and were illumined. Streets were covered with tar macadam and sidewalks had been installed for the first time. Gas light at night had drastically altered the habits of the city, the nocturnal life of the boulevards and the theatres. The development of railroads was only one aspect of a new life of luxury and pleasure.

This was the moment when Baudelaire inherited 75,000 francs, and momentarily thought in terms of a noble destiny, of a life that would be lived in alliance with beauty, in accordance with the dreams of a superior dandy. He lived successively on the quai de Béthune, on the rue Vaneau, on the île Saint-Louis in the hôtel Pimodan, the first choice of residence for the Bohemian princes of the day. He cultivated an attitude of detachment and indifference. As a member of *la bohème dorée,* which included such figures as Gautier and Nerval, Baudelaire tried by means of art and artifice to correct all natural imperfections, all imperious instincts. Nature was the original sin, in his creed of dandy. *Ce qui est naturel est abominable.*

The new types of the period were being observed by the writers and the artists, as they emerged and distinguished themselves by speech and dress: *le garde national,* for example, *le concierge, la lorette.* The artists in particular, a Gavarni and a Daumier, and the apprentice-artist, called *un rapin,* were quick to seize upon the comic trait and underscore it. Joseph Prudhomme, a character of Monnier, and the type of narrow-minded bourgeois, was the real enemy of the artist and the dandy. Joseph Prudhomme and the pharmacist Homais in Flaubert's *Madame Bovary* stupidly believed in the concept of progress. On this score, Baudelaire's vituperations were ferocious. In countless aphorisms, he flailed the doctrine of progress as being a deceit, a vast dupery. In his role of dandy writer, he was determined to avoid all sentimentality, all facility in writing, all turgid use of common sense. What attracted him, what he insisted on cultivating in himself, was a new form of beauty characterized by the strange, the bizarre, the abnormal. Dandyism permitted Baudelaire to scoff and blaspheme. He thereby affirmed a bondage with some of the arch-romantic heroes of a generation or two generations earlier: Goethe's Werther, Chateaubriand's René, Byron's Manfred.

There are passions peculiar to each period. Baudelaire looked upon the heroes of Balzac, a Vautrin and a Rastignac, whose passions are explicable by the social condition of the Restoration, as comparable to the heroes of the *Iliad.* The heroes of Paris represent new human drives, in harmony with their age, but the power and drama of these drives have as much beauty and universal significance as that in heroes of other centuries.

Baudelaire is the modern poet in the fullest sense who rediscovered for poetry its real destiny. The goal of poetry is itself, its own intrinsic beauty. As the Greeks once taught, poetry is a delectation for the spirit, a ravishment of the soul. Whereas Théophile Gautier tended to restrict and limit the poet's role in making him a prisoner of appearances, in turning him into a spectator of the visible world of objects and landscapes and animals, Baudelaire became the *voyant*, the seer looking for and finding the meaning of things. Gautier was a sculptor in words, who build up pictures with words. But Baudelaire was a singer, a magician who was dissatisfied with his verses unless they possessed an incantatory power.

At the age of eighteen, Baudelaire began to take possession of Paris, to see the city in its multiple aspects of horror and beauty. He was no Rastignac whose will was to possess the city. He had none of the dangerous exuberance of the Balzac hero, none of the overpowering drive to exploit the city for his own material gains. Far more complex than the provincial Eugène de Rastignac, Charles Baudelaire was a native Parisian whose curiosity about vice became a mode of investigation, and essentially an investigation of himself. During the early years, everything led him back to the poems he was writing, to the book he was planning to publish eventually. The themes of his work, which may seem limited, had so many variations, that behind the apparent sterility he spoke of so often, there was in reality a veritable fecundity. Every walk he took along the Seine and in the streets of Paris furnished him with images he was to use in his writing. No book is more a quintessence of life, a condensation of life than *Les Fleurs du Mal* (1857). The art offered to him by the city often became the source of his poem: a painting of Delacroix inspired *Don Juan aux enfers*, a statue of Ernest Christophe inspired *Le Masque*, a drawing of an unknown artist inspired *Une Martyre*. Literature was also used: a line of Gérard de Nerval is at the genesis of *Voyage à Cythère*. Slight incidents counted too: the sound of wood being chopped in a courtyard is recorded in *Chant d'automne*.

This poem, one of the most solemn canticles of Baudelaire, is a supreme example of his art, where there is no narrative, no preaching, no doctrine, where every line is a condensation of an impassioned man. Pure passion without sentimentality.

In the opening stanza,

> *Bientôt nous plongerons dans les froides ténèbres;*
> *Adieu, vive clarté de nos étés trop c̓ourts!*
> *J'entends déjà tomber avec des chocs funèbres,*
> *Le bois retentissant sur le pavé des cours. . . .*

time is materialized in the pieces of wood resounding as they
strike against the pavement. We are in between the violent seasons of the year: summer with its brightness and the cold gloom
of winter. The falling wood beats out the seconds of time. This
sound which marks the passing of time, announces death, at the
end of time, and the opening verb, *nous plongerons,* announces
the dizzying plunge of the poet into the cold of winter, which is
the cold of death.

The entire poem is the moment of pause on the brink of a great
change. After the intense life and light of summer will come,
swiftly, almost with the close of the poem, the opposite experience of cold and immobility. Winter is far more than a season: it
is the symbol of growing old, the sign of the drying up of energy
and life. The logs of wood that fall, *"chaque bûche qui tombe,"*
expand into the full dimension of metaphor. They are the minutes
that tick by, the beating of the heart, and they evoke the gallows
and the battering ram in its act of causing a tower to collapse.
The poet's mind is so obsessed with death that the repetitive
sounds he hears come from the nailing of a coffin and he wonders
for whom the coffin is being built. Death is the most mysterious
of all departures, and the sound of the echoing wood has something of that mystery:

> *Ce bruit mystérieux sonne comme un départ.*

This coffin in its metaphorical power represents the burial of
more than one thing: of summer, perhaps, of youth, of the poet
himself, of time. This autumn song is a synchronization of many
elements. The sun shining on the sea is so brief an experience for
the poet that it calls up the images of death: the setting sun and
the tomb waiting for the end. Each word in the poem is a part
of the whole, in the same way that autumn involves the summer
that preceded it and the winter that is to follow it. A log being
cut in a Paris courtyard for a fireplace becomes the gallows, and a

battering ram, and a coffin. The poet's obsession has found a word, a sign, capable of depicting it.

Paris is both real for Baudelaire and endlessly changing. He sees it and he sees beyond it because it is fertile in its power to stir his imagination. In the second edition of *Les Fleurs du Mal*, of 1861, a new section appeared, called *Tableaux parisiens*, of which *Le Cygne* is perhaps Baudelaire's major piece on Paris. It is dedicated to Victor Hugo, who at the time of its publication, was in exile from Paris. Exile is the principal theme of the poem and Paris is precisely the city that stimulates the poet's fertile memory of exiles. He is crossing the new Carrousel, an esplanade constructed in the Second Empire, situated between the Louvre and the Tuileries. Baudelaire is thinking of one of the famous exiles of antiquity: Andromache, a captive in the palace of Pyrrhus, and exiled from Troy and the river Simois beside which she lamented Hector's death. The poem opens with her name,

> *Andromaque, je pense à vous!*

and ends with the word *captifs* and a general reference to all those who suffer in humiliating captivity,

> *Je pense*
> *Aux captifs, aux vaincus* . . .

The poem celebrates the deepening power of Baudelaire's psychic experience. In his walk near the Louvre, in a section of the city where a work of demolition is going on, and débris is everywhere, he invokes the solemn majesty of Andromaque weeping beside the ridiculously small Simois. This spot was once the site of a menagerie and the poet recalls a poignantly dramatic incident he had once observed there: a swan, having escaped from its cage, was dragging its white plumage in the dust of a dried-up gutter. It turned its head toward the sky as if it reproached God for not sending rain. The swan was in exile from its native lake, as Andromaque was in exile from the Trojan Simois. Both a queen and a bird testified to the strange fatal myth of exile that preoccupies and disturbs the poet as he walks through Paris which alters its appearance faster than the heart of a man changes his fidelities.

The opening of the second part of *Le Cygne*, stanza eight, recapitulates the first part, by stating again the changes in the city and the steadfastness of the poet's sadness:

> *Paris change! mais rien dans ma mélancolie*
> *N'a bougé.*

The city itself has become the myth. The myth, everything that the city suggests, has become more concrete than the buildings, those that stand and those that are partly demolished:

> *tout pour moi devient allégorie.*

The thought of exile, with which the poem opened, like a vibrant chord of music,

> *Andromaque, je pense à vous!,*

has become more real and more solid than the granite of the buildings in the real landscape,

> *Et mes chers souvenirs sont plus lourds que des rocs.*

The transformation is now total: the swan returns with its vain movements and Andromaque bends over an empty tomb she had constructed for a funeral offering. By association, another vision rises up—that of a negress walking through the mud and fog of the northern city and trying to see the coconut trees of Africa that are not there.

> *Je pense à la négresse,*
> *Piétinant dans la boue, et cherchant*
> *Les cocotiers absents de la superbe Afrique . . .*

These memories grow in such strength and pervasiveness, that Paris, in the final stanza of the poem, becomes a forest and the memories become the piercing notes of a hunting horn:

> *Un vieux Souvenir sonne à plein souffle du cor!*

This forest is the poet's exile:

> *Ainsi dans la forêt où mon esprit s'exile.*

The list of imaginary exiles of *Le Cygne:* Andromaque, the swan, the negress, concludes with the poet as the exile in Paris. But in a theological sense, all of mankind are in exile. The allegory of the city is all-inclusive, and the great exiled writers have testified to this: Dante, Joyce, Claudel, Saint-John Perse. Baudelaire in Paris is exiled from it by the power of transformation. The images in his memory expand as the real Paris around him contracts. He remembers a world more real than the real world.

Before Mallarmé, Baudelaire is the poet of absences. In abolishing the exterior world, he substitutes for it: the native lake of the swan, Africa of the negress, the empty tomb of Hector. The poem narrates the poet's walk across the place du Carrousel and a voyage through his memory.

This same kind of transformation takes place in *Rêve parisien* where the city is idealized into an infinite palace of metal and marble and water, from which vegetation has been abolished. Paris is Babel and the poet is the architect of this dream world. In the *spleen* sonnet which begins *Pluviôse, irrité contre la ville entière*, Paris and the poet's room in Paris are the site of a series of transformations and substitutions: the dead in the cemetery receive the rain, implied in such a word as *Pluviôse;* the soul of a dead poet walks as if alive along the rooftops; a bell has the human characteristic of a lament; a smoking log wheezes like a human; the Jack of Hearts and the Queen of Spades in a dirty pack of cards engage in a sinister conversation concerning their former passion. In such a poem, life and death are seen as merged or confused. Inanimate objects are animated and given human characteristics. The transformation involving matter and spirit is phantasmagoria.

The poet is a wayfarer, an intercessor, an intermediary, because of whom we are able to feel related to forces that surpass our minds. Because of him, the universe perceived by our senses: seasons and cities, men and their wretchedness, are loved attentively and fervently and knowingly. Charles Baudelaire, one hundred years after his death, remains one of our witnesses. He continues to speak for men today in their name.

Toward the middle of the nineteenth century, Baudelaire was representative of a certain number of elements which the spiritual make-up of France did not possess at that time, and which, since Baudelaire's age, have been studied and explored with an ever renewed critical acumen. Every page in his writings celebrates the imagination as man's noblest faculty. He possessed the indispensable gift for the writing of poetry: the analysis, the lucidity and the affirmation of the self. He nurtured the impassioned plan to rediscover authentic human values and to oppose those forms of stagnation which in each generation man invents for his own misery.

Baudelaire was never a militant member of any group. Somewhat distant and somewhat secretive, but with an intellectual firmness that caused him to be respected and even feared, he studied problems that have dominated the critical conscience and poetic creativity in Europe and America during the last one hundred years. His art represents an awareness of man's situation in the modern world, and his example has taught subsequent poets that it is necessary to find a new language, a language adequate to transmit the feelings of modern man. The poet's first obligation is to create a language that is his, in order not to lose his identity of a poet.

The period of time beginning with Baudelaire's career as a poet and extending to today is a century of European and American civilization, of which the principal characteristic is, according to Baudelaire and to some contemporary poets, such as T. S. Eliot, disorder. Disorder in every domain. Baudelaire was the inventor of a significant attitude, an outlook on the disorder he saw everywhere. He was also the inventor of a way of feeling, a way of understanding disorder. For he was, at the dawn of modern poetry, the writer who claimed that all first-rate poetry is preoccupied with morality. If Baudelaire discovered for himself certain religious values; humility, for example, the need for prayer, the notion of original sin—his obligation as a poet was, not to practice Christianity as a religion, but to make its necessity felt in the modern world.

The initial impulse of poetry is the emotion the poet feels in his relationship with himself, in his relationship with others, with the world around him, and also with his past, with childhood, with the dead. This theme is central in Baudelaire as it is also in Eliot, who tells us at the end of *Little Gidding:*

> *We are born with the dead*
>
> . . . .
>
> *The moment of the rose and the moment of the yew-tree*
> *Are of equal duration.*

The poet's work is truly the quest and exploration of the past. In examining certain works of art, Baudelaire wrote that he often experienced a vision of the childhood of the artists. In one sentence in particular, he announces a principle associated today with Proust, concerning a child's sorrow, which when enlarged,

may become in the adult of a marked sensitivity, the foundation
of a work of art. *Tel petit chagrin, telle petite jouissance de
l'enfant, démesurément grossis par une exquise sensibilité, devien-
nent plus tard dans l'homme adulte, même à son insu, le principe
d'une oeuvre d'art.* This passage, of great importance for Baudelaire's aesthetics, ends with the celebrated formula: "genius is
childhood distinctly formulated" (*le génie n'est que l'enfance
nettement formulée*).

Baudelaire's greatness is in the degree of intensity to which he
elevated poetic imagery. His renovation of poetic language was
accompanied by a renovation of his attitude toward life. In his
aesthetics, the slightest object may be magnified by the poet. He
taught that there is poetry and beauty in the most trivial aspects
of modern life: a swan escaping from its cage and dragging its
white plumage through all the dust of the street, an old man
walking down a city street, a multitude of people deadened by
pleasure. . . .

It would be possible to write a long study on the close relationship between the prolonged metaphor of Baudelaire, in which the
idea and the image are miraculously fused (*La Chevelure*, for
example) and the "objective correlative" of Eliot, or the image
capable of translating and supporting a significant human experience, and the "memory-sensation" of Proust, that sensorial experience that permits a man to recover a feeling by which he was
once animated. Eliot, in *Ash Wednesday* and *Four Quartets*, and
Proust listening to Vinteuil's music, or tasting a madeleine cake
dipped in tea, rediscover places and privileged moments. They
are nontemporal moments. A half-century earlier, Baudelaire, in a
poem such as *Le Balcon*, had announced the principle of that
mnemonic art.

> *Je sais l'art d'évoquer les minutes heureuses*
> *Et revis mon passé blotti dans tes genoux.*

Time recalled is not time for Eliot:

> *Time past and time future*
> *What might have been and what has been*
> *Point to one end, which is always present.*
>   (*Burnt Norton*)

The happiness which invades Marcel as he drinks the cup of
linden tea makes of him a being freed from contingencies: he

ceases being accidental and even mediocre. This is exactly what Baudelaire had said in the last stanza of *Le Balcon*, in the form of an interrogation:

> *Ces serments, ces parfums, ces baisers infinis*
> *Renaîtront-ils d'un gouffre interdit à nos sondes?*

Proust in Paris, and Eliot in London, discovered almost at the same time a Baudelairian principle concerning time and the way in which a writer interprets time. Baudelaire, in translating the feeling of spleen, has said:

> *J'ai plus de souvenirs que si j'avais mille ans.*

And Proust, in *Le Temps Retrouvé*, says in one of his most profound sentences:

> *Une heure n'est pas qu'une heure, c'est un vase rempli de parfums, de sons, de projets et de climats!*

And Eliot, in his fervent meditation on time, says, at the end of *Burnt Norton:*

> *Even while the dust moves*
> *There rises the hidden laughter*
> *Of children in the foliage*
> *Quick now, here, now, always—*
> *Ridiculous the waste sad time*
> *Stretching before and after.*

The artist is the man who narrates himself and at the same time narrates the customs of his contemporaries. When the writer tells his dreams, his fantasies, his loves, he is telling the dreams, fantasies, and loves of other men. To be the interpreter of his age is a first duty for the poet, but it is not a comfortable duty when the poet is embittered by the ugliness of contemporary life. The meaning of history is indispensable for the man who wants to remain a poet. The meaning of history is also the meaning of myths, the meaning of antiquity. Eliot, in *The Waste Land*, underscores the parallelism between the contemporary event and the myths of antiquity. It is the principal procedure used by Joyce in *Ulysses*. And Baudelaire, in his major poem on Paris, the city where everything changes, when he sees a swan escaped from its cage, thinks of the great exiled figures of history, and especially of

> *Andromaque, des bras d'un grand époux tombée,*
> *Auprès d'un tombeau vide en extase courbée.*

The overture section of *The Waste Land, Burial of the Dead*, has four verses that evoke London today:

> *Unreal City,*
> *Under the brown fog of a winter dawn,*
> *A crowd flowed over London Bridge, so many,*
> *I had not thought death had undone so many.*

Eliot himself in his notes gives the two sources of this passage: the third canto of Dante's *Inferno*,

> *si lunga tratta di gente,*

and the Baudelaire poem, *Les sept vieillards*, which begins

> *Fourmillante cité, cité pleine de rêves,*
> *Où le spectre en plein jour raccroche le passant.*

Baudelaire's poem is a walk through the streets of Paris, and during this walk the city becomes the setting for an eruption of demonic forces. The city takes on a human form. Baudelaire calls it a colossus (*un colosse puissant*). At the beginning of the poem where the narrow streets (*les canaux étroits*) become arteries, the circulatory system of the giant, the reality of the exterior is destroyed. The city loses its shape and the old man coming into the vision of the poet is seen as hostile to the universe. This *sinistre vieillard* is doubled and multiplied. The one real action in this part of the city, shaken by the noise of tumbrill carts, is an inner Satanic action taking place in the poet's imagination.

In the composition of *The Waste Land*, the poet incorporates this expansion of reality of which Dante and Baudelaire had been, according to Eliot, the principal artisans. In his first essay on the French poet, Eliot says: "All first-rate poetry is occupied with morality: this is the lesson of Baudelaire." The phantom city, *Unreal City*, is first the city that Baudelaire had sung of in *Les sept vieillards, cité pleine de rêves*, and then Dante's limbo where we see those dead who had led a perfectly neutral life. The judgment of the world in *Burial of the Dead* is very harsh, and the poet does not exclude himself from this judgment. The passage ends with a line of Baudelaire:

> *Hypocrite lecteur! mon semblable! mon frère!*

The verse, quoted in French in Eliot's text, evokes more clearly than a translation could have done, the theme of modern ennui, which is the central subject of the poem, *Au lecteur*. *Ennui*, called by Baudelaire the ugliest of our vices, explains the atmosphere of *The Waste Land*, the mournful, neutralized atmosphere that comes from a universe of evil, and even from the diabolical universe of *Les sept vieillards*.

Eliot's arid earth, the hardened calcined reign from which all life has withdrawn,

> *And the dry stone no sound of water,*

was called by Baudelaire in *Un voyage à Cythère*,

> *Un désert rocailleux troublé par des cris aigres.*

Whether it is Baudelaire's Paris of the swan escaped from its cage or the sinister old man, or the London of Eliot and the crowd on London Bridge,

> *And each man fixed his eyes before his feet—*

whether it is the *désert rocailleux* of *Cythère* or *this stony rubbish* of *The Waste Land*, the poet's art is the use of the sensible world. The two poets speak of the death inherent in each life, but especially of the spiritual death of modern man. The poet renders this present sterility, thanks to the poetic process which Baudelaire called *sortilège* or *sorcellerie évocatoire*.

Eliot saw in Baudelaire the example of a writer for whom criticism and poetry are converging aspects of the same literary process. The books of each one represent the search for a form of analysis capable of translating the consciousness of an age, when it is a question of poetic creation, or a form of analysis capable of translating the consciousness of an objective work, when it is a question of criticism. Whether it is a poem or a critical essay, the definitive result recapitulates a personal reaction in which the intelligence of the writer and his sensibility are similarly engaged.

Le Voyage of Baudelaire and *Gerontion* of Eliot are poems that can be explained in terms of a cultural context. For Baudelaire, the world has become so small that it is reduced to what a single man sees, to the image of the inner life of a man:

> *Amer savoir, celui qu'on tire d'un voyage!*
> *Le monde, monotone et petit, aujourd'hui,*
> *Hier, demain, toujours, nous fait voir notre image . . .*

The same motifs of time, of consciousness of evil, and of spatial and chronological ambiguities are to be found in *Gerontion:*

> *After such knowledge, what forgiveness? Think now*
> *History has many cunning passages . . .*

These two poems are so deeply rooted in the meaning of an historical period that they defy any ordinary analysis. Baudelaire's voyager is the man who sets out for the pure joy of leaving his familiar world, and he is also the child who does not leave, who is in love with maps and pictures:

> *l'enfant amoureux de cartes et d'estampes.*

The character in Eliot's poem,

> *An old man in a draughty house,*

finds it difficult to return to former experiences and to comprehend them. But the minds of Eliot's old man and of Baudelaire's voyager contain the universe. There is a moment at the end of each poem when the protagonist experiences the intoxication and the exaltation of the infinite:

> *Gull against the wind, in the windy straits*
> *Of Belle Isle . . .*
> *Nos coeurs que tu connais sont remplis de rayons!*

Each of these poets has sung of the aridity of contemporary life, and each one also has sung of the same aspiration toward purity, the same search for humility. Each offers the example of the creative and the critical intelligence. In reading the measured verses of these two poets we become accomplices of extreme sentiments. This poetry does not reassure us. It does not engulf us with illusions.

There are many themes common to Baudelaire and Eliot: the strong attraction to the sea, an obsession with the city and its populous neighborhoods, spleen, a tone of derision, and especially perhaps the theme of anguish, comparable to the anguish studied by Jean-Paul Sartre in *La Nausée.* There is still to be studied an art, specifically Baudelairian, which Eliot learned from the French poet and perfected in accordance with his own aptitude and talent. It is the art of evoking a memory, and often a distant memory, deliberately and willfully, the art of associating the sensation of this memory with the spirit and the intellect, and at the same time excluding all sentimentality.

In the specific pages on Paris, and in many other pages throughout his work, Baudelaire reveals an attraction to the exaggerated and the absolute, a taste for the extreme which is not central in the French tradition. The directions in poetry proposed by *Les Fleurs du Mal* were followed by Rimbaud and Mallarmé, and somewhat later by Valéry in France and Eliot in England. These directions included a renewal of classical form in poetry. As a meticulous craftsman, Baudelaire opposed the ancient concept of inspiration and the verbal prolixity which romanticism permitted. In keeping with the classical tradition of a Racine, the formal aspects of Baudelaire's art are severe and simple, and the universe within the poems is extreme in its depiction of the irreparable, the irremediable, remorse, horror, death, nightmares, assassinations.

In his will to extract beauty from evil (*les fleurs du mal*), Baudelaire first gave the impression of a will to scandalize and shock. This was true in only the most superficial sense, and Théophile Gautier, in his preface to *Les Fleurs du Mal*, as early as 1868, defended Baudelaire against the reproach that the work was bizarre and original in a histrionic sense. Baudelaire's descent into himself does not appear today as a search for the abnormal or the unusual, but rather as a search for his childhood, for that indestructible purity in terms of which he saw all the later catastrophes and failures: his illness, the censorship of some of the poems, his abortive attempt to enter the Académie Française. The sensibility of a child in its lucidity and poignancy, the fleeting sadness of a childhood experience—these, for Baudelaire, became later, principles of his art. *Le vert paradis* of his earliest loves was a world intact and inexhaustible from which the poet could always draw as efficaciously as he could construct and impose an imaginary world on the real world on Paris. Baudelaire's greatest love was for what he believed he had lost: the innocence of his childhood, *le vert paradis des amours enfantines*, and his strongest sentiment of hate was for that form of evil that had deprived him of happiness: *l'obscur Ennemi qui nous ronge le coeur*.

Brunetière's indictment of Baudelaire as the poet extolling debauchery and immorality, illustrates the attitude of most of the first critics. Baudelaire was indeed looked upon as the man who took particular enjoyment in depicting evil. Such a thesis seems today in direct contradiction to the real meaning and spirit of the book: the antagonism between good and evil, that spiritual and physical struggle implicit in the subtitle given to the longest section of the book: *spleen et idéal*. The meaning of such a poem as *La Charogne* is not in the revolting picture of putrefaction but in the biblical warning that the body of man is but dust and returns to dust: *pulvis es*.

In the major lyric tradition of France, the language of Baudelaire bears a strong resemblance to that of Ronsard and Racine and Hugo, but as a poet, in the subject matter of his book, he waged far more desperately than they did an uninterrupted struggle with the nothingness of man, with that part of us which at all times is seeking to annihilate life.

That particular struggle was Baudelaire's life struggle and all the major aspects of his biography are related to it. No poet, unless it was Villon, was more attached to Paris than Baudelaire, and yet no poet was ever less nationalistic than Baudelaire. Paris was the city for him, the only city, but he made it into the site of his personal struggle in which he recapitulated the oldest tragedy of man, the humblest of all tragedies: the combat between the greatness of his mind and aspiration, and the fatal weakness of his will where the daily routine of suffering and humiliation won out. The specific characteristics of the tragedy of this man who died at the age of forty-seven, are in his early poem *L'Albatros*, the bird in exile on the deck of a boat. Not only is the sense of exile translated in the poem, but its ludicrous aspect is emphasized. The huge impotent wings of the albatross—the source of the bird's power and beauty—literally prevent its rising from the deck into the air. Its movements are grotesque and they are mocked by the sailors. The allegory, quite comparable to the swan in the Paris street, is applicable not only to the poet, unable to translate his vision or his dream, but also to every man impeded in his self-realization and who, like Job, ends by being the solitary figure crying out to the invisible God.

The key to Baudelaire's book is the meaning he gives to the word *evil: les fleurs du mal*. What is evil for him? This is perhaps the hardest question to answer concerning Baudelaire, and the most important. It may be possible to reach this answer by considering his temperament, that trait which, more than any other, distinguishes his temperament: Baudelaire's despair. As in the case of Dante, whose tendency to anger is somewhat explained by his pride, by his certainty of Paradise and of the triumph of a just and loving God, so Baudelaire's tendency to despair may be explained by his humility, by his disgust for himself, by his feeling that a world was collapsing around him, by his experience of a suffering God. Evil, then, for Baudelaire, would be his consciousness of the world, his ever present awareness of the physical forces around him that lead to change and destruction and annihilation.

But everything is difficult to define in Baudelaire, because everything is complex, in the modern sense: his sentiment of love as well as his experience of despair. Some of the greatest are surely the love poems, and they are different from the love poems of other French poets. Whether it is to Jeanne he is speaking, or to Marie, or to la Présidente, or to his mother, Baudelaire is concerned with some totally complex form of desire which grows and deepens in him as fear of being satisfied grows and deepens. Baudelaire is the most chaste of the love poets. In his garden of evil, he contemplates the flowers, smells their perfumes and condemns them. The very greatness and limitlessness of passion turns him away from it and converts him into a solitary figure who feels indulgent toward very few beings in the world, and very few works of art.

The creation of art was his life. The labor he spent on rewriting and perfecting his verses was his search for the absolute and his morality. He believed that genuis has to sever the connection with the norm. The pain of living and the desire to live became identical in Baudelaire. The barrenness of life was insufferable for him. Some form of ornamentation is therefore indispensable. Poetry is the loftiest form of ornamentation, because its beauty is metaphysics. In such a simple title as *Paradis artificiels*, Baudelaire states his creed as a poet. The need for ornamentation is the same as the need for escape. Exoticism and eroticism are both inexhaustible for Baudelaire, and they both have to do with the inner life and the former life (*vie intérieure* and *vie antérieure*): deserts, passion, the tropics, desires, oceans, and oases.

As Dante was supremely concentrated on dogma, so Baudelaire was supremely concentrated on his inner life. His attitude of nonchalance and indifference was exterior. At the dawn of modern poetry, slightly more than one hundred years ago, Baudelaire refined his instincts and his thoughts by meditation. In speaking directly to his reader, Baudelaire, for the first time in French poetry, threatened that he would curse him if he did not show him pity:

Plains-moi, sinon, je te maudis!

2. Lautréamont's Epic

LES CHANTS DE MALDOROR appears today a work of imitation, with countless literary echoes and allusions, composed in an almost declamatory style. The title *chants* (cantos) announces the genre of the epic, of the poetic narratives with scenes of violence and war. This is adhered to, to some extent. But an aspect of romanticism is also present throughout the work: a predilection for verbal eloquence, for blasphemy, for imprecation, for the turbulent atmosphere of the Gothic tale.

Although the first edition of *Les Chants* appeared in 1869, it was destined to exert no influence on the nineteenth century. But it became, in the twentieth century, with the writings of Rimbaud, composed at the same time, a work that has counted considerably in the literary consciousness of the modern period. Isidore Ducasse (comte de Lautréamont) and Arthur Rimbaud wrote in their late adolescence, and a generation later, André Breton and Philippe Soupault were in their twenties when they wrote their first collaborative work, *Les Champs magnétiques*. In their revelation of the subconscious, Lautréamont and Rimbaud indicated certain directions that modern poetry was to follow, and such a work as *Les Champs magnétiques*, while inferior to

Maldoror and *Une saison en enfer*, is among the first to reflect literary form and themes characteristic of our age.

Rimbaud's legacy has been exploited far more than Lautréamont's, not only because of the greater originality and power of his writing, but because of his life story, because of his human adventure and personality. Rimbaud's power of invention, his power to expand what he invented, and his ultimate demolition of literature, gave to his work and his example an extraordinary uniqueness. He established a relationship with forms of anxiety which reappear virulent and provocative in the twentieth century. These anxieties, in a histrionic and highly stylized manifestation, are the subject matter of *Les Chants de Maldoror*. The macabre is deliberately cultivated in the themes of lycanthropy, vampirism, murder, bestiality. The hero's name Maldoror would seem to be *aurore du mal*, "dawn of evil." We are at the beginning of time, because each human being, in his subconscious, relives the history of man. The fears of primitive man are orchestrated by Lautréamont in his stanzas; all the instinctive impulses of sexuality and egoism are celebrated as if they were necessary rites of purification. Monsters of the sea, animals of prey, insects, and vermin are everywhere on these pages. Pictorially they appear as they would in the imagination of a child, but they symbolize the basic drives of man in his destructiveness. They are used by Lautréamont in asking philosophy's great questions. Who is man? Why is he evil? The first syllable of the hero's name: *mal*, announces this preoccupation with the problem of evil. Lautréamont remains close to the tradition of Baudelaire in the analysis he offers of the perverse pleasure taken in perpetrating acts of evil. These acts would not be called evil if Baudelaire and Lautréamont did not believe in the existence of God.

Isidore Ducasse was born in Montevideo, Uruguay, in 1846 and was baptised in the cathedral, on November 16, 1847. After studying at the *collège impérial* of Tarbes, where he met Georges Dazet, a friend who became the source of much of the information about the writer's early years, and briefly at the lycée de Pau, he arrived in Paris, in 1867, soon after Baudelaire's death. He lived first in a hotel on the rue Notre Dame des Victoires, and later in another hotel on the rue Vivienne, in the neighborhood of the Bibliothèque Nationale. There he died, at the age of twenty-four, on November 24, 1870, a few months before the revolutionary movement of the Commune. All trace of his bodily remains and of his manuscripts was lost. The mysteriousness of Isidore Ducasse's life is quite in keeping with the sinister mysteries of the writings of le comte de Lautréamont.

To attach an absolute value to *Les Chants de Maldoror*, or to any book, for that matter, would be futile. Literary value is imponderable. But it would be difficult to exaggerate the moral and the aesthetic use that the book had for a generation of French writers and artists, those who worked approximately in the second quarter of the twentieth century. In addition to the themes specifically announced and elaborated in *Maldoror*, the book is also about the reasons for literary creation, about the madness itself of writing. The term of madness, in its medical sense, was used by early critics of Lautréamont, by Léon Bloy, for example, to explain the behavior and the writings of this young man, but today such an explanation would appear too facile and erroneous.

Lautréamont unquestionably had the conviction that the artist must be different from other men, must live in some other way than in accordance with the fixed standards of the bourgeoisie. His writings represent an attack on the traditional poses of romanticism, on the languorous and sentimental attitudes of the poets, on the moonlit scenes of peacefulness and meditations. He followed and exalted the more vigorous romanticism of a Berlioz, in his resounding periods and inflated style, and of a Delacroix, in the rich colors of his scenes. He was the youthful writer, who, with Rimbaud, felt he had been cheated and tricked by destiny. He refused, during the brief span of his writer's career, to compromise with society or with any of the forces that habitually promise success to the aspiring artist. In this regard, Rimbaud and Lautréamont closely resembled one another.

But the meditations of Lautréamont on humanity culminated in a greater sense of disgust and hate, and the literary influences on him were quite different from the influence of the poets that Rimbaud felt. There were undoubtedly English influences on Lautréamont: Edward Young, Anne Radcliffe, Lewis. And in addition to these, there was the prevailing influence of the Marquis de Sade, and a few more purely literary influences, such as Dante and Baudelaire. The book was written during a brief period of time and was the product of an intense intellectual fervor in a personality that would be traditionally classified as highly abnor-

mal. Rousseau would seem to be the forerunner of literary giants
whose abnormalities encouraged an enormous capacity for work
and vision: Sade, Baudelaire, and Rimbaud in France; Hölderlin
and Nietzsche in Germany; Dostoievsky in Russia. Other literary
giants of the nineteenth century, Hugo and Zola, for example, of
a much more normal constitution, have not had the same pronounced effect on twentieth-century literature as such *maudits* as
Baudelaire, Rimbaud, and Lautréamont.

From the example of Rousseau, and from their own personal
lives, these three French writers felt society to be a constraining
force and turned their backs on what the world calls sociability,
or social intercourse. They possessed a genius for solitude. By
comparison with them, the early romantic writers, Chateaubri-
and, Lamartine, Hugo, Musset, and even Vigny, were social
beings, habitués of the *salons* of their day. In his systematic visions, in his tone of scorn and sarcasm for what is human, Lautréamont revived and prolonged the romanticism of despair and
revolt, a resonant lyricism more reminiscent of Byron than of
anything French. *Les Chants de Maldoror* is the work of an
unhappy and even desperate adolescent. In the beauty of his writings, he derived some degree of satisfaction by demolishing the
world, by upsetting the moral values of the world. In his experience of solitude, Lautréamont saw only himself and his Creator.
All the scenes he depicted have to do with the epic struggle, the
oldest struggle of mankind, between man himself and God.

What meaning can be given to this work? The exterior literal
meaning of the various episodes is not sufficient. The narrative,
with its multiple literary echoes, is in reality a study of man's
fundamental complexes.

In the first canto, stanza nine, the elaborate apostrophe to the
ocean offers one of the principal clues to the work as a whole.
After five brief introductory stanzas on violence, hate, wickedness, genius, and the absence of good in all men; and three stanzas
which are scenes—the torturing of an adolescent boy, the firefly
(*le ver luisant*) and the house of prostitution, the dog fight where
the animals tear one another to bits—the solemn hymn to the
ocean breaks out: *je me propose de déclamer à grande voix la
strophe sérieuse et froide que vous allez entendre.*

The passage is both a salutation in the epic style, *je te salue, vieil océan!* and the history of man whose real nature is oceanic. This nature, which is abiding and imperturbable and vast because it is so deep, is the subsconscious. Lautréamont is going to evoke the subconscious throughout *Les Chants de Maldoror* by means of oceans and vessels, storms at sea, and sea monsters, half-concealed reefs, and shipwrecks. The ocean is the symbol of identity in its invariableness and perpetuity:

Vieil océan, tu es le symbole de l'identité: toujours égal à toi-même.

The ocean depths are comparable to the depths of the heart. The celibacy of the ocean (*Vieil océan, ô grand célibataire!*) implies the promiscuousness of man's nature, the waves of passion that break over him and disappear. The subconscious of man, that part of his nature that contains everything, is therefore oceanic, and his conscious nature is terrestrial.

The sea also is the mother of man (*la mer, la mère*). The basic Freudian complex is quite apparent in *Les Chants de Maldoror* when the child encounters first his parents and where his sexual interest is first fixed on one of the parents, according to his sex: the son who will hate his father and love his mother; and the daughter who will love her father and hate her mother. God, the symbol of the father, is ceaselessly attacked throughout all six cantos. He is called by all the familiar names for the Divinity: God, Creator, Almighty, Lord, Supreme Being, and even by some less familiar names, such as Heavenly Bandit (*Céleste Bandit*).

The ocean stanza dominates the first canto which describes the prenatal life of the child, in the sea-imagery of the mother. It is the appropriate introduction to the life story of the epic hero Maldoror, and especially to the second canto which is on infancy and childhood. Evil is in man from the very beginning. The purpose of the book is announced in the opening struggle: the will to strip man of all the sublime lies with which he had deceived himself. This is the longest and most varied canto, with sixteen stanzas, and appropriately so because the principal traits of a man's personality are fixed during early childhood. In keeping with the epic tradition as well as the psychoanalytic tradition, episodes of the hero's childhood are related, and they are all episodes of violence: either violence observed, as in scenes of paternal anger, or violence perpetrated in scenes of infantile sadism or plottings of murder.

The hallucinatory fourth stanza, scene of the omnibus that goes between the Bastille and the Madeleine, shows a group of people resembling a family comfortably seated in the omnibus, impervious to a wretched child of eight who implores help as he stands on the street. Lautréamont asks if this is human charity and denounces the race of men: *race stupide et idiote.* Stanza seven, on the hermaphrodite, is a lyrical interval, an evocation of a beautiful figure half-male, half-female, sleeping in a grove. But he is attacked and beaten by four masked men. After the lesson of violence, the hermaphrodite persists in remaining alone, in refusing the advances of the world, in living completely within a narcissistic dream of himself. This phase of self-love is a protection from the world's hostility, and Lautréamont does not hesitate to urge reclusion and sleep and separation from the world's ferocity:

> *Ne te réveille pas, hermaphrodite . . . Dors,*
> *dors toujours . . . n'ouvre pas tes yeux . . .*

The ninth stanza, an amazing story of lice, is one of the hardest to interpret. It is an invocation to the power of lice to multiply so rapidly that they can set up their own régime and control the world. Lautréamont imagines a reign, a dynasty of lice, so powerful that he would have to rise above the earth on angel wings in order to contemplate the spectacle. In the life story of the hero, this episode is puberty and the multiplying lice are the spermatozoa, the sexual excess of the youth who is amazed at the power of his fertility. The waste of sperm and the obsession with sperm are transcribed by the nightmare about lice and their domination of the world.

The tenth stanza which solemnly begins with the words

> *O mathématiques sévères, je ne vous ai pas oubliées,*

and which is in a literal sense an apostrophe to mathematics, to its power and splendor, to the services it renders mankind, has more clues than the lice stanza to its symbolic meaning. It is a passage on the hero's mother, the first development of the Oedipus complex, in which mathematics is called the source and the fortifying milk which the hero drinks. Mathematics or the mother appears as chaos out of whose entrails a treasure will be brought forth. The multiplication of cells during the period of gestation is implied in the choice of this symbol, and supplementary images, pyramids and labyrinths, reinforce the image of the maternal womb in whose darkness the hero first discovered the meaning of evil:

> *Le premier, je découvris, dans les ténèbres de ses*
> *entrailles, ce vice néfaste, le mal!*

The maternal image, in its sacred imperturbable manifestation of mathematics, is the consolation for the wickedness of man and the injustice of God. This is the ultimate sentence of the stanza, the ultimate exhortation: *O mathématiques saintes!*

As might be expected, the following stanza, the eleventh, is on the hero's relationship to the father, which is basically the Oedipus complex of hatred for the father. And here again, Lautréamont has invented an intriguing image to designate the father, and a scene of violence to designate the son's murder of the father. The hero is watching a silver lamp in a cathedral. It shines in the dark colonnades of the basilica as if it were choosing its victims among the kneeling penitents. The lamp so irritates Maldoror that he wishes it would turn into a man so that he could attack it. The wish is granted and the lamp turns into the figure of an angel. A fight ensues and Maldoror strangles the Lord's emissary.

With the twelfth stanza, we have reached the hero's age of puberty, where the prayers he had learned as a child sadden and irritate him because he is learning another kind of prayer, the offering up of himself in the practice of onanism. Many elements in the stanza point to this as the new experience for the boy: the tormenting dreams he has, the rights that his nature claims, his feelings that repeatedly lead him to this inclination (*vers cette pente*). The other boys around him are having the same experience which he contrasts with the sterile repetition of his childish prayers.

Again, in logical sequence, the following stanza, an elaborate episode of action, is the narrative of Maldoror's first love (*mon premier amour*, he calls it in the last words of the stanza) or rather his first sexual experience after the practice of masturbation. This is one of the most powerful and shocking passages in *Les Chants de Maldoror*. In order to depict incest in the life story of Maldoror, the hero's first knowledge of sexual love, which will be with his mother, in keeping with the ancient myth of Oedipus, Lautréamont imagines the hero seated on a rock near the sea. He watches a storm rise up and a ship strike against a reef and sink. He watches the death agony of the shipwrecked passengers with a sadistic voluptuousness. Six sharks swim into the mêlée and devour the survivors. A huge female shark then enters the fray and kills three of the sharks. Maldoror shoots another of the monsters and then, armed with a knife, leaps into the water. Maldoror and the female shark easily destroy the two remaining sharks, and then begin in the water an amazing scene of admiration and veneration. They embrace tenderly and then unite sexually. The union is pure and hideous, and the hero no longer feels alone. He is face to face with his first love. This is the act of incest in the life story of the hero. Since the ocean is the mother image, the female shark symbolizes the mother, and the union of the son and the mother takes place in the ocean depths:

> *vers les profondeurs de l'abîme, ils se réunirent*
> *dans un accouplement long, chaste et hideux!*

The act is described as the accomplishment of a primordial instinct of humanity. The shark and the young man are attracted to one another like two magnets:

ils tombèrent brusquement l'un contre l'autre, comme deux aimants . . .

If the book is read as the life story of a man, of the epic hero, canto III would be the initiation to life, which follows the prenatal life (canto I) and childhood (canto II). The opening stanza is mysterious. Two brothers are riding horseback side by side. They might be looked upon as the two selves of Maldoror, the genie of the earth and the genie of the sea, the male and the female principles. The first initiation is the separation from the mother, the emergence from the sea (*source, mer*) and the first experience on the solid earth. The two brothers could easily be, in terms of the entire work, the subconscious (*la mer*) and the conscious (*la terre*) which now exist side by side as the two horses gallop along the shore. During the ride they experience a premonition of distaste, a vision of life as being a wound: *j'ai reçu la vie comme une blessure*. It is an epic passage of movement and speed, a prelude to the battle which announces the ferociousness of the second stanza.

It is a scene closely modeled on a typical scene in the novels of
Sade where Maldoror brutally rapes a little girl who is then raped
by a bull dog. The pornography is traditional and the physiological details of the passage are capable of arousing readers with
certain temperaments.

The entire canto is a preparation for the final scene in the fifth
stanza, a scene of debauchery in a bordello where the hero encounters his father who is depicted as the supreme profligate.
This is the lowest, the most shameful initiation to life that Lautréamont was able to conceive: the vilification of the father, the
one to whom the hero owes his life. Outside the building, an inscription on a pillar, in Hebrew letters, warns the passerby not to
enter. It has the ring of Dante's warning (*Voi, ch'entrate*): *Vous,
qui passez sur ce pont, n'y allez pas.*

The horror and strangeness of a Dante-like scene begins when
the hero is in the room and sees what he believes to be a blond
stick (*un bâton blond*) moving about and walking. He compares
it to a battering ram (*un bélier*) striking against the gates of a besieged city. On closer examination, the moving object is a hair (*un
cheveu*) which had fallen from the head of the Supreme Being
when he had come to the house of prostitution (as once Jupiter
had assumed the form of a swan to possess Leda). The obviously
phallic object speaks of his abandonment in the room. In a clap of
thunder and a phosphorescent light, God reenters the room and
places the hair back on his head. The hero is the spectator of this
degrading scene. He listens to the Creator speak of his eternal
shame, he listens to the hair forgiving the Creator, and is overcome with sadness at having such an enemy as an ancestor. This
scene of an avowed attack against the father, in which he had
witnessed the degradation of the father, as the sons of Noah had
once witnessed their father's nakedness, parallels the scene of
physical union with the mother, at the end of the second canto.

In the fourth canto, the hero appears as one emerging from
adolescence and entering upon his maturity. The images of mature genital life prevail, and symbols of sexuality: towers, pins,
pillars. Man, in his sexuality, is shown as being humiliated and
rejected by woman. There are strong echoes of Baudelaire (*Bénédiction* and *Voyage à Cythère*) in the third stanza where a man is
hanging from a gallows and being tortured by his mother and his
wife because he refused to have sexual intercourse with his

mother. The episode recalls the crucifixion, with the suffering God and the Women at the foot of the cross. As in *Voyage à Cythère*, the spectator (Maldoror) is also the figure being tortured.

The following stanza, the fourth, is in close relationship with the third, because here the body of the man is dessecrated and metamorphosed, as in passages of Dante's *Inferno*. Those parts of his body associated with sexuality, penis, testicles, anus, buttocks, are inhabited and metamorphosed by a viper, two small herons, a crab, and two jelly fish. All the familiar anxieties associated with both adolescence and maturity in the hero's life, follow one another. The fear of castration is part of the obsessions in the third and fourth stanzas, but in the fifth it is predominant. In his mirror, the hero sees himself as scalped and his head encircled by rapacious birds. The bald head is a classical symbol for the fear of castration. Without hair the hero resembles a Red Skin (the word *Peau Rouge* is used as it will be by Rimbaud in *Le Bateau ivre*). In order to put an end to the obsession, he smashes the mirror. He realizes that his eyes can bring on death.

Each of the remaining stanzas, six, seven, and eight, is related to the mature sexual life of man, or rather to the obsessions, the complexes that derive from sexuality. The dream described in stanza six is one of bestiality. Maldoror is a pig, living in filth, outside of humanity, and in such a condition that even the animals move off from him. In the dream he is isolated on a cliff and calls his experience a metamorphosis.

The theme is bestiality and metamorphosis is continued in stanza seven, one of the "story" stanzas, and one of the most important of this canto. It is a plunge backward in time to an earlier existence when his body possessed an amphibious nature. This is the story of the amphibian (*amphibie*), man and animal in one body, a monster living in the water like a sea-horse (*hippocampe*), in the air like a sea-hawk (*orfraie*), under the earth like a mole (*taupe*). In his earliest memories he sees himself with a twin brother. But he was so handsome that his brother hated him and lied about him to their parents. Because of this betrayal he was thrown into prison by his parents and tortured. There he knew solitude of body and soul. From there he made his escape to the sea shore, and ultimately to the sea itself where he lived at peace with the fish. The amphibian is the monarch of the fish.

One after the other, Maldoror revives the archtypal dreams, dreams of escape into other forms and other existences which offset the immediate constraints of life. In the final stanza, the fear-of-castration dream is more pronounced than ever. This time Maldoror evokes a more recent past, when he was fifteen years old, and attracted to a blond youth of fourteen, called Falmer. The image of thick blond hair alternates with the image of a bald head, as bare as the shell of a turtle:

> *Eloignez donc cette tête sans chevelure, polie comme*
> *la carapace de la tortue.*

The desire to attack Falmer sexually or mortally is confused, in the evolving of this memory, with the fear of losing his virility.

Throughout the fifth canto there is a stronger sense of age and maturity, and a growing need for abnormal behavior, for abnormal ways of satisfying desires. The obsessions are denser and more persistent. They are symbolized at the beginning of the canto by the flock of starlings (*étourneaux*). These birds reproduce the cyclical return of obsessions whose blackness blots out everything else in the world. The son's relationship with his parents is now anthropophagia. For food, he rips out the arms of his mother, cuts them into pieces and eats them.

Dominating the second stanza are two figures: a beetle (*un scarabée*) as large as a cow, and a man with the head of a pelican. The passage is difficult and deliberately confused. Maldoror himself sees imperfectly. The pelican-headed man and the beetle would seem to symbolize the secrets of the double organism: male and female. A brief story of a wife's infidelity is interpolated.

Sleeplessness is a theme in stanza three where the recurring obsessions each night are related to birth and death for Maldoror. He stands erect at his window throughout the night and looks out at the stars. Dawn finds him in this position. To the sleeper his body is a corpse, and the sheets of his bed a shroud. Maldoror's endless meditation on himself (*ma subjectivité*) and on the Creator is too much for his mind to bear. His conscience, in stanza four, appears in various forms: as a python with its ever moving coils, a boa, a basilisk. His sense of remorse is confused with murmurings and plottings.

The apostrophe of stanza five is addressed this time to pederasts, and Lautréamont describes the prostitution of those men who offer themselves to the first comer. And as always, Maldoror becomes one of those he apostrophizes, as if, in order to fulfill his hero's destiny, he must know all the aberrations of mankind. The Creator engages also in this office, and, in the last line of the stanza, opens his door to a pederast.

As is frequent in Lautréamont's art, a sudden change of scene occurs with stanza six, and we see a funeral procession for a ten-year-old boy. This is the occasion for a meditation on the death-instinct, or the death-wish, which is closely allied with a feeling of impotence. Maldoror watches the burial, and then gallops away. The apocalyptic horse returns frequently in the work. This time he is described as a twisting cyclone. Lautréamont ends the stanza by stating his conviction that the dead boy is in reality living and that the strange figure on horseback is dead.

The betrayal of friendship is a persistent theme in *Les Chants de Maldoror*, and in the final stanza of Canto V it is more deliberately developed than elsewhere. Maldoror's distrust of friendship, or his incapacity for friendship, goes very far in explaining his solitude. At the beginning of the stanza, as a prelude, is the episode of the old spider that emerges from a hole in the floor to suck Maldoror's blood every night when he is asleep. The spider is the symbol of friendship because from its belly emerge the two friends: Elseneur and Réginald. (The English names recall the Gothic tales which are among the literary sources of *Les Chants*.) The suffering inflicted on Maldoror by his friends is implicit in the story of the attack made on Réginald when his right wrist is severed from his body. The Lord, who is never absent for long from the narration, had ordered the metamorphosis of the two friends into the spider destined to haunt Maldoror's bed and symbolize the failure of friendship.

Throughout the final canto, the author intervenes more constantly than heretofore, in direct speech to the reader, to explain and justify the work. The opening stanza is this kind of communication in which *Les Chants de Maldoror* is defined as an insult to man, to the Creator, and to Lautréamont! The purpose of the writing is to attack man and his Creator. The author has no intention of retracting his words. He announces a story of thirty pages which will enable the reader to comprehend better Lautréamont's position of renegade and the diabolical influences on him: *la préface du renégat, à la figure fuligineuse.*

With the second stanza, the genre of the work is acknowledged in the behavior of the hero. Maldoror cannot be seized. He
changes his form constantly. He is ubiquitous. Agents, spies, disguises characterize the world of *notre héros*. He can turn into a
cricket in the Paris sewers. One day he is in Madrid, the next day
in Saint Petersburg, and the day before in Peking. He is the type
of hero, the adventurer, who has appeared in every age. He is the
magician of the medieval tale, the sadist of the Gothic tale, Robin
Hood, James Bond, one of the witches in Sade's *Juliette*, Dr. Fu
Manchu, Batman, Superman, Jesse James. The list is endless,
because man's dream of liberation is endless, and his hope of
transcending laws, both physical and moral, and his determination to change his human fate.

The story then begins. It will occupy eight chapters and conclude the work. The story of Mervyn and Maldoror: the story of
a spiritual seduction and a physical assassination, which is probably a disguise for what Lautréamont had in mind: a physical
seduction and a spiritual assassination.

There is great geographical precision in the Paris that is evoked
in this story. It begins on the rue Vivienne, in the vicinity of the
Bibliothèque Nationale and the Bourse. Night is falling. Shutters
are being closed. Solitude and darkness are settling over the city.
Against this setting appears a sixteen-year-old boy, Mervyn, who
is on his way home. His beauty is such that language is inade-
quate to describe it, but the shock that his beauty creates is put
into a sentence that was destined to attract the surrealists and
Breton especially: the encounter on a dissecting table of a sewing
machine and an umbrella . . . *comme la rencontre fortuite sur une
table de dissection d'une machine à coudre et d'un parapluie!*
Mervyn is being followed by Maldoror. The boy feels the presence of some malefic influence. The infernal machine is at work.

Maldoror, for the pursuit of evil, has given up everything and
lives mysteriously alone. But Mervyn has everything: the love of
his parents, a beautiful home, elegant clothes. This evening the
boy appears changed, listless, inattentive. The parents fear a spell
is on him. But then the crisis seems to be over, and the physician
promises that all is well again. Late that night, Mervyn reads a
strange letter that Maldoror had left for him. It is a call to embrace love and adventure and fixes an early morning rendezvous
in two days on the Pont du Carrousel. With the reading of this

letter (all the melodramatic effects are called into use in this episode), Mervyn's bewitchment deepens. He writes an answer to his unknown admirer and consents to the rendezvous. It is hard for him to understand the attachment he feels for this stranger and the feeling of guilt he has in welcoming his solicitations.

The narrative itself is here interrupted by two brief passages which are related to Mervyn's fate, but only in a general sense. The first is on Maldoror's duality: the beauty of his vice and the demonic powers of his magic. His power now allows him to challenge the Creator who is permitting him to descend the river of his destiny. The words he uses are almost the same that Rimbaud uses in the first line of *Le Bateau ivre:*

> *que le Créateur me laisse descendre le fleuve*
> *de ma destinée!*

The second passage is a complicated allusion to a figure called Aghone who seems to execute the order of Maldoror.

From this point on until the end, during which the action mounts to monstrous proportions, the lips of Maldoror are often described and always with a different color: *bronze, jaspe, saphir, soufre.* The metallic hardness of his lips seems to symbolize his skill of demon. The real prelude to the final episode on the place Vendôme is God's attempt to save the adolescent boy. He sends his archangel in the form of a *crabe-tourteau.* Maldoror hurls a stick at the crab and slays it. Faithful to the rendezvous on the Pont du Carrousel, Mervyn is overpowered by Maldoror and stuffed head first into a bag. When he continues to struggle, Maldoror strikes the bag against the parapet. The bag is given to a butcher who is told it contains a mad dog that must be slaughtered. Mervyn is rescued and comes back to consciousness only to be given over to Aghone who attaches him to a rope and dangles him from the top of the Vendôme column. The body then is swung back and forth over Paris, like a comet, and strikes against the dome of the Panthéon.

Everything is presented as enigmatic in the long series of episodes which compose *Les Chants de Maldoror:* dreams, myths, symbols, realistic effects. The son's hostility toward his father (or man's effort to liberate himself from his Creator) is the most apparent theme of the work. There are several examples of the traumatic experience of a child being brutally separated from his family: in the second canto, the child running after the omnibus; in the fourth canto, the child taking refuge in the ocean and being transformed into an amphibian; and the story of Mervyn in the sixth canto.

The exaggeration of this violence as it is narrated in *Maldoror* exists in the few facts that are known about the life of Isidore Ducasse. At fifteen he was sent from Uruguay to France, where, rather than living with his family, he lived in a school dormitory. After the exultant experience of the ocean, he knew the solitude of the *collège*. After the freedom of the ocean, the prison of school, with surveillance and the constant fear of punishment. The passage on Falmer in the fourth canto appears as a childhood memory of school, when Ducasse was fifteen and Falmer fourteen, and where the memory evoked is one of punishment. Male and female components are both here in the thick head of hair of Falmer, in the threat of being scalped (or castrated). It is to be wondered whether the name Falmer is itself the conjugation of male and female: *fal—phall* or *phallus*, and *mer—mère*.

Literature is primarily a movement of discovery, of self-discovery. In its extreme examples—*Les Chants de Maldoror* is one of these—the discovery of the individual is almost equivalent to the beginning of madness. To know oneself is dangerous, and this danger is emphasized throughout the cantos. The symbolic presentation of the writing, where it is impossible to fix on one meaning alone, where several interpretations occur to the reader, is a way of disguising the danger. The immediate literal interpretation is the shock of melodrama that holds the attention of the reader only momentarily. Then the plethora of possible meanings form a kind of net in which the reader is caught. He flounders about trying to find his way out, trying to widen one of the meshes that will permit him to escape. The libidinous tendencies and the death wishes of the subconscious are so numerous and so urgent that the reading of such a work as *Les Chants de Maldoror* provides an almost too exact representation of them. It is difficult to bear the power of the subconscious when it is cast into recognizable forms of violence. Lautréamont is telling us that the individual first recognizes himself as such in his relationship with his father, both his human father and his supernatural Creator. But as soon as this recognition takes place, a combat ensues. A combat for survival, which will challenge all the powers of a man. The long genital life of an adolescent, as he grows and develops, will constantly recapitulate this combat. Mervyn's story is both his renouncing of his father and his search for a father.

Infrequently Lautréamont alludes to the strong words of "minotaur" and "labyrinth," striking symbols for his conception of the life of an individual. Life is not static. It is constantly moving, both progressing and retrogressing. In his subconscious, man creates his own labyrinth, and then in his conscious life he tries to explore it. Each man therefore plays the two roles of Minotaur, of monster for whom the labyrinth is designed, and Theseus, who heroically tries to encounter the Minotaur and slay him. *Les Chants de Maldoror* is the meeting between Theseus-Lautréamont and the Minotaur-Maldoror. The cantos are the labyrinth. They are the literary expression of man seen in his labyrinthine ways.

As a writer, Lautréamont is totally conscious in his labors of reconstructing the labyrinth, classically logical in the ordering of his sentences and in their transitions. But behind these formal aspects, he is searching for the obscure forces of a psyche, searching in his movements toward the future and toward the past for the meaning of the drives and the emotions in a man's life. The danger of such an exploration is that of losing one's way, of complete alienation from conscious life. But in the labyrinth of *Les Chants*, in each phase of the search, the hero finds his way, even if it is momentarily, as in the popular horror story, of the *série noire* type: Fantômas, James Bond, Fu Manchu. Whenever Lautréamont speaks directly to the reader about his work, he emphasizes his logic and his prudence in the way in which he reveals the unusual and the fantastic. In order to approximate the great reason for life, he procedes reasonably.

It is indeed reasonable to look upon sleep and nightmares as experiences that reveal the subconscious. Sleep, madness, and death are states where the deepest ego comes to life. A conscious effort to see clearly into oneself is quite different from the vision provided by the subconscious. Lautréamont is both analyst and psychoanalyst: analyst in the lucidity of his form, and psychoanalyst in the obscurity of his meaning.

The writer is always to some degree the recreator of myths. In the figure of Maldoror, whose name could easily mean the dawn, the light of evil, one can see the recreation of the Christian myth of Lucifer, of the fallen archangel whose name means light. And in the name Ducasse chose for himself, Lautréamont, some critics believe they can see L'autre Amon, or Amon-Râ, the Egyptian sun god, the other sun. The defiance of Maldoror is of such proportions, the violence of his actions and his thoughts is so extreme, that he becomes the personification of evil, an epic figure in the very greatness of that which he opposes.

The psychoanalysis of a character reveals what Maldoror reveals in a literary form: the close relationship existing between the subconscious and the symbol. The labyrinth and the desert can easily symbolize the subconscious; the one composed of too many conflicting paths, and the other, pathless. From Greece and from Egypt come the two myths of the minotaur and the sphinx, two figures who complement one another: the minotaur with the animal head and the human male body, the sphinx with the female head and the animal's body.

Maldoror encounters the minotaur in the numerous episodes of bestiality, and the sphinx in his efforts to explain the enigmas of existence. The supernatural powers he manifests, the swiftness of his movements, his ubiquity make him appear as an archangel hesitating between good and evil, fearful of God and wanting to be God.

The literary creation of Maldoror, and the writer Lautréamont are also the young man Isidore Ducasse, alone in his room on the fifth floor of a Paris hotel. At almost the same time, the author of *Les Illuminations* was a young boy in his room at the top floor of a hotel on the rue Monsieur-le-Prince. And just before that time, Ducasse was a student imprisoned in the collège de Tarbes in the Pyrénées, and Rimbaud a student prisoner in Charleville, in the northern Ardennes.

3. Rimbaud's Season

ARTHUR RIMBAUD WAS only one among several poets in the nineteenth century who examined the nature of poetry and who,
by restoring to poetry certain prophetic powers claimed by the
Ancients, ascribed to the poet his role of seer. Hugo and Nerval
in France, Poe in America, Blake in England, Novalis in Germany, all contributed to this reassignment of the poetic vision.
Rimbaud, without always possessing the knowledge of the history of poetry and orphism which some critics have claimed for
him, did establish at moments in his work an extraordinary con-
cordance between his own poetic experience and the wisdom
which tradition allocates to the poet in every age.

Rimbaud's practices of a poet, in his use of analogy and symbol
and parable do not have to come from readings in older metaphysical systems of man. They are natural to poets, they are
inherent in the poetic process when the poet, often without
realizing it, participates in the past. In his efforts to find his own
position in the universe, the poet reveals, unconsciously, traces of
great myths of the past which themselves were attempts to describe the true nature of man and the poet.

The experiences of violent revolt which Rimbaud lived through as he passed from adolescence to young manhood, were recast in his writing and there became means of understanding the conditions and the necessity of revolt. The expression given to his adolescent experiences was their solution in the sense that it was Rimbaud's means of understanding the imperious demands of his nature. In claiming in his *Lettre du Voyant* that Baudelaire was a true god, he acknowledged his alliance with all poets and the continuity of the poet's experience throughout the ages.

In a fundamental sense, therefore, the tradition from which Rimbaud comes is that which leads the poet to create his own universe. In *Une Saison en Enfer*, Rimbaud speaks of the Orient and of his return to the original wisdom of the Orient.

> *Je retournais à l'Orient et à la sagesse première*
> *et éternelle* (*L'Impossible*)

There are traces in his writings of Plato's idealism, traces also of the occult tradition, of the initiate in the Kabbalistic and alchemist traditions. But far more than in the fragmentary allusions to Plato and the occult, Rimbaud's knowledge of himself and of the world is to be found quite simply in the ancient discovery and practice of poetry. The writing of poetry can be a way to knowledge and it usually involves a metaphysical and an esoteric approach to an understanding of man and his universe.

Arthur Rimbaud was, at a very early age, a sufferer and a rebel. The city of Charleville, where he grew up, in the Ardennes in northern France, was a stifling prison, the site of perpetual penance for him, and where all the elements of authority—school, mother, and church—seemed ludicrous and bent upon crushing his spirit. His one escape was, what he calls in *Les Poètes de sept ans*, "vision," the willed discovery of an obscure world beyond the immediate world. He cultivated the moments of vision avidly, because during the rest of the time, he cultivated feelings of disgust for teachers, parents, priests. These feelings grew until they forced him to leave Charleville abruptly, melodramatically, in an invincible need for freedom and purity. But he always had to return to Charleville, penniless and sheepish, and try to forget the escapes, as he walked in the streets of Charleville, read in the public library, or drank beer in the bistrots of the place Ducale, with his friends Delahaye and Bretagne.

Everything he observed about him encouraged and flattered his determination to destroy. Passages in his earliest poetry speak of Rimbaud's desire to reach the absolute, to move beyond the tawdry restrictions of his Charleville life, into a region where his spirit will be free. He acknowledges, in *Soleil et chair*, his desire to explore and know,

L'Homme veut tout sonder, et savoir . . . ;

but the reasonableness of his insipid life conceals the infinite from him,

Notre pâle raison nous cache l'infini . . .

The violence of Rimbaud's sentiments is all the more intense because of the secret drive in him to discover the world's unity, to understand the correspondences between the life of the spirit and the life of matter. He will enact, once again, the oldest struggle of man: his rivalry with God, that principle of individualism which at times appears a defiance of God. What Rimbaud saw in Christianity was a materialistic system, corroded by the lowest motives of man. He was willing to believe, with other prophetic spirits of his age, that it is incumbent on man to recreate God. Like the mystics, he understood the law by which man has to die to visible things in order to mount to invisible things.

The famous letter written to Demeny on May 15, 1871, is the basic text for an understanding of Rimbaud's method. He offers in it a brief history of poetry, and then describes the ways by which a poet becomes a *voyant*. Rimbaud followed the age-old habit of poets, namely the discovery of a system or of a belief, a way to make something out of mystery. The gifted, youthful poet, such as a Rimbaud, begins with scandal and ends with metaphysics. Or rather, he makes metaphysics out of scandal. Violence, when the poet attempts to express it, is inevitably converted into an understanding of violence. The poet abandons his human role of rebel and destroyer when he engages in the creative act of poetry. He emerges from the experience of what might be called the reason for poetry and enters upon the experience of the *vates*, which is the power of poetry.

As all the usual hostilities toward the world grew in Rimbaud, his personality of an adolescent grew into a closed universe. His poems were the spiritual struggle of his ego and at the same time

the ancient effort of the human race to follow, not the narrow
confines of dogmatism, but the freedom of thought. The oneness
of God which Rimbaud had learned of in catechism class, he
experienced in his longing to come upon the unity in the world.
The Word of God creating the universe was the ever present
proof that multiplicity of the world derives from One.

In acknowledging the oneness of God and the spirit of the
Orient, Rimbaud was claiming that it is not necessary to choose
between spirit and matter. They are joined and primarily by the
artist who discovers a form for the spirit. The poet translates into
words the upheavals and drives of the spirit. Rimbaud's use of the
words number (*nombre*) and harmony (*harmonie*) indicates his
alliance with Orphism. He knew fragmentarily of systems and
beliefs, and from them he had to reach his own system which
he named *la voyance*. This was not a vision deriving from the
study of books. All the formulas of Rimbaud are those of an
adept, of a believer in that part of himself, his "soul" as he calls it,
which is the source of real knowledge, of that power that will
lead him to the reality of things.

"The reasoned derangement of all the senses," is the formula
for this method and Rimbaud insists on its lengthiness and its
vastness (*un long, immense et raisonné dérèglement de tous les
sens*). It would be difficult to know what Rimbaud meant by *dérèglement* if he had not explained the word in the same passage of
the *Lettre* by the three experiences of love, suffering, and madness. These are the aspects of violence, the derangements which
train the soul and lead it to the "unknown," to that state of
detachment from daily realities which tend to deaden the soul.
Violence was for Rimbaud a regimen of asceticism. In a very
moving letter to Delahaye, written from Paris, from his room in
the rue Monsieur-le-Prince, Rimbaud describes in detail his regimen: an all-night vigil of study, the coming of dawn, his fast, his
descent into the street at the earliest moment when he could
purchase bread, the return to his room, his sense of detachment
from the city. To be able to write poetry, Rimbaud believed in a
way of life that was made up of privations, chastity, fasting. By
the age of sixteen, and largely by his own intuition and thanks
to his own practices and discoveries, poetry was for him a way of
knowledge, a means of knowing himself and the world. By the
time he had reached that age, he knew the importance of premo-

nitions, of dreams, of psychic phenomena which have always belonged to the tradition of poetry. He welcomed certain drives in him that transfigured his being and his life. These were forms of exaltation, ascetic experiences of the *voyant* which go very far in explaining the most successful of his poems, where sensual habits are named: *Fêtes de la Faim, Comédie de la Soif.*

> *Si j'ai du goût, ce n'est guère*
> *Que pour la terre et les pierres*

His ancestors tell him that man has to drink:

> *Que faut-il à l'homme? Boire.*

Friends urge him to join hands with them, but he is alone with the image of an ideal country where he will drink contentedly:

> *Peut-être un soir m'attend*
> *Où je boirai tranquille*
> *En quelque vieille ville.*

These poems of asceticism, of obstacles in the way, of ancestors and friends, of a fictional countryside where the poet hears voices and sees castles are the richest that Rimbaud wrote, the most subtle in their pure lyric fervor, in their impulse toward the world, toward union with the world whereby the poet may come upon the key to love (*quelque chose comme la clef de l'amour* [*Vie*]).

These poems pose the problems that are recapitulated in many of *Les Illuminations*. Is physical love the way to fulfillment or is detachment from the world of the senses the better way? (cf. *Sonnet*). Poetry is the means by which its primitive purity may be restored to humanity. The monstrousness of Rimbaud's ambition is clear in such a text as *Génie* where the poet is god, or at least a supernatural envoy. Even in the celebrated phrase of the *Lettre: Je est un autre*, Rimbaud may well be identifying himself with God.

Rimbaud knew as deeply and as tragically as any of the major poets the perils of exposure, the failures to which his mind was exposed. His first and only contact with the established Parisian writers was a disaster. He was rigorously excluded or admitted derisively. After the Brussels drama and the return to his mother's farm, at Roche, in July, 1873, Rimbaud was despondent,

discouraged, humiliated. Most of *Une Saison en Enfer* was composed at that time. The text is a kind of morality play where
reminiscences immediate and distant are juxtaposed with inpulses
to rebellion and outbursts of exuberance. References are made to
the poet's discovery of Oriental wisdom, to his rejection of
Catholicism, and to his ambitions of a prophet.

In the prologue of the work, Rimbaud's scorn is directed
against art and social systems and religious constraints. Later, in
Mauvais Sang, he calls upon his executioners in a moment of
rage, when his desire for the absolute seems to equate the void.
Perfection is perhaps to be found in negativism, or at least in an
exaltation of the primitive. Rimbaud elevates the convict, the
man who is intractable in the eyes of the social order: *le forçat
intraitable*. The savage must have been devoid of the hypocrisies
of civilized society. Rimbaud prefers to be primitive: *je suis une
bête*. Let him sink into the occidental marshes.

Throughout *Une Saison*, Rimbaud alternates between a desire
to merge himself with the cosmos, with the world consciousness,
and the desire for some kind of permanent individuality. When
he feels defeat in one of these beliefs, he turns in the other
direction, with the courage of a hero and without indulgence
for himself. He sees himself on the open road, in all kinds of
weather, and totally sober:

> *la grande route par tous les temps . . . sobre naturellement . . .*

Ascetic loneliness is his way of life. He claims pride in having
no country and no friends. He moves easily between extremes of
feeling, between a child's innocence and a Promethean pride.
Rimbaud is trapped by eternity which he calls hell. Eternity
is precisely hell when it is felt to be a trap.

The poet's revolt against his early training is total, as narrated
in the brilliant autobiographical poem *Les poètes de sept ans*. His
attack is against the catechism, against the Bible, read on the bleak
December Sunday afternoons, against the moral code of his
mother. During his three or four years as a practicing poet, he
fought against all that, in an effort to eradicate the memories of
his early years. But the *voyant* also sees the past. Bible images are
everywhere in *Une Saison en Enfer*, and memories of the catechism class. They form a religious climate for the work, as strong
and as impenetrable as the vituperation against religion. He re-

turns to Christ and then refuses him. He moves back and forth between acknowledgement of paganism in his distant past (*le sang païen*) and phrases of the Gospel (*L'Evangile*). He calls upon God to be free of God: *De profundis, Domine*, and concludes that the sacrament of baptism left on him an indelible mark: *je suis l'esclave de mon baptême*. Nowhere does he accept Catholicism as such. He fights against all traditions and refuses them one after the other in strongly rhythmical enumerations. He stammers words spoken as by a child, especially in the section *L'Impossible*, which is an important synthesis of his rebellion.

M. Prudhomme, the type of narrow-minded bourgeois, insensitive to values of art and morality, was born with Christ, according to Rimbaud, who flails his civilization, especially in the strong sentence: *M. Prudhomme est né avec le Christ*. The Church, then, is responsible for the civilization he detests and which is totally different from what he believes the Orient to be.

Pitilessly Rimbaud flails his own pride. The real *voyant* can stand any degree of self-debasement. He sees himslf in every age, in a variety of roles. He knows what it is to be a Christian, at an earlier epoch when Christianity was ardent and generous and charitable. But to be that today would be pretentious. The *voyant* has moved beyond pretention and vanity. Verlaine, in his role of "Vierge folle" in *Une Saison*, undertook to restore Rimbaud to his state of *fils du soleil*. But how could Rimbaud live up to such a vocation? Not even Verlaine was able to comprehend him!

His climate is extremes: ferociousness and charity, revolt and love. The poet's delirium of *Délires II* seems to be a madness brought on from living in extreme states of feeling, from the double vocation of poet and prophet. Neither one was able to hold Rimbaud exclusively, and he broke under the weight of the two. How can an adolescent live simultaneously as poet and metaphysician? As the creator of language, he is proud of writing down the inexpressible: *J'écrivais des silences . . . je notais l'inexprimable*. The incantatory power of language is referred to by all the mythic religions, and Rimbaud, like many poets of the nineteenth century was fascinated by the Logos or the Word as it appears in Genesis and in the Gospel of Saint John. Is not the poet's myth the same as that of the Tower of Babel? Is not human speech one means of reaching the divine in the universe? Are not the Pentacostal tongues of fire aspects of the same tradition?

These are questions posed as themes throughout *Une Saison en Enfer*, and which became, later in the twentieth century, in the writings of the surrealists, poetic beliefs. Language, in its power of communication, is a return to a lost unity. Poetry is a means by which a single man participates in the world. The goal of surrealist practices, which Rimbaud discusses in *Une Saison*, is a magical union of an idea with a word, of the mind with language. Such a union is a realization of man's primitive innocence, of his participation in the world when he experiences an interpenetration of things,

> *la mer mêlée*
> *au soleil,*

and when time is one,

> *Plus de lendemain.*

By the communication of his art, the poet becomes one with those with whom he communicates.

In a letter to Ernest Delahaye, Rimbaud spoke of the importance of *Une Saison en Enfer*. He claimed his life depended upon it: *mon sort dépend de ce livre*. The season he spent in hell is narrated as a rebellion against Christianity (*ma sale éducation d'enfance*) and as a series of attempts to reach some other belief, some other experience. He moved from city to city, from one experience to another, plagued by defeat, and returning at last to the earth (*rendu au sol*) and to his state of a peasant (*paysan!*) where he was alone, cut off from everyone and from every belief. The poignancy of the phrase *pas une main amie* is all the greater after the ambitions and the visions (*un grand vaisseau d'or*) that were Rimbaud's. At every turn in his life, and especially during the three or four years of his career as poet, but also during the varied experiences of Rimbaud's other life after 1875, he encountered total incomprehension.

The life story of Rimbaud, as well as the story of his life as narrated in his writings, is that of a man trying to escape his fate. He called it once, in *Une Saison*, *la fatalité du bonheur*. But one does not escape fate, one is consumed by it. Unsuccessful in playing any role other than his own, the rebel is in the very deepest sense, the rebel against the fate of man, against the finiteness and the mortality of man who longs for the absolute and for perfection. Rimbaud is a rebel because he is so lucidly cognizant of the gift of his spirit, the gift of speech, of language in its pristine form after it has passed through all the trials of the cliché and the verbal approximation.

The most extraordinary aspect of Rimbaud's case is the closeness, the identity perhaps, between the life of the rebel poet and the poetry he wrote. The deliberate cultivation of the monstrous which Rimbaud discusses in his *Lettre du voyant* and in *Alchimie du verbe* of *Une Saison* is both the action of the rebel against the static, familiar, and dishonest forms of life, and the willed hallucinations which are transcribed in the poems. The source of vision is an organic disorder. The poet in Rimbaud kept close surveillance over the functioning of his mind. He directed it and recorded the results. But in doing this, he exposed himself as a martyr. To reach the degree of knowledge which Rimbaud possessed, he had to pass through states of illness, according to the world (*le grand malade*), and states of ostracism (*le grand maudit*). There is no literary coquettishness in these solemn phrases of the *Lettre*. Literature was an enterprise involving his body and his mind in a perilous adventure which ended in failure, as judged by human standards.

At times, key words used by Rimbaud were threateningly abstract. *Je tiens système!* for example. How can the system be interpreted? It must mean something like the dissolution of relationships or of barriers. Is the system a ruse? Is it the need to travel and thus distract his mind? Is it the ability to see other lives that are owing to each life? A gentleman, for example, Rimbaud calls an angel in *Alchimie du verbe?* Or a family he calls a *nichée de chiens?*

Readings, memories, images picked up at random turn into visions. The poet indulges in a telescoping of words, taken out of context, and converts them into something monstrous. The combining of the real and the unreal in his writing makes it inexhaustible. A poem of Baudelaire is intact, self-contained, a closed metaphysical system. It is an art that has gone past the experimental stage and one that reaches the calculated effect within the limits of prosody and metaphor. A page of Rimbaud is far more open. The music of the lines creates secret affinities between the parts. The poetry is successful as judged from other criteria, from the criteria of its limitlessness, from the elements that are incomprehensible in terms of organized and recorded experience. A poem of Baudelaire contains all that can be communicated from a given moment of the poet's consciousness. An *illumination* of Rimbaud is a force able to promote visions outside of itself. It is a laboratory in itself where the power of words is experimented with, where warnings are implicit in all the nascent images.

The major lesson of Rimbaud, both in his life and writing, is the revelation of a strong resemblance between the poet and the novelist: the moral preoccupation and the aesthetic preoccupation are similar, even if each has a different subject matter. The novelist (and the playwright) are concerned with the meaning of acts and events, with something that can be called a narration. The poet is not concerned with actions, but with the universe where actions occur. In terms of subject matter, the poet does not suffer from constraint, as compared with the novelist.

The art of the poet may well lead into the art of the camera, which has not yet begun to realize itself. The peril for the poet is the very limitlessness of his subject matter which stifles almost every poet. Only a few survive. Only a few poets are able to write poems. The art of the poet is gratuitous as compared to that of the novelist. The art without constraint of Rimbaud will now be reconsidered and felt more deeply, thanks to Beckett and Genet, and the films of Resnais and Truffaut and Godard.

At this point in the history of aesthetics, a whole revision is needed. How exasperating the absolute is, for the eye of a poet and the eye of a camera! The best poems of Jean Cocteau, and the best scenes of his film *Orphée* have something of the gratuitousness of Rimbaud's writing, where the universe is celebrated, where the whole is never sacrificed to a meager part. What would be action in a novel, Julien's entrance, for example, into the bedroom of Mathilde de la Môle, is, in *Les Illuminations* and *L'Ange Heurtebise* the celebration of poetic knowledge. Such a celebration could not have been carried out without moral considerations of man's actions and the poet's skill with the sound and the rhythm of words.

The power of verbal expression alone has never satisfied a

major poet. The courage demonstrated by Rimbaud at moments of moral crisis and metaphysical dilemmas gives him a place among the moralists of his age, as important, for example, as the place of Dostoievsky. The relationship between man and the world, and between man and the absolute, is as integral a part of *Une Saison en Enfer* as it is in Stendhal's *Le Rouge et le Noir*. The rational will and the irrational impulses in man are looked upon by Rimbaud as if they may be closer than is usually believed. *Une Saison* represents a revolution in the history of literary genres. Without its example, it would be difficult to account for some aspects of Proust's writing, of Ionesco's plays, of Resnais' films. Poetry turned to prose in Proust; and prose turned to poetry in such a work as Gide's *Les Nourritures Terrestres*.

The art of prose in the novel still remains largely the narration of events, of a succession of events. *Une Saison en Enfer* is not the narration of events, but the answers to events that have taken place, the reactions to these events. It is a work devoid of rhetorical logic, a work without the ordered rhetoric of prose. It is a text of the meeting of words in poetry, of the infinite number of suggestions that come from these encounters.

La vraie vie est absente, writes Rimbaud in *Une Saison* ("Real life is absent"). Such a phrase is a new seizure of reality. It is not expressed logically, and is, in fact, a defiance of logic. It is an opening out to systems and philosophies, to moments in *Le Soulier de satin* of Claudel, of *Fin de Partie* of Beckett, of Breton's *Nadja*. In such a sentence, the limitless action of the mind takes precedence over the physical action of man.

On the two levels of formal expression and analysis of man's conduct in moral and metaphysical spheres, *Une Saison en Enfer* has had an effect impossible to measure. It set the style for brief lapidary phrases (such as the just quoted *La vraie vie est absente*) that congeal intuitive flashes. Such a style has outmoded the elaborate oratorical commonplaces of the romantics where lengthiness is out of proportion to thought. The hard reduced phrases of Rimbaud helped to throw into disrepute the traditional syllabic verse of French poetry. Since Valéry, few poets have used the alexandrine or decasyllabic line except Cocteau, from time to time, and Aragon. But Char, Ponge, Jacob, and Saint-John Perse are among those whose poetic form is reminiscent of *Les Illuminations*.

Rimbaud's intuitions concerning the world and man's relation-ship to the world, his belief concerning the function of poetry and the art of poetry are also present in the work of writers who came after him. They have continued to explore the uncertainty of the world and to use poetry as a means of revolting against language, against that kind of language which transcribes an ordered universe when such a universe does not exist. Rimbaud made poetry into a wager. Is it possible to express an emotion in a language that can be communicated? This problem is still upper-most in poets and prose writers alike who avoid purely descrip-tive and narrative language, and language that describes only generalized sentiments.

Human reason tends always, with a certain degree of preten-tiousness, to define everything, to impose an order or an orderli-ness on everything. But the subject matter of *Une Saison* is the indefinable experience of a man's mind. It cannot be captured as the failure of common sense. Habitually the language of poetry is the narration of sensibility and emotion, but Rimbaud expresses a direct contact of a sensibility with the universe. He makes of poetic language an adventure of knowledge, an experience that is not planned, not organized, but one which comes about at random. The goal is unknown, and the means of reaching the goal are also unknown.

Rimbaud seems almost to have instituted a new requirement for the poet: a belief in an unknown world. The writing of poetry will then be the authenticity given to the existence of such a world. How different this conception of poetry is from the traditional view that poetry is ornamentation and embellishment, that it is an adornment for an idea or an emotion! The poet wills to see what is invisible. He is concerned with *revelation*, which implies, when used in this quasi-mystical sense, the revealing of what is obscure and illogical. The divine furies Plato speaks of in *The Phaedrus* are revived by Rimbaud and reasserted by him: the poet-prophet as inspired by Apollo, the poet-lover as inspired by Aphrodite and the poet-mystic as inspired by Bacchus. These are experiences of madness only when judged from an ordered existence of reason.

In his practice of poetry, that is neither exclusively sentiment nor music, Rimbaud laid the basis for a new opening out onto a supernatural world and a surreal world, an art that will be associated with a Claudel and a Char. The novelists also, a Cocteau and a Gracq, explore an unknown universe beyond the common order. In the mind's search for the absolute, which began with Baudelaire and Nerval, and continued in diverse ways with Rimbaud, Mallarmé, Claudel, and Apollinaire, poetry changed from an art of lyricism to one of inquiry and exasperation, to a search for values and metaphysical assurances. The basis is the charter as set forth in *Correspondances:* the visible world is the image of a secret universe. How can such a universe be apprehended and pierced? The *alchemy* Rimbaud alludes to is one term for an age-long quest for certainty, the survival of a tradition which parallels the history of mankind and is diffused throughout history. Man has to learn how to work back from the visible to the invisible.

Today the traditional romanticism of such poems as *Le Vallon, Moïse, Souvenir,* and such a play as *Ruy Blas,* seems inferior to the sonnets of Nerval, the stories of Nodier and *Une Saison en Enfer.* The influence of Rimbaud fashioned the future of literature and refashioned the past. The new evaluations of Nerval, Baudelaire, Balzac, and Hugo are in large part due to Rimbaud and the study that has been made of Rimbaud's texts. *Les Chants de Maldoror* are far more startling for us today, far more significant than *Jocelyn* or the *Nuit de mai.*

Between the time when the poems of Rimbaud were written and certain texts of Valéry on poetry were composed, that is, during the fifty year span of 1870 to 1920, quite literally a revolution took place in poetry, in the way poetry was looked upon. By the end of this period and at the beginning of the era when our contemporary poets today began writing, poetry was considered an essence in itself, a world in itself, separated from other essences, containing its own beauty, its own explanation, its own moral order.

The new poetry has been called a return to purity. This is not a restatement of "art for art's sake" (*l'art pour l'art*), because the goal of the new poetry is nothing that can glibly be called "aesthetic." It might be defined as the creation of a new reality. The search for the unknown, motivating the poem, is more important than the finished poem. Even Mallarmé would subscribe to this doctrine. Because of the belief that there is a reality beyond the real, the literary work will be a reflection of it, but will not be equivalent to it. This new poetic practice always seems to be on the margin of religion, always seems to testify to a religious origin.

Yes, from all the claims made by the poets themselves, there seems to be no rigid doctrine save the one belief that the invisible world exists behind the visible, and there the solutions are to be found. There the two worlds may be joined, the barriers effaced, the antinomies eliminated, the relationships established. In *Une Saison en Enfer*, the crimes that are referred to, and the vices and the anguish, are due to the absence of this relationship which poets can bring about. Poetry is therefore a belief and one that is not at all outside of what is usually called moral philosophy.

The daily habits of thought and action, the mechanically carried-out routines of life are the obstacles to what Rimbaud called the cultivation of the monstrous and what subsequent poets will name the seizure of the real and the unknown. The poet must literally learn to see a world that is invisible to most men. He will be able then to give a new meaning, a truer meaning to everything. This is the function and the revelation of the poem, and it is comparable to the revolution in the realms of the novel and the theatre where such emphasis has been placed on the unmasking of social behavior, on the lies of the human comedy that most men play in their conventional relationships.

Rimbaud first, and especially in the boldest passages of *Une Saison*, taught that art is the antidote of the familiar, the habitual, despite the fact that familiar objects are used in his poems, as they are used in still-lifes of Picasso and Braque. Poetry, in the sense that Rimbaud gives it, demolishes our useful conventions, our comfortable but false amenities. A boat speaks, in his most famous poem, and the reader senses from the start that this is no usual boat. By the end of the voyage, the boat has turned into a paper boat in a mud puddle, and the reader has moved far away from the familiar confines of his world.

Le Bateau ivre was designed to trouble, to upset, to discontent. It is in opposition to the familiar relationships we establish or that have been established for us. And it creates new relationships for our mind that reveal unsuspected meanings that henceforth we will attach to such a commonplace object as a boat. *Le Bateau ivre* illustrates the limitlessness of poetry. Poetry is what we habitually neglect, a world of limitless proportions by comparison with the limited contained world in which we live.

The word that seems out of its usual place in a poem of Rimbaud—in *Mémoire*, such words as *la soie en foule, la sphère rose, dragueur*—is there as an aid, as something we can hold on to, as on to a buoy in the sea, as an island that is stable. The principle of the esoteric presides over all poetry, and the poet is knowing or unknowing of this principle. To give meaning is a magic process: the meaning of a drunken boat, of a flight from home, of a first communion, of a buffet, of the delousing of a boy's head of hair. The absolute is unintelligible, from our limited viewpoint, but the poet plunges into it, utilizes it and finds there his freedom and the game of poetry.

Rimbaud unquestionably felt the perils of this enterprise, of this plunge into the unknown, into the absolute, and the only sound explanation of his flight from literature, is this sense of peril. He realized that poetry, which ultimately is the control of words, is initially the loss of control of a man's faculties. It is an experience of madness, an entrance into what Baudelaire called *la surnature*. It is impossible to estimate the scruples felt by Rimbaud over the poetic experience that forced him to abandon it. Mallarmé's contemplation of the white page, of that wordless absolute, is comparable to Rimbaud's sterility that followed so closely upon his career as a poet.

Other poets were able to circumvent this peril and live with it, even when they were fully aware of its reality—a Claudel, for example, and a Valéry. But all of the poets, in the wake of Rimbaud, felt the peril. Poetry does lead to a discovery of the absolute, and this can discourage poetic expression. To penetrate into the unknown is to reach a place where expression is not necessary. The adventure is what counts and not its narrative. Rimbaud stopped at a point of greatness and courage, whereas others fall back from such a point in order to remain poets.

The experience of delirium is usually followed by the ambition to write. The traces of a great struggle are in Rimbaud's writings, of a man's confrontation with mystery, of the prophet who came face to face with the unspeakable. As a *voyant*, Rimbaud destroyed all appearances, and as a poet he wrote down some of his hallucinations. But this method leads straight to madness, in terms of the world.

Rimbaud fixed the definition of poetry which the best poets

have followed since his day. Poetry is not ornamentation. It is something more than even metaphorical beauty. It is the discovery of a new relationship between things. This is more of a revolution in human conduct than has been realized, because the relationship in question is one between man and the world, between man and man, and between man and God. All of these relationships are revised and reconsidered in the art of the poet-*voyant.*

PART II

Transcendence of Language

4. Mallarmé's Purity

THE DIFFERENCE BETWEEN what Mallarmé represented to the world at the time of his death, in 1898, and what he represents today, seventy years later, has the proportions of an almost miraculous change. It is an alteration that justifies and illuminates Mallarmé's celebrated line about Poe and any poet who is finally changed into himself by eternity: *Tel qu'en lui-même enfin l'Eternité le change.*

For the academic world in 1898, Stéphane Mallarmé was a teacher of English in the lycées of Paris, who had asked in 1894 for an early retirement, to the relief of his officers and superiors. He was granted his retirement after thirty years of teaching and a pedagogic record which, in all fairness, can be summarized only as mediocre. For the general public in Paris, interested in literature and art, and for the journalist critics, those called in French *critiques du boulevard*, Mallarmé was a dreamer, a dilettante, an aesthete (to use only the polite names) who willfully obscured his infrequent publications in order to make them incomprehensible to any normally minded, normally constituted reader.

But fortunately there remained a third group, far more restricted in numbers than the other two: the circle of devoted friends, most of whom were either poets or painters. Many of them attended the Tuesday evening gatherings in Mallarmé's apartment on the rue de Rome. A few of them, especially a few of the painters, such as Manet, Whistler, Berthe Morisot, he called on regularly in their own studios. These rare individuals found Mallarmé to be a loyal warm friend, whose speech, whose conversation was unsurpassed in brilliance in a capital already famed for the verbal wit and profundity of its inhabitants. Those who were closest to him and who heard him from week to week, knew that this brilliant speaker was a kind of contemplative who meditated and actually thought before speaking. One after the other, both those belonging to the older group of friends, Dujardin, Fontainas, Mockel, and the younger disciples, Gide, Valéry, Gauguin, and Vuillard, acknowledged that the speech of Mallarmé and his comprehending devotion had helped to teach them who they were and what they were capable of. After the creation of his own work, Mallarmé's greatest role was the revealer of genius. If he was not an able pedagogue in the classroom, he was surely a pedagogue in one of the highest senses of the calling, the gentle attentive pedagogue for some of the most gifted poets and painters in the late nineteenth century.

When, in the second decade of this century, Albert Thibaudet requested permission to present a thesis on Mallarmé at the Sorbonne, he was turned down as if he had perpetrated a bad joke. But independently of the Sorbonne, he did publish his study—a true pioneer work on Mallarmé—in 1925. Since that time, during the last forty years, theses, books, and articles on him have multiplied. There is today a vast literature on Mallarmé, almost exclusively concerned with an effort to interpret his poetry. By his most penetrating critics, his work is seen to represent the final stage and perhaps the most dazzling achievement in a veritable revolution concerning the meaning and the interpretation of poetry.

What counts the most in the art of poetry is the spiritual state, the lucid state of enthusiasm or even of delirium, which it is able to create or which was present at its origins. Poetry therefore becomes for man a remarkable instrument of discovery of what is most secret in him, of what the mystics refer to as the inner life or what the psychologists refer to as the subconscious or even repressed life. It is the life in man which his reason does not know or acknowledge, and which his ordinary speech, the language he uses daily, is unable to express. All this is to say—Mallarmé enunciated this belief in many ways and on many occasions—that poetry is something akin to magic. It is a talisman which may open up the way to a metaphysical life in man. After passing through the two phases of individualistic and social poetry with the early romantics and Victor Hugo, it became, especially with Mallarmé, a metaphysical exercise. It is certain that Mallarmé would not have reached this high position in modern poetry without the examples before him of Hugo, Baudelaire, Nerval, and Rimbaud.

Mallarmé married the arts without hesitation. His defense of the new painting in his day was undertaken with as much fervor as his defense of the new poetry. He used the metaphor in a congenital kind of familiarity and it mattered very little whether he was speaking of a poem or of a painting. Once the symbolist poet André Fontainas approached Mallarmé at a gathering and spoke to him about a magnificent tree in a painting of Claude Monet, which he had just seen exhibited in the window of a gallery. Mallarmé concurred in enthusiasm on the new painting of the tree, and said, "Yes, it's a superb Monet, a peacock burning the landscape with its spread-out tail." (*Ce Monet superbe, un paon brûlant le paysage de sa queue étalée.*) This analogy was startling, in the good Mallarmé tradition, but a bystander, overhearing it, chided the poet. "Come now, Mallarmé," he said, "is the picture a peacock or is it a tree? What possible relationship can there be?" The art of Claude Monet had a very special appeal for Mallarmé. It is personal, like Mallarmé's own art, very willful, fragmentary, fleeting, with its ecstatic play of light on fields, stones, water. Once, in speaking with Mme Berthe Morisot, Mallarmé said he was happy to live in the same period in history as Monet. (*Je suis heureux de vivre à la même époque que Monet.*)

Victor Hugo addressed Mallarmé with the words, *mon cher poète impressionniste*, not only because the poet was a friend of impressionist painters, notably Manet, but because his art bears relationship with theirs. The exterior world, for the impressionists, is knowable within the limitation of man's sensorial perceptions. The "impressions" which they wished to give on their canvases were the immediate result without adulteration of a visual perception at one time. The word "sensation" describes more accurately than "impression" the more complex experience which Mallarmé wanted to translate and communicate in his verse. But both the painting and the poem are created with a full awareness of the fleetingness of our sensations. The notations will be rapid, the shadings will be delicate and faint. What counts for both poet and painter is the first vision which was the real experience, the vision which revealed in a flash a new meaning of the world or of some part of the world.

The authority accorded to the "line" in the paintings of Ingres, and the authority accorded to the "color" in the paintings of Delacroix correspond in a rather striking way to the art of the Parnassian poets, predecessors and contemporaries of Mallarmé, who emphasized the contour of the material object they described, who rendered it with as much precision and accuracy as language could afford and whose colors were as strong and dramatic as the corresponding colors on the canvases of Delacroix. The substitution for line and color was what the impressionists called the divisioning of color, the new prestige they found in the infinite number of possible accents or accentuations of pure pigment. The art of symbolist poetry, as formulated by Stéphane Mallarmé, strives for the same kind of subtlety in nuance, of suggestiveness in the impression rendered.

The value and even the beauty of the object itself underwent a radical change, a degradation from the viewpoint of the earlier painters. The object, as it had been painted by an Ingres or a Delacroix lost its immediate significance and began serving as a mere pretext for the rendering of light or luminosity surrounding the object. The painter became the lover of light and air. He learned how to depict an object by means of the numberless reflections of light on the object. Likewise, in the art of Mallarmé, the object, no matter what it was initially, a swan, a fan, a vase, a room, ended by being almost concealed or diminished by the sensations created by the language and generated by the verbal expression of the metaphor.

The object exists in an impressionist painting and in a Mallarmé sonnet, but it does not exist for and by itself. It creates, in the art of painting, a luminous concept, an "impression" coming from the object and reducing the object's importance in the fleeting lights and shadings it is composed of. This hope of painting the very instability of matter and of capturing a single moment in its varied tonalities of light, was far too ambitious in its absolute sense. And likewise, the goal of Mallarmé, to discover and write the mysterious Orphic meaning of the world, was destined to failure according to his own measurement and realizations. Both painters and poets alike embarked upon a veritable renovation of technique. Whether it was the flesh of a nude or the grass of a field, the total effect in its reflections and shadows was one of mobility. "Every landscape is a state of the soul," was an impressionist maxim which would have a very real significance for Mallarmé.

Soon after the turn of the century, Mallarmé's influence was felt on the new poetry, about the time when Cézanne began influencing the new painters. These two artists who hardly knew one another have probably exerted the most telling influences on modern art. Cubism, particularly, owed a great deal to the plastic forms in Cézanne's paintings, and the importance which Mallarmé paid to signs or symbols in his poems encouraged a comparable boldness in the cubist painters. In its richest period, cubism demonstrated that painting was a kind of writing for which new signs had to be invented.

The central lesson in Mallarmé's aesthetics concerns the incantatory power of words. He placed a veritable faith in the magic quality of words and the cubists placed a comparable faith in the inventions of their colored signs as creations of reality. In his very important two-page essay called *Magie*, Mallarmé points out that the medieval study of alchemy, when it disappeared with the Middle Ages, left in its wake, for the modern mind, two ways of thought or two studies: aesthetics, on the one hand, and economics, on the other (*économie politique*). Without hesitation he claims that alchemy was the "glorious and mysterious forerunner of economics." The philosophical stone, referred to so often in the Middle Ages, whose function was to produce gold, announced, according to Mallarmé's interpretation, in the new world of finance what is called credit and what precedes capital or reduces it to the humble state of mere money!

The poet goes on to acknowledge that, contrary to the practices and beliefs of his contemporaries, he has on many occasions announced the secret equivalence that has always been maintained between poetry and witchcraft. What the poet does in effect is very close to a magical creation. In a deliberate darkness he calls up an object that has been silenced, by means of words that are allusive and not direct. Then what happens next is truly magic. By the enchantment of letters, placed by the mysterious recipe of the poet's art and the poet's game, the words begin to glow and mean until the illusion they evoke is equivalent to what the eyes of a man can see in the material world. *Le vers, trait incantatoire*, Mallarmé calls it. "The verse, an act of incantation." The occupation of the poet, quite in keeping with the ancient occupation of the alchemist, is the measuring or dosage of essences, of what we sometimes call sentiments, whether they be wicked or good. The medieval book of magic would mean nothing to the uninitiate. Only the magician or the alchemist was able to apply the formula and concoct the potions. In the same way, the secret of modern poems is printed on the pages of the book and the illiterate will make nothing out of that human artifice, called, for example, a sonnet. But the leaves of the poet's book, insists Mallarmé, are the "dispensers of the charm." And he uses the word "charm" in its full magical connotation.

Recent critics and biographers of Mallarmé have tried to discover the philosophical books and authors that might have served as the foundation of his aesthetics. But Mallarmé was probably not an assiduous reader of the German metaphysicians, not even of Fichte and Hegel, with whom his name has been associated. The opening line of one of his early poems, *Brise Marine*, is not at all to be taken in its literal sense:

> *La chair est triste, hélas, et j'ai lu tous les livres.*

He doubtless read very little of technical philosophy, and had no characteristics of the erudite, which Flaubert, for example, possessed. He was of course aware of the philosophical concepts current in his day, but his mind deepened by means of perceptions rather than dialectics. Pascal would have called Mallarmé *un esprit de finesse*. Like his friends the painters, he thought more readily with images than with ideas. The series of seemingly unrelated or discontinuous images which many of his poems demonstrate place them beside the work of postimpressionists, cubists, and surrealists.

The comparatively few poems he published, his avoidance of clichés and of verbal facility, his unwillingness to hasten the writing of any line or of any stanza were elements of his exessive scrupulosity. Unlike those writers for whom writing was a constant career, a Voltaire or a Victor Hugo, Mallarmé was one of those poets, men like Baudelaire and Valéry, whose far rarer productions were the result of certain privileged moments in a lifetime. As with the painters who were his friends, and with the great painters who followed him, Mallarmé had only a few subjects in his poems. Like a portrait painter, he waited for commissions. His poems were of circumstances.

In the early years, what seemed to him poetic sterility, or lack of material, was the cause of a great personal anxiety. It became one of the personal principles of his aesthetics. Poems like *Le Pitre châtié*, *L'Azur*, *Les Fenêtres*, all testify to the merging of a personal anguish with an aesthetic belief. The flowers, referred to at the beginning of *L'Azur*, have a despairing kind of beauty about them because the poet is incapable of incorporating it in his verse. The poet's struggle with the white page is comparable to the painter's struggle with the white canvas. The actual reference, again in *L'Azur*, to the "empty jar of rouge" with which the poet might have painted the "tragic idea," is borrowed from the practice of the painter. The infrequent sonnets of Mallarmé and the still-lifes of a Braque, for example, represent a difficult attitude toward nature and the familiar objects of a room. The newer artist, both poet and painter, is more isolated from the world in his almost obsessive treatment of a few familiar objects and figures and scenes. The often-recurring treatment of the same objects in the sonnets of Mallarmé and the paintings of Picasso lent itself to the art of deforming the presences and the objects.

Symbolism and impressionism both were reactions against the data, the given subject material, the rigor in order and composition of an Ingres or a Leconte de Lisle. The so-called cult of obscurity, as opposed to an oratorical or expository art, is certainly to some degree the art of doubt and nuance, an art based upon a predilection for ellipsis, which was long ago defined by Boileau as a precept for classical art: "The secret of boring the reader is to tell him everything." Mallarmé, in the very title of his collected essays, *Divagations*, warns that he will turn the reader's mind from the usual ways and channels. He was fully aware that his poetry was an arduous exercise for the mind and a delicate testing of the sensibility.

Mallarmé's habit of living in his apartment more than in the world parallels his withdrawal from popular literature and his creation of a highly esoteric poetry. The fans, vases, books, and bibelots of his parlor helped to constitute the scene of a refuge not unlike the "blue room" of Mme de Rambouillet, where manners and the art of poetry were preserved from the roughness of the court of Henri IV. Beyond any doubt, Stéphane Mallarmé believed that the highest or the purest expressions of art were accessible to very few. His faith in the potential power of the solitary poet almost equates him with the philosopher. He is an idealist in the very simple sense that he idealizes whatever he sees: a book, a painting, a ballet. Poetry is not composed by naming objects but by realizing a synthesis between silence and speech. The symbol, rather than describing the object, suggests it by creating a net of analogies and relationships. A similar treatment of objects is apparent in postimpressionist painting in France. Both poet and painter call upon the creative activity of the reader and spectator to conceive the fullness of these analogies and relationships.

Words have familiar meanings, and this fact represented for Mallarmé the constant trap or obstacle to the creation of his kind of poem. Likewise, the objects painted by Braque and Matisse were all recognizable. Yet the goal, for both kinds of artists, was to suggest rather than signify. Mallarmé turned more and more to the negative word, the word of absence, as in his toast sonnet,

> *Rien, cette écume, vierge vers*
> (*Salut*),

and the use of a series of seemingly disjointed or discontinuous images, as in the sonnet on Baudelaire's tomb. The successive images, flaming and fulgurant, in *La Chevelure vol d'une flamme*, present a solemn exercise of relationships which have to be seized by the reader. Such demands on the reader are not unlike the demands on the spectator implied in such a painting as *Les demoiselles d'Avignon* of Picasso.

What the symbol really is in poetry is lucidly apparent in Mallarmé's faun: a search for reality in its total aspect which is distant, elusive, inaccessible perhaps. The far-off nudity of the nymphs as they appear either in the real forest or in the forest of the faun's dream illustrates the inner vision of poetry in its almost despairing purity.

The difficult and often painful existence of the poet and the artist, such as we associate with a Baudelaire, a Mallarmé, a Cézanne, and a Van Gogh, with its failures, exile, sadness, seem a necessary part of the scheme whereby he will see the purer, more spiritual vision of things and their relationships. Proust has spoken in detail about the disparity between the artist's life and his work. Alfred de Vigny's ivory tower is the symbol of the poet's suffering and dignity. Mallarmé's salon and Verlaine's café were in one sense their ivory tower.

Mallarmé's critical pages on the different arts are surprisingly precise and analytical. He begins always with the art object itself, whether it be the theatre, painting, poetry, ballet. He does not discuss the idea of the art or generalities about the art before he analyzes specific works and examples. And he always starts with the contemporary art of his own time which he considered more devoutly and profoundly than other aestheticians. Each art expresses, in its own way and with its own means, the total universe. Each art is therefore capable of reaching truth. In one of his pages on the art of dance, Mallarmé says that with every step and every pose of the dancer, the spectator has the right to ask, "What does that mean?" The ballerina in the execution of her dance is able to reveal the bareness of concepts. Art is an opening out on to the universe, a surpassing or a transmutation of the immediate or the sensible or the material.

The thought of the poet and painter, for Mallarmé the idealist, tends to become eternal as it releases itself from the material world. The contradiction of all art, as visible in a sonnet of Mallarmé as in a painting of Renoir, is the need to express the eternal by means of the material. But in the final work, art reaches truth and the artist moves beyond his condition of man relentlessly depicted in his sleep and in his death. The sensitivity of the poet and the vision of the artist isolate a few aspects of the world of matter and give them an expression. They are the flowers not one of which will fade. *Fleurs dont nulle ne se fane. (Toast funèbre.)* Mallarmé affirms, and Proust affirms the same thought in his pages on the painter Elstir, that what has not been expressed in art will in the course of time return to the void.

In the history of poetry, and specifically of French poetry, Mallarmé represents today a turning point, and a point of achievement. His art and his theory are of such a nature that his

moment has the significance of the *trobar clus* of the troubadours
in the twelfth century, of the Platonist poets of the Renaissance,
of romanticism and the Parnassian ideal which immediately preceded him in the nineteenth century. By his concentration of
language, by his skill with ellipsis, he utilized language and
purified it. Only the most efficacious words remained in the
finished line to designate the object and the way in which
the object was seen. This purification of language was such,
that the object revealed was elevated to a metaphysical value:
the swan, the punished clown, the helmet of the girl em-
press, reach meanings far beyond the usual. This is Mallarmé's
angelism: the flight of words, the experience of Icarus, in their
effort to reach a purified region nearer the source of language.

A poem is a privileged moment when words are revealed in a
new context, in an unusual lighting, an unusual drama: the sun-
flooded room of faun, in the forest, or the cold midnight of Hérodiade in her tower. But whatever the object, a lascivious faun, an
hieratic princess, a garden of irises, an empty bibelot, the theme
of the poem is always the same, the poetic act. The making of a
poem, that is, the conversion of human experience or thought
into words, is equally present in Mallarmé's art, with the ultimate
discovery of a metaphor which translates and supports the experience. Baudelaire was undoubtedly a master for Mallarmé in this
process in which the work itself and the thought concerning the
work are fused. The hair of Baudelaire's Jeanne is a black ocean
containing dreams of sails and masts:

> *Tu contiens, mer d'ébène, un éblouissant rêve*
> *De voiles, de rameurs, de flammes et de mâts.*

And the hair of the girl Mallarmé celebrates is the flight of a
flame, a torch of desire:

> *vol d'une flamme à l'extrême*
> *Occident de désirs.*

The words, pressed one against the other, in a tight formula,
sustain the object and multiply its beauty, as they separate it in
the poem from everything else. With them, the poet lives differently. The limitlessness of sensation, the waywardness of experience are converted into a verbal unity. Even the rhythm of the
formula and the rhyme are aids in this unifying process of poetry

because they too answer immemorial needs of the poet to reach some form of oneness. This dream of the poet is his torment, this realization of experiences that are fleeting and fragmentary and dispersed. The poem is not their proof but a witness to them.

The language which the poet discovers and creates is a bond between himself, his own consciousness, and the consciousness of the world about him. The uncertainty of human action is made into the firm fixed language of metaphor, and there the poet welcomes and strengthens all the hesitancies, all the uncertainties, all the torments of human experience. When the poem is achieved, that which is most personal in a poet enters into a strange impersonal work. T. S. Eliot in his early essay *Tradition and the Individual Talent,* gives firm expression to this belief concerning poetry, to which the major poems of Mallarmé are brilliant testimonials. Poetry is at once a deeply personal art and the art by means of which the poet moves out of himself to others, and in which he demonstrates not only himself but the stranger that is in himself. The poet is the one whom others welcome because he ends always, in that chemistry his art represents, by saying something he had not proposed saying. He opens up to the world a mysterious richness of forms, canals, waterways that lead from some invisible source to the arid lands of our minds.

In his letter to Verlaine, in 1885, the important text called *Autobiographie*, Mallarmé calls the book, the ideal book he hopes to write: "the Orphic explanation of the earth." (*Le Livre, explication orphique de la Terre.*) Metaphors are in reality metamorphoses and transmutations, and thus the poet, creator of metaphors, is a kind of alchemist and magician. Mallarmé's ambitions in the early years of his career, between 1865 and 1870, were of such a nature, that they induced in him the beginnings of a form of madness. The attempt to recreate the world, by means of the poetic word, is a quasi-divine ambition. Such a dream is a peril. Any poetic enterprise as vast as Mallarmé's is a mental hazard.

The problem of being (*être*) tormented Mallarmé as much as it has anyone. The problem of how to be in the world, how to live in the world, was of such a torment that he had to find some way by which to trick the ironic challenge. Poetry was the way he chose. He believed that the words of a poet, their necessity, might cover up the endless irony deriving from the conflict between the aspirations of man to the absolute and the obstacles of mortality. The finiteness of man and the world remain as permanent mockeries of man's spirit in its flight upward. *L'Azur*, one of the early poems, is on this mockery, which is Mallarmé's personal drama:

> *Où fuir? Et quelle nuit hagarde*
> *Jeter, lambeaux, jeter sur ce mépris navrant?*

Mallarmé will not feel differently when writing the rich sonnets in the latter part of his life.

Poetry is a purification of language, and it comes about also as intermediary between man and the abundance of things that surround him and even obsess him. Objects in the world multiply in an hallucinatory rhythm. Their excess may block off the vision of the original object. In *Prose pour des Esseintes*, Mallarmé focuses on this drama of growth, of bigness and encumbrance which threatens the poet's vision and which hides the name of beauty, *Pulchérie*, as he calls it in the text. The flowers that multiply in the island garden testify to this threat of the physical world, of its impingement on the spirit, and they testify also to the words that press on the poet, that multiply in their effort to speak endlessly things that have already been said, and fill the hours of living with repetitions. The poet is the man practicing a strict surveillance over words, who arrests their spontaneous hallucinatory growth, in order to make of them a single word, a new and total poem which will appear foreign to man's habitual language, strange and incantatory: *un mot total, neuf, étranger à la langue et comme incantatoire.*

Existence has its obvious limitations for man, but Mallarmé queries whether art has any limitations. The absolute which haunts his mind he looks for in poetry. In a letter to Aubanel, he compares his early poems to the strands of a spider's web: they represent the permanent themes and preoccupations of his life work. In the image he describes, he will be the spider who will merely continue strengthening the same threads, embroidering with fuller designs those already established. This prediction in the letter was accurate. The early themes, recognizably Baudelairian, continued to be used by Mallarmé: *l'azur*, for example, designating the ideal, the unknowable dream and hence the anguish of never reaching the ideal or of never filling the void. *L'Azur* is related to the pane of glass (*la vitre*) in *Fenêtres*, and to the water image of *Le Pitre châtié*.

Such a major theme as *l'azur* is supported by clusters of related themes which give to the poems a kinship, a significant relatedness. "Wing" (*aile*), "swan" (*cygne*), "flight" (*vol*), as well as "water" (*eau*) and "plunge" (*plongeon*) bear evident relationships. The poem *Hérodiade*, as many interpreters of Mallarmé have pointed out, is an arsenal of themes because the princess feels herself exiled from the absolute, from the totality of things. Mallarmé's art is based upon secret affinities between words. As such a word *fleur* ("flower") leads to "flower collection" (*herbier*), and from there to the "Word" (*le Verbe*) and the "book of magic" (*le grimoire*) and the "books of rituals" (*le rituel*); the poet's center, his ego, grows more and more impersonal. The quest for language replaces the initial anguish, of an ontological nature, which had instigated the quest. Mallarmé renewed the dogma of language as the creative word. As this Word grows into its own power and luminosity, it is destined to exclude all the torments and joys of the human spirit. The romantic elements in the poem disappear, and the formal elements claim the attention of the reader. The theme ends by becoming the poem, the joy of the Word.

Mallarmé is fully conscious of the immemorial prestige of words: the meanings they have today in their human context, and the more esoteric meanings that still cling to them from their uses in a remote past. The moral theme, so strong in *Les Fleurs du Mal* diminishes in Mallarmé's poems. The theory of verbal incantation, defined by Baudelaire, is more fully applied by Mallarmé, until the power of the words, with their associations and their relatedness replace the moral allusions. This would be a major distinction between Baudelaire's *Le Voyage*, where the various kinds of voyage are moral quests, and Mallarmé's *Prose pour des Esseintes*, where the island voyage is the poet's quest for beauty. The reality of Paris in such a poem as *Le Cygne* is the basis of Baudelaire's art, whereas the real world is nullified in *Toast funèbre* as Mallarmé celebrates the poetic universe created by the poet.

If the obsessions of the poet are similar in Baudelaire and Mallarmé, they are far more disguised in Mallarmé where the words,

like masks, form a network of images. The drama of poetic creation is bare in Baudelaire, but in Mallarmé it is projected into the
forest scene of the nymphs where the faun, playing his pipes,
wonders whether he can perpetuate his desire with music or
satisfy his desire by separating the nymphs one from the other. In
Bénédiction, Baudelaire adumbrates the poet's drama almost in
the form of biography, whereas in *L'Après-midi d'un faune*, it is
recast into the age-old myth of the soul eager to know itself.
Mallarmé is not a metaphysician in any literal sense, but he is a
poet haunted by metaphysics.

The duality of man's nature and the conflicts that arise from
this duality are present in most of the poems. The violence of the
combat existed before the action of the poem, but it pervades
the poem which is the *dénouement* of the action, the failure of the
struggle. The duality is clearly announced in *Prose pour des Esseintes*, as a duality of actors:

> *Nous fûmes deux, je le maintiens.*

It is the duality of human nature in the swan who remembers
his neglected duty of flight, of soaring into space,

> *vols qui n'ont pas fui,*

and yet who looks scornfully at his prison of ice,

> *Il s'immobilise au songe froid de mépris.*

The ambition to reach the absolute is a predestined failure. The
irises (*iridées*, both *iris* and *idées*) multiply and grow to such an
extent that the will of the poet in his island adventure of *Prose* is
frustrated. The warm hour of noon for the faun-musician is in
reality an hour of sterility when he sings of passion rather than
experiences passion. The violence of passion preceded the faun's
afternoon, and the violence of quest preceded the moment of
the swan's immobilization in the icy lake. The counterpoint of
words, of Mallarmé's words, is the final trap, the final capitula-
tion, where action is held in a steadfast grip and the cry of
passion is modulated into a single clear melodic line. The darkness
and the silence of evening are always just beyond the poem's last
line. They are waiting for the last line to be said. They are
waiting to take over.

But Mallarmé translated into his poems a human experience and not a system of metaphysics. He understood the full implications of the poetic doctrine as defined by Baudelaire and Poe: of poetry believed to be the object of beauty, of a poem to be looked upon as the search for an effect. Such a poetic doctrine, however important it is, would not fully account for the great poems of Mallarmé. The personal crisis of 1866, which seems to have been largely of a metaphysical nature, plays a vital role in the creation of the future poems. The discovery of such a concept as the void (*le néant*) is as important as Mallarmé's decision to avoid in his poems mere analyses of impressions and depictions of sentiments.

To the experience of sterility, evident in such a poem as *l'Azur*, succeeded the experience of purity. *Hériodade* is perhaps the work that best designates this very marked change in Mallarmé's poetic process. What had once been for the romantics and even for Verlaine, poetry of the ephemeral, became, for Mallarmé, an experience cast in the form of a drama, a drama of the mind in its search for the absolute.

The dreams of the mind can represent on the one hand a splendor of form and dazzling exterior beauty, but they represent, on the other hand, the void. The beauty of the world and its absence are fused into the subject matter of Mallarmé's poems. The poem is the dream, at once real and unreal. To recall a dream is to blow it up, as the faun blows into the empty skin of the grape after he has sucked out the juice. The notes of his flute are the drops of cool water falling over the forest scene. His own breath in the instrument takes the place of real wind in the scene of the poem's action. The music played by the faun in the forest sustains his dream of reduction which has vanished, and in exactly the same way the poem sustains and prolongs the poet's dream that has vanished. A poem is inevitably, for Mallarmé, a poem of absence. The paradox of all poetry is thus clearly defined: the words chosen by the poet for the rhythm of his verse give the impression of life, but in reality they celebrate the exaltation of a dream.

Igitur is probably Mallarmé's most profound commentary on his personal crisis of 1866. No other text of his evokes so much with so little. Mallarmé trains his reader to imagine the poem's action. This poet of sterility is the richest because his art leads the reader to the confines of the mind, of philosophical thought, of that limitless realm that lies beyond the real world. Whereas the typical romantic poet, Hugo, for example, practices the fecundity of words, Mallarmé practices, with a sparseness of words, the fecundity of the imagination.

Visions spring from words. A poem is a human invention. When it is read sympathetically, it begins the extraordinary adventure of recreating itself, and of creating what is beyond itself. Whatever object is the symbol is merely a kind of investiture, and from it something unreal emerges which is the real poem. A vase, for example, as in Mallarmé's sonnet, calls up the idea of a flower.

> *Surgi de la croupe et du bond*
> *D'une verrerie éphémère.*

The absence of the flower is a poem created by the mind of the reader. But the poet's poem remains on the page after the dream of the reader, or the vision, or the experience destined to disappear.

> *Une rose dans les ténèbres.*

The poet sees this rose in the vase that has no flower. As in the silence of his inner self, he hears the poem before he writes it. The kind of sonnet Mallarmé created comes after many births that did not take place.

The poems of Mallarmé and his teaching about poetry mark a drastic change in the history of an art. There is French poetry before Mallarmé and French poetry after him. Poetry before him, on the whole, translated sentiments and ideas, and usually without ambiguity. Poetry after him is more difficult because it conforms to other powers of language, because it is the expression of mysterious aspects of existence. The charm and the processes of Mallarmé are visible in such different and original poets as Apollinaire, Valéry, Claudel, Eluard. He created an art form that is antioratorical and antisocial. By writing a poetry in which the concrete is always vanishing, he created what might be called a countercreation. The flower he holds up in his verse is not a flower, it is the one absent from all bouquets: *l'absente de tous bouquets.*

5. Valéry's Dream of Narcissus

THE SOURCE and the explanation of every significant poem are the entire life of the poet and his reactions to the world about him. The meaningful lines of a major poem are answers to problems that the poet has asked himself and that the world has asked him; or they are echoes of phrases often repeated by his subconscious self or persistent sentences that have guided his conscience.

The art, the temperament, the intellect, and struggles of Paul Valéry are all present in *Fragments du Narcisse*. Composed between 1919 and 1922, and published in *Charmes* of 1922, it is an exercise, and one of the most brilliant he ever wrote, on a theme that obsessed him throughout his life, both in the narrow sense of the Greek myth and in the broader philosophical sense of the "self." There is an earlier text and a later text on the subject of Narcissus. *Narcisse parle*, a sonnet of 1890, went through many versions before it was published in *Album de vers anciens*, in 1920. Almost at the end of his life, he wrote *Cantate du Narcisse* for the composer Germaine Taillefer, in 1938. These poems, and especially *Fragments du Narcisse*, and the comments Valéry made on them, and his more general observations on the study of the self, form his autobiography, the kind of autobiography, devoid of specific details of dates and events, that he would have approved.

Between 1890 and 1891, Valéry was a law student in Montpellier, but his passion for poetry dominated his life. His first meetings with Pierre Louÿs and André Gide, which have been described in many books, were significant events in the history of French poetry, because the young Paris esthetes encouraged Valéry in his love for poetry, and soon introduced him to Mallarmé who became, avowedly, his master. Gide, in his *Nourritures Terrestres*, speaks of the Jardin des Plantes in Montpellier where he and his friend Ambroise (Paul-Ambroise Valéry) used to walk and discuss poetry. The self, *le moi*, was a central theme in their conversation, a notion that fascinated both, and which both, in very different ways, were to explore in their writings. Whereas Gide will tend to explore the ego and reach some knowledge of it, some awareness of his deepest motives and desires, Valéry will tend to look upon the unity of the self as something that is foreign to his conscious self. In the domain of consciousness, Valéry will always be struck by the principle of the multiple uncertainties that form and inhabit the self. But *le moi* is a commodious notion for him. He will always cherish it. He will always be drawn to the dangerous beauty of self-knowledge.

Such a word as "dangerous" imposes itself because self-knowledge appears vain. On the one hand, knowledge is godlike and serene and stable; whereas the nature of man is always human and restless and variable. Knowledge, or the hope of reaching knowledge, is vain because of the antinomy between the inaccessibility of absolute knowledge and the variability of human nature.

But Valéry is not only a thinker, he is also a poet, and he has written extensively on poetry as a craft and a technique, on what poetic composition means, on what meaning such a word as inspiration has for him, on the purpose of poetry and on its limitations. Central among the leading articles of his belief is his commentary on the principal source or inspiration for a poem. He claims that inspiration for a poem does not come to him from an emotion, but rather from an idea that flashes through his mind spontaneously and that can be provoked by the most banal type of happening: the poet's encounter with a man carrying a ladder, or his encounter with a woman returning from the market.

It is comparatively easy to classify Valéry as a moralist, as a theorist, and as a technician in those passages of his work where he is obviously that. The function of Valéry as poet, and the way in which he undertakes the writing of poetry, are infinitely more difficult to understand. Landscapes, the shape and the poses of the human body, the impulses of the psyche are themes in the poems of Valéry. His poetic method would involve a study of the way in which he has observed these subjects and the way in which he has transcribed them in an art that is always recognizably his. Valéry is constantly establishing an opposition between life and the, mind of the poet observing life. But he is also constantly establishing a connection between life and the poet's mind. Life never comes to a completion (until, of course, the event of death) and a poem is therefore never completed, until the poet's death arrests all future work on it. Valéry is always tempted to look upon his anxiety as his real profession, which precedes the writing of a poem, which helps in the writing and which continues after every stage of composition the poem reaches. *Angoisse, mon véritable métier!*

The very personal incidents in Valéry's life are not known with any certainty. In 1892, he suffered over love for a woman, but there is no trace of this passion in his early poems. There is probably some trace of it in *Fragments du Narcisse*, in the second part of the poem, but this is so universalized and transposed that it is not the autobiography of Paul Valéry, but a poet's creation. Valéry, always showed scorn for the trivia in a man's life, for the incidental and the transitory. At any rate, it would seem that the summer night in Genoa, in 1892, when the young poet underwent a moment of illumination, did mark a change in him and resulted in a decision to give up everything, including the writing of poetry, in order to make progress in self-knowledge (*pour l'avancement en soi-même*). He began a period of study, of self-analysis, of rigorous introspection, in order to answer the general question of who he was and Nietzsche's question of "what is the potentiality of man?"

The inner life of a man thus becomes a kind of spectacle which he observes as a spectator and in which he is the subject of the play and the actor. This is precisely the complex triple drama of Narcissus. What began for Valéry as an exercise of meditation and contemplation was ultimately converted into a literary work, and notably into such a poem as *Fragments du Narcisse*. As the

method of contemplation developed and matured, so did the desire to recast what was seen. Such a desire, for a poet, is his
"poetics," his method of giving reality to the creatures and the
creations of his mind. A poem is destined, not to the poet, but to
the reader in any age to come. And the reader is in a far more
advantageous position to understand the secrets of the poem than
the poet himself. The composition of the poem, which is the
bringing to life of a secretive vision of the self, forces the poet to
revelations of which he may be quite unaware. A self-portrait is a
portrait which the author will not fully recognize, but which will
reveal him to the reader or the spectator.

The poetic language used by Valéry in all the poems of
Charmes, where *Fragments du Narcisse* occupies a central position, is both a purified speech from which all unnecessary elements have been discarded, and a speech of liberation when
the sentiment is allowed to grow to its fullest intensity. In
Valéry's career, these poems followed his long silence and they
all testify to the intellectual ambition which was the reason for
the long silence. The idea of a poem, its theme, its subject matter,
is not its purpose. A poem must go beyond what it affirms, otherwise it is prose, language for mere communication. The
poems of Valéry demand the full creative powers of the reader.
He will have to reconstruct what has been said in the poem,
because of the many possibilities of meaning. This art is the summation of a rhetorical tradition which begins with Baudelaire and
continues with Mallarmé and Rimbaud in France.

When, in 1912, Gide asked his friends to collect Valéry's
poems and publish them in a volume, Valéry agreed and said he
wished to write one more poem to be included with the early
poems. Between 1912 and 1917, he worked on *La Jeune Parque*,
which was published separately in 1917. This "exercise" which
turned out longer than he had planned, had revived his taste for
the writing of poetry. *Album de vers anciens*, the collection of
early pieces, appeared in 1920. Between 1917 and 1922, Valéry
wrote the poems for which he used the general title *Charmes* and
which was published in 1922. The somewhat mysterious word
charmes, from the Latin *carmina*, means primarily poems, but
it also means magic or enchantment. It therefore designates the
primitive magical function of speech. A poem is a "charm," an
alliance of sound and meaning, destined to bewitch the reader's

senses and his mind. Valéry often referred to the chance accidents in life that sometimes determine a career or a work of art. Gide's request in 1912 that the poems be collected did precipitate a return to the writing of poetry and ultimately to the composition of *Charmes*.

In a corner of the Jardin des Plantes in Montpellier is an inscription: *narcissa placandis manibus* ("to appease the shades of Narcissa"), used by Valéry as an epigraph to his early poem *Narcisse parle*. This Narcissa was the daughter of the English poet Young who, suffering from tuberculosis, had come to Montpellier to consult with the eminent physicians of the medical faculty and enjoy the sunlight of Provence. She died soon after coming to Montpellier and a gardener dug her grave in an isolated corner of the public garden. In using this inscription for *Narcisse parle*, Valéry deliberately confused or fused the sad modern story of Young's daughter with the Greek myth of the youth who fell in love with his own reflection.

In his early years in Montpellier, the art and the secrets of poetry were unquestionably associated with Valéry's frequent walks and meditations in the Jardin des Plantes. In one of his later texts, *Lettre de Mme Emilie Teste*, he describes a fountain in the garden: *des bassins ronds et surhaussés*, as that place where he understood the sentiment of solitude, where he lived hours very different from his hours of sociability. The garden with its fountain was a secret place for him where he cultivated images that seemed to belong to his inner life. Gide understood the importance of this place for Valéry, and celebrates it briefly in his *Nourritures Terrestres*. In one sense, then, the source of *Fragments du Narcisse* is in a fountain of Montpellier, but in a deeper sense, it is in the intense secret life of the poet, in the silence where he learned to live. Valéry, known as the antiromantic, knew all the familiar storms of passion, but refused to transcribe them in his poems.

As epigraph to *Fragments du Narcisse*, Valéry used the Latin phrase: *Cur aliquid vidi?* ("Why did I see something?"). It is taken from Ovid's work *Tristes II*, but the story of Narcissus and the nymph Echo is related by Ovid in the third canto of the *Metamorphoses*. The real subject, however, of the Valéry poem had already been used in the prose work, *La Soirée avec Monsieur Teste*, of 1896. It is the subject of man's conscience. The attainment to lucidity about oneself, to a full awareness of one's motives and desires brings with it both pleasure and pain. What is seen (*Cur aliquid vidi?*) is both gratifying and terrifying. In the early *Narcisse parle*, in *Fragments* of *Charmes*, and at the end of his life, in *Cantate du Narcisse*, which concludes the volume *Mélange*, Valéry uses the hero Narcissus as the adolescent in love with himself, but especially as the man engaged in self-analysis, who comes to realize the inexhaustibility, the endlessness of the self, and the complex of conflicting sentiments which compose the self.

From a purely philosophical viewpoint, Valéry can believe only in himself. He is a unity separated from the world, who can know the world only as it is apprehended by his senses and by his mind. Beyond his physical body, his senses, and the powers of memory and reasoning of his mind, there is nothing. Such were Valéry's convictions from the beginning. And the practice of poetry was for him as a young man the means of transforming and illuminating the world perceived by his senses and his intellect. The semimystical experience he underwent during the night of October 5, 1892, determined him to give up the writing of poetry and devote his energies to the study of mathematics and allied subjects that might lead him to a more rigorous understanding of his mind, to a more lucid penetration of the self. On his return to poetry, in 1912, he had grown in self-knowledge but he had not basically changed his views about poetry. In writing *La Jeune Parque* and the poems that immediately followed it, Valéry was opposing, in his style and themes the current of popular poetry in France between 1918 and 1925. The intellectual rigor of Valéry's writing and the classical diction of his verse represented the culmination of symbolist poetry. But the idols of the day: Apollinaire, Max Jacob, Cocteau, and the surrealists Breton, Soupault, and Aragon, represented a completely different poetic practice, at odds with Valéry's, in the irrational tendencies of their verse.

Fragments du Narcisse is a long poem on the encounter of a young man with his own image. Whereas in the myth, the beauty of his face and his body is the cause of his wonderment, in Valéry's poem the cause of the wonderment and self-examination is more dominantly philosophical. The erotic attraction is certainly present but the protagonist is struck by the contrast between his uniqueness and his universality. In the *Cahiers*, Valéry names the two angels: Knowledge and Eros (*Connaissance et Eros*) and these preside in quite even power over the principal subject, which is fundamentally the properties of thought: its subtlety and its ever flowing quality. The poem is in three parts, each of which was published at different times. The first *fragment*, and the longest, of 148 lines, is a monologue spoken by Narcissus who has just come to the edge of the water. The daylight is changing into the first dark of evening. As he sees himself in the water, he hopes the nymphs will continue to sleep, because on awakening, they would disturb the water's surface and dispel his image which he wants to contemplate. But this contemplation does not bring peace to Narcissus. He is *l'inquiet Narcisse*, anxious and troubled. Much of the passage is on nature: the air, the forest smells, the reflections, the setting sun, but everything brings Narcissus back to his fever, to his memories, to his pride, and his impotency, to what he calls in the last two words of the passage: *inépuisable Moi*.

The second *fragment*, of 116 lines, opens with an apostrophe to the fountain. Momentarily Narcissus interrupts his self-examination in order to invoke the many dramas of love to which the fountain has been witness. The passionate intensity of love between two human beings is invoked, as well as the disappointments and bitterness that destroy the passion. This is a familiar theme in romantic poetry. Valéry acknowledged this but claimed he looked upon it as an exercise and a challenge. To the familiar story of love and its dissolution, Narcissus opposes his own drama of solitude.

The third *fragment*, of 50 lines, resumes and terminates the monologue. In it Narcissus acknowledges the impossibility of joining with the image he loves. He thereby underscores the great distance between the ephemeral and the profound part of his being. In wishing to join with his double, Narcissus shatters the image of his love.

These are the three moments or scenes of the meditation which Valéry, with great labor, made into his most poignant poem on the conscience and the consciousness of the self. Implicit from the beginning, and growing in intensity throughout the poem is the conviction that love and death are inseparable. In countless

ways this duality is sung of in the poem. It is in the changing
of day into night. It is in the confronting of the mind and the
body, the myth of the self and its appearance. It is in the presence
of Narcissus at the edge of the fountain and in the absence of
Narcissus in his reflection. It is in his desire and in the impossibility of his seizing the object of his desire.

During the unfolding of the myth, Valéry describes the calm
of the forest scene, the silence of the fountain, and Narcissus'
discovery of his image. As he remains immobile, his love grows in
him until it reaches a high point of fervor. As thus narrated, it is
also the myth of poetry, the discovery of poetry as it rises up in
the self when the self is immobilized and totally attentive to the
emotion that is forming in words. The happiness of the poet is the
tranquility of the self when he allows the image to form. So
Narcissus and his image are in reality the poet and his poem.
They are as totally separated one from the other as Narcissus is
separated from his image, but they are bound to one another in
the sense that one is dependent on the other, that one comes from
the other.

Fragment du Narcisse is a solemn monologue. A tragedy is
enacted in it, and one senses this tragedy at the beginning with
the change from daylight to darkness. Night falls over the scene
with the inevitability that is associated with tragedy. It is a sign
of the presence of the gods who are in control of the fate of
this youth. What is to happen will have to happen, and it will
happen to every man. The law is inexorable. As Valéry rehearses
faithfully the characteristics of the myth, he comes upon the
endless worlds contained in the myth, which are in a way myths
within the myth. The mind of Narcissus, in its tranquility, contains the world, as the water mirrors the forest. And in the world
is the body of Narcissus, which alone attracts him, and in the
body of Narcissus is his mind which discovers, restores, and prolongs his desire. Why is this enacted as tragedy? Because of the
ultimate discovery of introspection: that between the self that
loves and the object of his love, is the distance of infinity, a
separation of worlds, one as far apart from the other as day is
from night, as a real body is from its reflection. The inescapable
tragedy is the regular rhythm of verses composed with the absolute assurance of their musical properties, of words chosen for
their strength and delicacy which transcribe the emotions of the

poet as he watches nature itself lead him into the heart of the ego's tragedy. The tragedy is bearable because of the poem's formality. We follow our fate because of the mind's victory in comprehending fate.

The opening line is brilliantly conceived to demonstrate the two aspects of tragedy which will penetrate the entire poem. On the one hand, tragedy is an event which is safe and inevitable, and on the other hand, it is ambiguous because the mind refuses to believe or is unable to comprehend it. There is a finality (*enfin*) in the first line, and each word is ambiguous:

> *Que tu brilles enfin, terme pur de ma course!*

The entire phrase may be either hortatory ("May you . . .") or exclamatory ("How you . . ."). The object addressed, *tu . . . terme*, may be the literal end of the race through the forest or it may be death itself. And the adjective *pur* may refer to the limpid surface of the water as it shines (*brille*) or it may be the absolute of death. The entire line, therefore, may be the boy's expression of pleasure at seeing the fountain, or it may be an experience of his desire to behold the shining water. Suspended and separated from the rest of the poem, the line announces both a violent action: *ma course*, and a perfected or absolute ending (*terme pur*) of the action.

Then immediately, with the first long stanza of fifteen lines, the ambiguity vanishes and we are involved in a scene where the unnamed protagonist is compared to a deer (*cerf*) coming to the edge of the water to slake its thirst, and where the nymphs in the water are told to continue sleeping so that the surface of the water will be untroubled. We are in a world strongly reminiscent of Mallarmé's *L'Après-Midi d'un faune*, with the animal referred to, the nymphs, their sleep, and the forest setting. But whereas the faun's attraction to the nymphs was perfectly natural, here in Valéry's poem, the love of the protagonist is called "curious": *cette amour curieuse*. He prays for the continuance of stillness and of the nymphs' sleep, so that he can see and undergo the bewitchment:

> *Votre sommeil importe à mon enchantement.*

The self is mirrored and sees a face. And gradually the speech

becomes more direct. The protagonist speaks of his own beauty
and suffering (*ma beauté, ma douleur*). The water, where this
beauty is visible, is apostrophized, both its surface and its depths.
The figure is assured of his solitude, *Je suis seul!*, but he knows
that all about him the mysteries of the universe are attentive. He
speaks of the gods and the echoes and the ripples, and the atmosphere is not unlike the opening scene of *Phèdre* where the
suffering queen is aware of her ancestors the gods and where
the silence of Trézène is only a specious silence. Tragedy begins
at a great distance in time and space. The forces that plot against
man are mathematically calculated in some region beyond the
limits of his senses.

So, in a way, the solitude of this figure is not really that. The
stillness, as if personified, listens to the youth, and in that stillness
he listens to hope. The inner quest has begun which he will
pursue into the secrets revealed on the water, secrets that he fears
learning. The night air on his body seems to be telling him that
he loves this body:

> La nuit vient sur ma chair lui souffler que je l'aime.

In eight lines (48-55) which the poet once claimed were the
most perfect he had ever written, Valéry describes the sunset.
The comparison is with a woman who, after the act of love,
gradually loses the high coloration of her body and goes to sleep.
The sunset itself and the eroticism of the passage are both important for the following stanza (vss. 56-71) when the calm of night
is total, when the tyranny of the youth's body becomes a
stronger theme, and when he names himself for the first time. In
leaning over the water, he sees the disappearance of the ruddy
sky and looks for the picture of a god. But a swan has silently
moved off (could it be Jupiter?) and the naked body mirrored
gives not peace to Narcissus but worry and torment:

> Pour l'inquiet Narcisse, il n'est ici qu'ennui!

The seeming peace of the water makes him dizzy (*la paix vertigi-
neuse*) because he senses the limitless depths underneath the
image. He is dizzy from the vision which is "pure" in its shim-
mering surface and "fatal" at the same time. The two adjectives
fatal et pur describe the destiny of Narcissus which contains the
absolute and the knowledge of death.

With a change of rhythm (alexandrines alternating with octosyllabic lines), an incantation begins, addressed to the water, to
the depths which contain the dreams that are looking at Narcissus.
The beautiful ambiguity of the word *profondeur*, both water
and the deep secrets of the self,

> *Profondeur, profondeur, songes qui me voyez,*

leads to a passage on the beauty of the body, described as the
perfect prey (*cette parfaite proie*). The self, in this experience, is
both seducer and prey, both admirer and victim. The captive
could not be more a captive because it is identical to the pursuer.
But the beloved figure cannot be removed from its crystal world.
To extract him from the water would be to destroy him. The
dilemma is endless and fruitless. The image is like the echo of a
word, an experience of mockery. The nymph Echo is far away
from this Valéry scene. All the sounds—the wind and the birds—
mingle in an auspicious way and Narcissus feels them to be expressions of the gods who are speaking his secrets to the air. He is
held to this one spot by eternal forces of attraction. His fate is
truly inevitable. The naked body of the fiancé is formed on the
water, a demon both cold and desirable. The answer made to his
prayer is tragic.

The dilemma grows more and more implacable as the beauty
of the image becomes clearer and the desire more insistent. The
figure on the water is similar to Narcissus, his double in fact, but
more perfect than Narcissus and separated from him only by the
night. The increasing darkness forces Narcissus to lower his head
even closer to the surface. So close that he could drink the face
he watches:

> *Je suis si près de toi que je pourrais te boire,*
> *O visage.*

All of his senses are focused on the one sense of sight. In eight
lines (136-143) the infinitive *voir* is used four times with the
insistence of a prayer: to see not only the beauty of a face, but to
see also the secrets contained within the forehead that is mirrored. The long "fragment" ends with five lines that recapitulate
the dilemma and redefine it in the strongest terms. It begins with
the first person pronoun *Je* and ends with the pronoun turned
noun: *Moi*. The duality is clear: the "I" recording the experience

and the "self" that is undergoing the experience. All possible companions are rejected:

Nulle des nymphes, nulle amie, ne m'attire.

Solitude is necessary and august. Eroticism is indistinguishable from desire and it is inexhaustible. But this final adjective, *inépuisable*, is attached to the self (*Moi*). The self in its duality is both desire and the object of the desire. The ancient myth has at this point been fully recreated by Valéry, and partially interpreted also. But the interpretation continues in the second and the third fragments.

The intensity reached at the end of part I has to be relaxed. Part II is quite different. It is a necessary intervening scene where the love of man and woman is evoked in order to offset the extraordinary solipsism of the first fragment and create a pause, before returning to the drama of self-love.

The fountain is apostrophized now, serenely and in a manner that seems detached from the fountain-mirror:

Fontaine, ma fontaine, eau froidement présente.

The poet is reminded of the fountain's age, of the years that have gone by, and of all the beings that have stopped by the water's side. Nature (*roses*), time (*saisons*), and the physical experience of love (*les corps et leurs amours*) have been observed by the water. It is the witness to all of life. It has witnessed the greatest characteristic of life, that characteristic which gives to men their deepest desolation and anguish: the passing of life, the changes, and the disintegration. This applies even to the greatest of human experiences, to love itself:

L'amour passe et périt.

The generality is first stated, and then the fragment is given over to an analysis of love. Verses 171 to 191 form a passage of dense sensuality where the violence, the imperiousness of sexual love is described. The joining of the male and female makes one "monster" (a famous line of *Othello* at the beginning of the play comes to mind), after the caresses, the mounting of the blood, the lust, the kisses, the moaning, and the momentous climax. But the monster, once formed, dies. Physical love is a momentary exaltation. The fountain has watched it grow and dissolve countless times. The reeds around the fountain have heard the sighs of lovers year after year. The memories of happiness and unhappiness in love are attached to every spot in nature around the fountain: the cypress tree, the rose, the place where the sea air was strong. The lovers' desires and natures are fused in this passage that quite literally reproduces a major theme in Hugo's *Tristesse d'Olympio*. Valéry acknowledged that he wrote this passage of the second fragment as a challenge to himself: to write in accordance with a rigorous art lines that seem easy.

Before speaking again of himself, Narcissus—because the entire poem is a soliloquy—in a hard, carefully wrought stanza (vss. 211-230) speaks of the bitterness that follows love, of the emptiness that succeeds to exaltation, of the very paths in the forest that finally become for the lovers a labyrinth where the minotaur lives and curses the sun. The dream of love is still absolute, but the eyes are dry and the souls are embittered.

This passage on the separation from the intensity of love leads Narcissus back to himself, to his own form of love, which from this point on in the meditation becomes more philosophical. The youth is curious only about his own essence:

> *Mais moi, Narcisse aimé, je ne suis curieux*
> *Que de ma seule essence.*

The new tone of peaceful introspection (vss. 231 ff) contrasts with the erotic and hopeless violence of the preceding passages. How can the most handsome of mortals love anyone else save himself? This is not really a question now for Narcissus. It is a statement of conviction. He has accepted the concept of his solitude, of the one body that he possesses and that is his own:

> *cher corps, je n'ai que toi!*

He welcomes the infinite exchange between himself and his image which the faint light from the moon permits. The important words are *un échange infini:* an exchange which can go on for as long as there is visibility. Exchange and not union. The boy he watches is of the water and of himself. And he watches not only his image but his desire. He knows now that this other half of him is only light.

But such pure contemplation is exasperating. Narcissus wants the perils of love-making: the hands that join, the violence, the sobbings. He wants the silence to come to an end and hear words spoken by this inaccessible cruel youth depicted on the water with his grace and virility.

The relatively brief third fragment (vss. 265-314) recasts this violence with a series of questions to which the answers will be the final formulation of tragedy. The fountain is now called an abyss and the reflected image is the inhabitant of the abyss, the "specious host" of the sky that has been hurled down from the heavens. In the words *hôte si spécieux*, we read both the beauty of the image and the deception this beauty brings. The water's surface is likened to a dark sky because it bears a relationship with the heavens of the gods who have determined the fate of the protagonist. The full truth, thanks to these symbols, is going to emerge now. Narcissus has already acknowledged that the body he desires is a mere reflection on the surface of a deep fountain. He is about to learn that the real body that casts the reflection is similarly an abyss, bottomless, endless. Can it be that he too is but the reflection of a reflection?

The initial questions of this fragment conclude with the most significant of all: Who can love anything else save himself?

> *Et qui donc peut aimer autre chose*
> *Que soi-même? . . .*

In reaffirming his love for his own body, Narcissus goes one step farther which announces the poem's conclusion. He realizes now that his body is the one object that protects him against joining the company of the dead.

> *Je t'aime, unique objet qui me défends des morts!*

This line breaks off the meditation, and when it resumes, after a pause, the tone is more quiet, more resigned. The words are now a prayer addressed to the gods whose presiding presence we have felt from the beginning and who have been touched by this spec-tacle of so much love.

In one extraordinarily succinct phrase,

> *Pères des justes fraudes,*

these gods are called the "fathers of justified deceptions," because they have allowed the faint illumination of night to show to

Narcissus a figure toward which he is attracted, and they have allowed him to experience the torment of love and its impossibility. The entire action of the poem is recapitulated in the two words: *justes fraudes*, the deceptiveness of light and love.

The new closeness to the gods Narcissus finds permits him to utter for the last time his prayer that they arrest time and the change of light. His fate is immobility and adoration, provided that he bends down over the fountain. His torso has the smoothness of a stone, the stone of a temple where he lives. His body is the temple separating him from his divinity. Narcissus' concentration is now on his mouth, and with the word "kiss" (*baiser*), he invokes the verb "shatter" (*briser*), close in sound, and dramatically close in meaning. The distance between the lips of Narcissus and the lips he yearns to kiss is almost nothing, but it is also everything; it is the distance between himself and the water, between his soul and the gods, between life and death. The consummation of love is death.

Even as this thought is articulated, the darkness of the forest deepens, and Narcissus knows that soon he will not see the beloved image. The trees are separated one from the other by night. The death of the soul will be its joining with the dark, when nothing will exist between death and the self. There is no time left save that for the final act: the joining of Narcissus with his image by means of a kiss. He lowers his head, and with the fatal kiss, the water is shattered, Narcissus is shattered, and love takes flight:

> *L'insaisissable amour*
> *dans un frisson, brise Narcisse, et fuit . . .*

The final word *fuit*, which designates the collapse of self-love and death, is an echo of the first two lines of the poem: the *course*, the race through the forest, *la fuite*, the flight of the boy to the fountain's edge in the forest.

Nothing remains at the end. The verb *briser* makes of the water a crystal, a mirror that is shattered. And yet everything remains, because the poem is intact, composed of the tragedy of self-love.

What is, in its general lines, this tragedy? What is, in its contained meditative form, this violence?

Each of the three fragments begins with an invocation and

what is invoked becomes the central part of the development.

I. As soon as he is at the edge of the water, Narcissus invokes the nymphs who live in the water and urges them to continue sleeping:

Nymphes! si vous m'aimez, il faut toujours dormir!

Their sleep will assure the stillness of the water on whose surface Narcissus will behold his image. Sight is all important for the desired experience of love, and that is why so much of this opening poem is concerned with the sunset and the coming of night. The sky changing from a violent color to a subdued color and then to the first phases of night, is a symbol for the ecstasy of passion and the appeasement of passion. For Narcissus, it will be this experience reversed. He will first attentively, prayerfully study his traits in the water, his form, his mouth, and then the incitement to know this body will grow throughout the rest of the work.

II. Placed between the two poems on the solitude of Narcissus, the second fragment, with its invocation to the fountain, accentuates first the distance that separates him from the water's surface, from the object of his desire. His sensuality gives over to a mental activity as he remembers the lovers who must have stopped by the fountain and experienced on this spot the closeness of their love. His mind carries him even beyond, to the disappointment and the bitterness that can follow love.

III. The first word of the third fragment, *Ce corps,* is the invocation. Love, in its purely physical insistence, dominates the poem now. The body is desired but it is impossible to embrace this body. The end of the poem is the effort to join by a kiss the real body and its image. The union takes place in death.

Thus the cycle is completed. The poem moves from daylight to night and back again to the light of self-knowledge and experience. It moves from elation to despair, and back again to that elation which is the absolute of tragedy. It moves from the love of self to the love of two beings and back to solitude and death in solitude. The gods of tragedy are there in the fatal calm of the forest scene. Through them the violent feelings of Narcissus are foreseen and controlled. Man's fate is implacable.

6. Saint-John Perse's Quest

ABRUPTLY, with the announcement in the late fall of 1960 that Saint-John Perse had been awarded the Nobel Prize for literature, the work of a relatively obscure poet became a public concern. The work itself had been previously scrutinized and studied only by that small public that is devoted to the cause of poetry and aware of the poetic ambitions of our age, although to a wider public the name of Saint-John Perse was known, as were the few biographical details that have been rehearsed so often in print: the birth of Alexis Léger on a coral island near Guadeloupe in 1887, his education in France, his choice of the diplomatic service in 1914, his sojourn of seven years in China, his high post at the Quai d'Orsay in the Ministry of Foreign Affairs, his refusal to work for the Vichy government, and his arrival in the United States in 1940, where he lived for seventeen years, before returning to France.

With the honor of the Nobel Prize, which in a sense was the world's recognition of Saint-John Perse, the wide international public that follows literary matters, asked, with perfect justice,

Why this man? Why a poet? Why a French poet so soon after the award to Albert Camus? Why this particular poetic work? Does it bear a relationship to that cause of man associated with the Swedish Academy awards?

From his earliest poems, those published under the title *Eloges* in 1910, through *Anabase* of 1924 (translated by T. S. Eliot in 1930), and *Exil*, published in French in *Poetry Magazine* (Chicago) in 1942, and *Amers* ("Seamarks"), published in 1957 and *Oiseaux* of 1963, Saint-John Perse has continued to describe and analyze the condition of man in our time, the fate of man at this moment in history. His poetry has always had a singular effect in France. Yet no poetic work exists alone. The poetry of Saint-John Perse has affiliations with certain formal rhetorical aspects of Claudel's work, and with poetic theories of Mallarmé. However, and this is the miracle of every major poet, the work of Saint-John Perse is unique and incomparable.

Such a historical event as the Nobel Prize announcement indicated the need and the duty to reassess the function of poetry, to increase our understanding of the very notion of poetry. A great art comes from a precise moment in history, reflects it and testifies to it, and at the same time surpasses its historical moment. The virtue of transcendence has to inhabit every major work of art. The actual poetic work of Saint-John Perse is quite limited in its proportions, but it stands, in its modest totality, as a work that contains the full mystery of poetic form and utterance. It testifies to the mystery of poetic rhythm: the sheer weight and force of words, their resonance and their meaning. It is music, beyond a doubt, and it is more than music. It is an effort to rediscover the lost language of man.

When news of the Nobel Prize award reached M. Léger in his home in Giens, in southern France, his first statement expressed his satisfaction that it was poetry that was being honored. The award represented for him an act of confidence in the belief that a single line of poetry has the power to arouse awareness of the deepest problems of man, of the most difficult and persistent of his problems.

Poetry today is jealous and watchful of its secret. But this experience of jealousy and watchfulness is not new in the history of poetry. It is the ritual secrecy associated with early Orphic poetry. It is comparable to the youthful ambitions and pride of the French Renaissance poets, and to the esoteric theories of the symbolists. The poets today, as heirs of the oldest of poetic traditions, are fervently aware of the intangibility of their art, of the constant need to use disguises in the composing of their poems.

Why is this? Poetry has always been a protest. It has never been, in its great instances, a mere inoffensive diversion or entertainment. Poetry is that language out of harmony with social language. The poetic act is a testimonial to the insufficiency, first, of the poet himself, and then of all mankind. Poetry is always the compensation for some kind of distress. Saint-John Perse knows, as all his ancestors among the French poets knew, that man is made to live at peace with nature, that the first function of man is to establish a peaceful relationship between himself and the entire universe. The poetic act testifies both to the immediacy of this belief and to its imperfect, sometimes tragically imperfect, realizations.

And this is why, despite varying poetic theories and emphases throughout the centuries, poetry has always been a token for the future, a pledge and a sign for the future of man. Such a pledge is as audible in the poetry of the German Goethe, of the American Whitman, of the French Rimbaud, as it is in the work of Saint-John Perse.

It is well known that his early diplomatic career, had he pursued it, would have led him to one of the highest positions in the French government. But he chose the secret destiny of the poet. And even in this vocation, he has always refused to be the professional man of letters. The chronicle of his real life is in his work. It is a personal work, in the deepest sense, and yet it has no trace of the confession. He is both seer and visionary, both the man who has seen what the world is and the man who sees what the world may become. The poet is invulnerable. He is the man who reconstitutes himself after every blow, after very assault. Out of his private destiny, he is constantly formulating a protest. Poetry is the revelation of this man perpetually rehabilitated from the shocks and the clashes of his destiny.

In the same way, poetic theory is constantly being broken down, metamorphosed and annulled. For each poem, the theory demands reconstruction. In *Anabase*, in *Vents*, in *Amers*, the poet sought to express the wholeness of man, the integral forces of his life and his memory. Even more than that, he sought to project man ahead into the uncharted and the new, into a future that was impatient to live. It is not sufficient in the case of Saint-John Perse to say that rhythm and image constitute the essence of poetry. This definition applies, however, provided it is supported by the axiom that poetry is a creative impulse, a manifestation of human energy.

The many elements that compose a poem are not decomposable. This commonplace is admirably illustrated in the strong *verset* of Saint-John Perse where the form is one with the idea. There is no distance between the subject matter of the line and its expression, no distance between the periphery and the center, between the technique and the spirit. The miracle of poetry lies in this unique relationship, this fusion of art and its subject matter.

There is a dramatic movement everywhere in these poems where man, in his historical and natural environment, is playing the role of his existence. This sense of drama and the high nobility of the poet's language provoke from time to time a comparison with Racine. And yet the differences between the poetry of Racine and that of Saint-John Perse help to define the art of the twentieth-century poet.

In the tragedies of Racine, the universe is summarized and ennobled in the human figure. There is no sense of the world around the figure, and no sense of his past and his future. The human figure, the protagonist, is in the epic poems of Saint-John Perse: the conqueror in *Anabase*, the exiled poet in *Exil*, the lover in *Amers*. Whereas the Racinian protagonist has in his poetic utterances the elevation and the simplicity of his solitude in the world, the protagonist of the twentieth-century poems has the elevation and the nobility in his speech which are comparable to Racine's, and he also has the denseness and the richness of his memories of time and the natural world. The actors of Greek drama, the conquerors of the Renaissance, modern man in exile because of his wars, are the poet's protagonist portrayed in his dramatic intercourse with the world: with the deserts and seaports and oceans, with the erosions of time, with the abiding hope of the future.

This poet's work relates the secular and the spiritual efforts of man to see himself as a part of the natural world, to tame the hostile powers of the world, to worship the endlessly renewed beauty of the world, to conjugate his ambitions and dreams with the changes and modifications of time. One of his constant preoccupations is the will to approve of all the past attainments of man, and to magnify the work of man today as the heir of the past, as the only voice that can speak of the past and remember its accomplishments. This became especially clear in his last long work, *Amers*, a massive ceremonial poem that revealed an extraordinary sensibility to historic man.

The manner of *Amers* is a fuller development of the manner characteristic of the earlier poems. It involves all the diverse activities of man and states them in successive gestures. The world of this poetry has the freshness of a new creation. It is total and totally present. Whatever legendary elements remain are actualized in this poetry which is always praise, as the title of the first volume, *Eloges*, revealed.

Man's fate, throughout history, has always been a drama of violence. Conquest has almost always signified war and destruction. Even the spread of religious faiths has aroused hate and led to massacre. *Amers* is a poem that moves far beyond the violence of man's history in order to exalt the drama of his fate which is looked upon as a *march*, the march of all humanity. Saint-John Perse himself, in a very brief statement about his poem, calls it the march toward the sea (*la marche vers la mer*). The word sea (*la mer*) is in the title of seamarks (*amers*), those signs on the land, both natural and man-made, which guide navigators as they approach the coastline. Around the sea the action of the poem will take place.

The sea is both the real sea and a symbol. It is real, as the source of life, and it is symbolic as being the mirror reflecting the destiny of man. The march toward the sea is an image for the quest, for man's eternal search for some experience with the absolute. But this search, as it continues in *Amers*, is exaltation. Man, as the poet sees him, man in his role of poet, in fact, is exalted in his vocation of power and in his desire to know the absolute, to approach the divine. The image of power comes to him from the sea, and from the endless power of words. Covered with foam, the sea resembles a prophetess speaking the most secret, the most enigmatic words of the poet:

> *La Mer elle-même tout écume, comme Sibylle en*
> *fleurs sur sa chaise de fer . . .*

(The Sea itself all foam, like a Sibyl in
flower on her iron chair . . .)

From the opening passages, we realize that this poem will
contain all the images of man's dreams (of this poet's dreams)
and of his thoughts. Such matters have to be seen, have to be
reflected. The vastness of the sea, and its eternity, will allow this.
The poem has very little temporal sense. It is composed at some
distance from our time, from the specific history and problems of
our time. The characters referred to in the poem are dignitaries
and leaders: Tetrarchs, Patricians, Prophets, City founders,
Magicians, Conquerors. Greatness is being celebrated throughout
the work, because by greatness, man moves beyond violence. At
the very beginning, the poet is careful to tell us that the poem
sings not of the sea itself but of the reign of the sea in man:

> *Et de la Mer elle-même il ne sera question, mais de*
> *son règne au coeur de l'homme.*

> (And of the Sea itself it will not be question, but
> of its reign in the heart of man.)

At every point this greatness is allied with poetry, with the poem
that is being written and that celebrates greatness.

Thus the poetic adventure is on the same level as conquest, as
the march to the sea. To reach a lofty permanence, man will have
to merge with all the great forces in the world, both the spiritual
and physical forces. He has to engage in complicity with them
and with the sea. Man has to know both the culture of the past
and the power of the elements. But the elemental forces in
nature and the basic drives in man are expressions of violence.
By understanding them and using them and celebrating them, the
violence is diminished. *Amers* is the poem of victory over violence.

One of the key words of the work is *alliance*, which is precisely the concept named in opposition to violence. It occurs for
the first time in the fifth section of the *Invocation* where the poet
says he had nursed for a long time a taste for his poem:

> *mêlant à mes propos du jour toute cette alliance,*
> *au loin, d'un grand éclat de mer . . .*

> (mingling in my daily talk all that alliance, afar,
> of a great flash of sea . . .)

This word announces the fundamental unity of the world. The extensive knowledge of this poet permits him to celebrate the alliance of elemental forces with all the aspects of culture: history, geography, natural sciences, linguistics, religions, technology, ethnology, drama, symbolism, and finally, the greatest of all alliances, that of man with the sea.

In his Stockholm address, given on the occasion of the Nobel Prize award, Saint-John Perse used the word "surreality" in defining the poet's role, and pointed out that it is unlike the surreality of science. The order discovered by the poet is not an apparent order, a superficial order, but a profound, secretive cohesion. *Le poète s'investit d'une surréalité qui ne peut être celle de la Science.* The sought-after unity of the poetic work is first to be seen in the fundamental unity of creation. A religious thinker would say: in the oneness of God, in the oneness of his creation.

Thus the poet favors a union which he calls alliance. In his practice of poetry, the poet has to use figures of rhetoric: metaphor, antithesis, simile. These are all means of discovering alliances. In the Stockholm text, Saint-John Perse calls the thought of the poet and his art, analogical and symbolic. An image is a mediator. It throws its light far out into the obscurity of man's thought, and by the reactions it creates, by the associations it calls up, by its correspondences (as Baudelaire would say), it transmits life and movement, within its own means, which are far different from the means of science.

Throughout the centuries, civilization has made a constant effort to remove men from the great forces of nature, to protect them from the violence of nature and natural forces. The work of Saint-John Perse seems to be consecrated to pointing out a way to reconcile man with nature, and hence with himself. In *Anabase*, of 1924, man is seen confronting the burning of the desert sands; in *Vents*, of 1946, man confronts the violence of the winds, as he confronts the violence of the sea in *Amers*, of 1957. The poet is determined to reestablish contact with the elements. Not only in *Eloges* of 1910, but in all the subsequent poems, he praises the sky and sea, the earth and the winds, the snow and the rains. These are not fearful elemental forces, but forces loved by the poet.

All of creation speaks to this poet, and he speaks to it in the *verset* he uses in the writing of his poetry, and which, in *Exil*, he calls a long sentence forever unintelligible:

> *la longue phrase à jamais inintelligible.*

Unintelligible, surely not in the usual dogmatic sense of the word, but in the sense of irreducible to the usual processes of the intelligence. The learned words Saint-John Perse uses, and the technical words (*mots de métier*), are always charged with additional meanings.

What do the four sections of *Amers* represent in their thematic structure? The task of defining them is far from easy because of their richness and complexity.

I. *Invocation* is the poem's prologue. In it we see man turning to the sea, for a sense of freedom, for a liberation. The sea is at all times alive. It is constantly recreating itself. The sea is thus the great force in nature that will guide the poet and inspire him in the creation of his poem. In the six brief parts of *Invocation*, the sea is a festival (*la grande chose fériée*), a celebration which intoxicates the poet. From the very beginning of the poem, and throughout the long work, it is difficult to distinguish the sea from the poem. The singer is born out of what he sings. The sea reigns in his heart, and since it is the sea of every age, the poet is able to live in closeness with every age. In the beginning was the water. The sea is the source of our dreams. Such is the closeness between the sea and the poet, that he is the singer docile to the poem which is being born. The sea is wisdom, power, presence. Out of the sea will come all life and the poem itself.

II. *Strophe* is the body of the poem and is composed of nine parts. It is "strophe" in the ancient sense of movement and rhythm, of poetic speech which is action and which is different from the speech of prose. Part 1 is the introduction to the site of the poem's action: the cities bordering on the sea. They represent the chorus moving around the altar. The scene is a hemicycle of coastal cities. The eight sections following the introduction are each dominated by different actors, by different celebrants we might say, because the unfolding of the poem is at all times liturgical.

In part 2, the master of stars and navigation speaks words of the sea. He is called the Dark One. (*Ils m'ont appelé l'Obscur.*)

The tragediennes appear in part 3, and we see them hastening to the shores. They have come to reenact the drama of man, the drama of everything that is human, on the stone around the sea, and in full sight of the sea. The Patrician Women of part 4 are not actresses, but they too in their role of creatures of the earth, wish to come to the sea. The single woman of part 5, called "poetess," is language. She is the one by whom all things that are consumed close to the sea will be remembered. In part 6, another girl appears, a girl prophet among the poets. She speaks the prophecies that are too profound for an easy understanding. Then, in part 7, all the girls from the countryside leave their childhood and go toward the sea. These are the daughters, ready for love, the girls ready to assume their role as living women. Part 8 is a brief interlude between the coming of the girls to the sea, and the final part concerning the lovers. A Stranger appears, coming from the sea. He comes mysteriously, as if to consecrate the evening of love which is celebrated in the long part 9: *Etroits sont les vaisseaux* (Narrow are the vessels), composed in seven sections. This love song: part dialogue, part speech in unison, and part speech by the woman, describes a night of love. We witness the approach of the lovers, their union and ecstasy, and their repose after love. The poem is built on the alliance of the sea and love. The night of love is the sea night, and the passion of this love is total in its freedom and power and joy. In his own brief analysis of the themes of *Amers*, Saint-John Perse calls *Strophe* the hemicycle of marine cities (part 1) and eight figurations, evoked in their alliance with the sea.

III. *Choeur*, which opens with the solemn line,

> *Mer de Baal, Mer de Mammon—Mer de tout âge et de tout nom*
>
> (Sea of Baal, Sea of Mammon—Sea of every age and every name),

is a unified, somewhat abstract poem, a homage to the sea. It is a single lyric movement of exaltation, in which the people, the celebrant or the reciter, and the city itself, are united in their approach to the sea, in their desire to honor the sea. The sea is apostrophized as the measure of being. In making this identification, the poet is the leader of the chorus. His poem here is a sacred recitative.

IV. *Dédicace*, a brief page, is the conclusion of the long work, and the restitution of the poet to his normal life of man. In his role of poet he has sung of those forces that are beyond man, and he had now at last earned this moment of restitution, which is destitution, because he divests himself of his gold in honor of the sea,

se dévêt de son or en l'honneur de la Mer.

The poet has brought his work to its dual culmination: the full expression of his faith in man and his allegiance to the sea.

The opening passage of *Strophe*, the first two sections of *Des Villes Hautes s'éclairaient*, reveals the fundamental violence which the poet intends to transcend in his poem. The tall cities themselves bordering the sea, *des villes hautes*, are seamarks (*amers*). When they flame in the sun, they are visible to the mariner far out at sea, *in the golden salts of the open sea* (*dans les sels d'or du large*). The cities are characterized by their sea walls and ramps, by the stone concepts of their design. They stand between the sea and the land, a frontier architecture. Are they hostile countries, the sea and the land? The subject of the poem is precise here. They would be hostile, if the sea were a natural force feared by man, over which he has no control. Is man hiding behind the walls he has built? Are these fortifications destined to protect him against the sea? Are the jagged rocks lining the sea a natural protection for the men on land? Do the tall cities with their ramparts represent an age-old struggle of man against the elements? Deliberately, specifically, the poet announces the intention of his poem: to reveal or to bring about an alliance between the men on land and the sea that surrounds the land. A gold marriage ring is to be forged by the poet:

Trouve ton or, Poète, pour l'anneau d'alliance.

The passage opens on a bustling port scene. Port officers are in conference, and they are likened to frontier guards. It is this dangerous word frontier which implies hostility, that has to be changed. The people are crowded along the seawalls where they are waiting for Plenipotentiaries of the high sea, hoping that the alliance will be offered. Thus the words frontier and alliance are opposed. There seems to be a delay in the arrival, a delay perhaps caused by an erroneous reading of signs, such as the moon and the tides. Nature is not at fault, but man's incapacity to read nature and comprehend its signs.

The will to reach an alliance comes from the people. They are praying to both the sea and the land to bring about an exchange. Work carried on in a harbor, concerns necessarily both the land and the sea. *Travaux mixtes des ports.* The sea is apostrophized by the people as mediatrix: *Mer mitoyenne,* and the land is called the land of Abel (*Terre d'Abel*). It is the earth loved and tilled by the second son whose sacrifice will be fruitful. In their prayer,

> *Nous vous prions, Mer mitoyenne, et vous, Terre*
> *d'Abel,*

the people reason out why the alliance must be made, why the marriage ring must be forged, and the alloys formed for the bells that will ring in the pilot lanes,

> *et tes alliages pour les cloches, aux avenues de*
> *pilotage.*

The reason is everywhere: in the sea breeze that comes to every door in the city, and the sea itself which is at the end of every street. The breeze from the sea, and the sea, are in the bits of wisdom by which the people live, and in the earliest form of their laws by means of which they live at peace with one another.

> *C'est brise de mer dans nos maximes et la naissance*
> *de nos lois . . .*

The very air they breathe is from the sea. The water they need for themselves and for their work, is held on hire in their shelters, and this water is in secret alliance with the sea water.

The last three lines of the passage are a brilliant transcription of this indispensable alliance which the people understand secretly and which the poet is able to expose. On the outer harbor is an escutcheon of a winged beast, chosen by the ancestors of these people. This very symbol of *bête ailée* represents an alliance of beast and bird, of land and sea. The pierhead (*musoir*) has a male ring (*anneau mâle*) to which boats can be attached. The words recall a horse or beast whose muzzle is pierced by a ring. This figurative horse, the *bête ailée* attached to the pierhead, with its ring, is conceived of by the poet as dreaming of distant relays (*lointains relais*) "where foam flies from other manes" (*où fument d'autres encolures*). The fabulous horse (Pegasus) passing in flight over the sea, is witness to the joining of the elements.

Everything in the passage seems associated with the need to unite, to reunite. The men of the port cities are priests of commerce (*Prêtres du Commerce*) and commerce always suggests sinister insinuations of war. The male element of commerce and conquest signifies closeness to the land. But the sea, more powerful and more enduring than the land, is female. A woman's body, a Patrician Woman, is the highest luxury. Yes, the sea is female in its fluidity and grace. The Patrician Woman will pacify. Just preceeding the final image of the winged beast is a line describing the sea in an image that is feminine and at the same time evocative of the creation of poetry. Spasmodically the sea unfolds its answers, golden answers in the sun, "in great luminous phrases" (*par grandes phrases lumineuses*). The waves of the sea are thus compared to the assembling of words in a poem. A poem is a creation that transcends the mere sound of words. It is a force of alliance, of a reuniting in which the human being (the creature) finds his place in the universe (creation).

In his speech at Stockholm, Saint-John Perse emphasized the power of this adventure called poetry and claimed it is not inferior to the great dramatic adventures of science. The title word *amers*, in its most eloquent meaning, has nothing about it that is "bitter." It should not evoke the meaning of the familiar French adjective. Rather than on bitterness, the poem is built on hopefulness, on enthusiasm and optimism. The course of the mariner can be guided by the seamarks (*les amers*). The poet's purpose is to consecrate the alliance between man and the creation, and he needs the seamarks to show that the alliance takes place when the land recognizes its relationship of vassal to the sea. If the sea is female in its self-perpetuation and fluidity and spasmodic undulations, the poem is male. It is the ring in the muzzle of the beast, it is the force that will direct and lead and explain. The end of the alliance is unity when man is integrated with the creation.

This is Saint-John Perse's answer to the violence in the world. The image of *relay*, used in the metaphor of the winged horse, is a way of demonstrating the continuing forces of life. Poetry itself is a kind of *relay:* it picks up and sustains the element of the divine, when religious belief weakens, and when mythologies no longer function as explanations for disasters and catastrophes.

When Saint-John Perse speaks of the "sea of every age and every name," at the beginning of *Choeur,* and of the long time he had been nursing a taste for this poem of the sea, in *Invocation,* he may well have been thinking of the long history of the sea in poetry, of the power the sea possesses to call up the poet and create him. The Homeric voyage might have been in his mind. At the beginning of *Etroits sont les vaisseaux,* he evokes magnificently the unity of history and time with the words:

> . . . *Une même vague par le monde, une même vague depuis Troie*
> *Roule sa hanche jusqu'à nous.*

> . . . One same wave throughout the world, one same wave since Troy
> Rolls its haunch toward us.

The sea was important in the medieval voyage of Tristan and the quest voyages for the Holy Grail. And more immediately, many French poets of the nineteenth and twentieth centuries had sung of the sea: Victor Hugo in *Oceano Nox;* Baudelaire whose *Voyage* alludes to the adventure of Ulysses and the voyage taken by the imagination of a child as he pores over maps and prints; Arthur Rimbaud, whose *Bateau Ivre* is, in a way, an answer to Baudelaire's question, *Dites, qu'avez-vous vu?;* Lautréamont, whose sea violence is matched by the sadism of Maldoror; Corbière, the Breton poet, inspired by the sea and who chose the name of Tristan for himself; Valéry, the Mediterranean poet who found in the sea, contemplated from his cemetery at Sète, an incitement to life; Claudel, who like Saint-John Perse, frequently crossed the oceans of the world, in diplomatic missions and who analyzed the religious meaning of water in his ode *L'Esprit et l'Eau.*

In *Amers,* the sea has reminiscences of all of these uses of the sea metaphor. With no trace of metaphysical torment, it is celebrated as that place of meeting where all the paths taken by men in every age will converge. It is the goal of the march of mankind. It is the one image and the one reality able to sustain all the themes and unite them: the reality of the sea, the limitless power of life that is best transcribed by the sea, the eternity of man in his continuous action, the personal themes of man's solitude and freedom and love, and finally the poet's creation: the image of the poem. In its ceremonial walk around the sea, the movement of the chorus is compared to the circuit of the strophe. Whatever the Reciter says is in honor of the sea. The sea itself is comparable to the web of poetry (*l'immense trame prosodique*). The endlessness of poetry is the nameless prolixity of the sea:

> . . . *mer innombrable du récit, ô mer prolixité sans nom!*

Passage after passage, especially in *Choeur*, evokes the violence of the sea in its relationship to the history of man:

ô Mer violence du Barbare (O Sea violence of the Barbarian)

Mer agressive de nos Marches (aggressive Sea of our Marches)

Mer de violence, et de mer ivre, parmi tes grandes roses de bitume (Sea of violence, Sea drunk with sea, in the midst of your large roses of bitumen).

All fables and incarnations of history are in the sea and in the lofty ode of the poet's homage. The *Chorus* sings of alliances and progressions. In the love-song of *Strophe*, the most personal, the most intimate experience of man's nature is related in terms of the sea. At the moment of union, the lovers obey the sea's rhythm without fully understanding it. The lover, when she speaks, identifies herself with the sea. She is both woman and sea, and the night of love is a sea night. It is difficult to keep in mind that during the violence of passion and during the long moment of appeasement after passion, the poet himself, in the power of his language, is recreating the sea and recreating his lover. From the beginning to the end of *Amers*, the sea is the sign of the poet's irrepressible need to create.

The usual dimensions of poetry, in length, in meter, in theme, are surpassed in *Amers*, because the vastness of the sea is reflected in it. The enumerations are not mere lists or proliferations. They are in the poem because man in the poem is the figuration and the witness of the history of the earth. He is both a single secret presence on the earth, and an ensemble of all wars and revolutions, of the endless surging of mankind, of the choral celebration of mankind—a solitary man who finds himself in the midst of life and desirous of understanding it. Man, facing the sea, is a power that has to be spent. He is a potentiality, or a vital tension that refuses the concept of tragedy. His fate is not death, but a merging with the continuous life of the universe. His love song has no trace of narcissism, no trace of facile sentimentality. He raises the image of love to the hyberbolic level of a cosmic force. In the experience of love, when man is usually centered upon himself, he is, in *Amers*, seeking to identify himself with the vastness and the prolixity of the sea.

Although the fury of violence is at times the subject of this sea-poem, the fury is controlled by a poetics fully conscious of its method. At all times, the Reciter is serene. The sea he celebrates is the sea of language. The seamarks are those signs that regulate chaos, because they are the instruments of man's knowledge. As it is sung, the poem reveals the coherence of life. The experiences behind the poet are often the violence of nature and the violence of man's life in nature, but the poem is the celebration of the mysteries of this violence. No matter what its subject, language has the dignity of ritual. The poetic act is solemnity articulated.

PART III
In the Wake of Symbolism

7. Proust: Analysis of the Heart and Society

W HEN THE FIFTIETH ANNIVERSARY of the publication of *Du côté de chez Swann* was celebrated in 1963, a certain amount of stocktaking was made, and what came to light was evidence of Proust's universality. It is awesome to think that in the course of merely fifty years, the landscape of Combray, the hawthorns of Méséglise, and certain expressions of Mme Verdurin have become familiar to countless readers throughout the world. The power of literature is this capacity to give common memories to many people of different races. Literature may well be, after religious belief, the greatest bond uniting people.

How can this writer's universality be explained? In his analysis of the subconscious, in his exploration of regions of the mind that are not usually explored, Proust has gone farther than most novelists. The reader's own drama, only partially understood by himself, his sense of anguish and unfulfillment, which is often obscure to him, may suddenly on the pages of Proust's novel, be-

[105]

come clear and decipherable. In following the experience of Marcel and Swann, who are the two protagonists in Proust, and who are, in a profound sense, the same protagonist, the reader may reach a new understanding of his own experience. The pages on childhood in the opening chapter of Combray, have a universal meaning. And the torture that Swann undergoes in his love for Odette, in the second chapter of *Un amour de Swann*, is, to some degree at least, the torture that every lover experiences in his most oppressive moments of jealousy.

Proust's novel is a repertory of sentiments and the analysis of these sentiments. Notably absent from this repertory is religious sentiment, but all the others seem to be here: the sentiment of love and desire, filial love, parental love, love of race and country, friendship, the sentiment for natural beauty and for aesthetic beauty, the sentiment of ambition both social and political, *snobisme*, timidity, pride, apprehension, fear, exaltation. The repertory is almost exhaustive. It is more complete than that found in any other literary work. To equate this repertory, Dante would have to be joined with Shakespeare and Balzac, and even then there would not be the detailed analysis of states of feeling and sentiment that Proust gives.

His universality is also apparent in the emergence of so many of his characters as types: Norpois the aging diplomat, Charlus the brilliant but unpredictable profligate, Françoise the devoted but tyrannical domestic, Oriane the impeccably dressed and self-centered aristocrat. These characters, and so many others, Odette, Bloch, Robert de Saint-Loup, Gilberte, are so portrayed by Proust that they are both distinctive and representative. During the long course of the novel, their personalities do not undergo radical changes, despite the affirmation to the contrary of some critics, but they continue to reveal new and sometimes unexpected traits of character. They become, thanks to that power a few literary masters have, not only characters in a novel, but characters who exist outside the novel, as representative men and women, as types who live on, often in the secret lives of readers, who inhabit personal regions we often close off from the world.

In *Du côté de chez Swann*, we see a young boy, whose name is used only once, and much later in the novel, but who is called Marcel by the critics, and who is to grow up into manhood as he looks for certain kinds of experience which represent happiness for him. But at the same time, and even in the earliest part of the novel, this youthful hero (who is also the narrator) is trying to find the subject for a book. He would like to be a writer. The subject matter, so ardently sought after, is not discovered until the end of the entire work, in *Le Temps Retrouvé*, at the very moment when the narrative of the life story comes to an end. At the end of the novel, the search for happiness suddenly becomes identical with the creation of the book, the very book that we have finished reading. The initial movement of Proust's novel, the narrative of a boy's life in his search for happiness, is progressive and is presented as a series of disappointments, as an almost despairing experience of disillusion.

Despite encouragement given to young Marcel by the writer Bergotte and by his friend Bloch, he terminates his ruminations about writing pessimistically, when he says that he is giving up literature forever. He is led to believe he has no aptitude for writing. This embittered decision has an important result for the general plan of the novel. Marcel will feel freer to attempt other experiences in life. He is liberated for other aspects of existence that attract him: friendship, love, society, art. And yet the scheme of the book depicts a gradual disappointment and even disillusionment with every aspect of life that Marcel will test in his search for satisfaction, in his search for happiness.

A la recherche du temps perdu is totally subjective. Proust deliberately and successfully attempted to reduce an entire world to himself. It is a puzzling fact that this novel in which there are so many characters, more than two hundred, and so many of whom are unforgettable, is in reality an epic of a single man's mind, the epic of the self. Gaeton Picon, one of the most recent critics to reevaluate Proust, looks upon his novel as the first work in French literature where the voice of Balzac and the voice of Baudelaire are fused and heard simultaneously. This would mean that in Proust's novel, we hear the voice of the historian, of the memorialist who depicts an entire age, as Balzac had once depicted the Restoration, and also the voice of the poet, of the man who feels the apprehensions and the anxieties of our modern world, as Baudelaire had felt them in the middle of the nineteenth century.

Proust's novel appears today as a kind of telescoping where

images and human beings, where periods of time and places are evoked and given firmness. Proustian time, a subject of a great deal of discussion, and often contradictory discussion, is characterized by the most recent commentator, M. Georges Poulet, as time which always takes the form of space. The favorite hour for this novelist would seem to be the hour when the sleeper awakens, and therefore the unity of place is the bedroom. There all the divinities presiding over a human life meet. There night becomes an accomplice in the quest for lost time. There a former personality of a man, a former self who had been forgotten, may rise up again and live again. In the centuries and the milleniums of humanity, as in the life of an individual, events that are notable or insignificant, may be spared from oblivion. Reminiscences that abolish time-gone-by, are for Proust, as they were for such a writer as Gérard de Nerval, the foundation of a work of art. In these reminiscences of the past—Marcel hears them in the little phrase of Vinteuil's sonata and septet—the creative geniuses reveal to us "the melody of their lost country" (*le chant de leur patrie perdue.*)

In the early years of the history of Proust's novel, certain contradictory elements were not apparent, which today go very far in explaining the book's power and beauty. On the one hand, Proust the writer is a man who reacts vibrantly to every experience, to every state of awareness, which he analyzes and savors in great detail. And on the other hand, Proust has no belief in any essential permanence of man. He records on countless occasions the experience of being fragmented by the minutes that tick by, the experience of being tortured by the passing of time. The courage, the heroism of Proust is these contradictory movements which his writing reflects. His first vision of nature and man is Heraclitean. One cannot bathe twice in the same river. Everything in the world, nature and man's consciousness, are in flux and condemned to change and dissolution. And yet there is also in man the principle of some inner fixity, of a permanence that gives to the ego its unity. Proust will claim that this unity is ultimately to be found in the creative act of the artist.

His art is the enlarging of the ego, the discovery of the deepest part of the ego, and even its purification. But this opening up of the ego is no guarantee for happiness. At best, it would be the consolation that comes from understanding, the consolation of lucidity. Some writers exalt the ego into a form of heroism. This would be true of Nietzsche, André Malraux, T. E. Lawrence. Others describe the ego as that part of man aspiring to God. Kierkegaard, Claudel, Bernanos, for example. For Proust, the ego is the duality of permanence and impermanence which he explores relentlessly and lyrically.

To some of his earliest critics, Proust appeared as the novelist-heir of Balzac, as the artist bent upon painting the huge fresco of an age in French history. Today the literary ancestors appear more numerous, and the critics are beginning to estimate how much he owes to such writers as Chateaubriand, Nerval, Baudelaire, and Mallarmé. These would seem to be the writers who taught Proust something concerning the art of transfiguring objects and human beings, the art of selecting and magnifying, which is the art of transfiguration.

By comparison with the traditional nineteenth-century novel, *A la recherche* seems a new form in which the psychological analysis is far more developed, but is not conclusive, not dogmatic. The patterns of human existence are not clear in Proust. So many mysteries remain after the psychological exploration of the characters, that they end by bearing some resemblance with allegories. Proust is a secretive writer. Despite the elaborate analysis of scenes and characters, we never learn his complete thought about the significance of a scene or his complete understanding of a personality. The novel as a whole is secret and esoteric, and the countless critics of Proust tend to be exegetes in their effort to explain the allegory, to pierce the secret of Proust and of his work.

It is difficult not only to explain the esoteric quality in Proust, but also why there is this quality and what its source is. A part of his book comes from his life and his observations of life, but another part comes from some other source, which might be called his genius, and which is infinitely difficult to name. Scholars have diligently searched for the models of the characters, for keys to their enigmas. Proust himself claimed there is no one key to a character, but several keys, several sources. Today, this kind of search, which has filled many critical studies, seems futile. To explain, for example, the character of Bergotte, the writer in the novel, who befriends the boy Marcel and whose death is memorable, it no longer seems useful to point

out his possible affiliations with Anatole France or Bourget
or Ernest Renan. It is more probable that Bergotte was born
out of Marcel Proust's reflections on what a writer is, on
what distinguishes a writer from all other men, on what characterizes the relationship between a writer's life and his work. No
model can adequately explain Bergotte. If he was born out of
Proust's meditations on the writer, we know that such a source,
by its very nature, is limitless.

Proust believed that the self a man exhibits in his daily habits,
in his social life, in his vices, is artificial and even false. His real
self is not easily exhibited. It is inner and concealed. If the man is
a writer, it will be exhibited in his books. Far more than in the
laborious and repetitious biographies of Marcel Proust, he is visible in his own novel. His real self is meticulously described in the
three major cycles of the novel, all of which engage in different
ways the personality of the protagonist Marcel: the cycle of
Swann, first, where we see the boy as an admirer of Swann the
esthete, the connoisseur of art and the father of Gilberte. Marcel
the social being is portrayed in what might be called the cycle of
the Guermantes, especially in his relationship with the duchesse
Oriane and the baron Charlus. The third cycle, that of Albertine,
is Marcel in love, going through all the tortured phases of love
we associate with Proust.

The anecdotal aspect of Proust's novel seems today far less
important than the elaborate projection of a personality. Proust's
ego is not only described, it is mortified and transcended in his
characters. The pompousness of Proust is expiated in Legrandin
the dilettante who sees in poetry only the spices of existence. The
idle amateur is chastised in Swann. The affectation of the esthete
is reproved in Mme Verdurin who, because of her extreme sensitivity to music, contracts a cold every time she hears Debussy's
quartet. Proust watches himself in all of his characters as if he
were Narcissus. He is of course predominantly in Marcel, but
very recognizable traits of Proust are in Swann, in Charlus, in
Bergotte. He is also in some of the female characters: in tante Léonie's hypocondria, in Oriane's skill at imitating people. He is
harsh on himself when he is harsh in his novel on dilettantism, on
snobbery, on the idolatry of esthetes. Three characters in *A la
recherche du temps perdu* are saved ultimately by their devotion
to creative work. They are the three artists: the writer Bergotte,

the composer Vinteuil, and the painter Elstir—three aspects of the same type of man whom Proust undoubtedly wished to be himself, or wished to emulate.

Through the years of a half century, the main character of Proust, this Marcel, has taken on the dimension of a hero, of an initiate whom we watch being submitted to trials, to tests. The hierarchy of society, the various circles of the Guermantes world are temptations of social power, tests of endurance and skill, related to all the pleasures of worldliness. One after the other, Marcel savors each, is disillusioned, and passes on to the next. Before he enters it, each salon is foreign and terrifying to him. But when he knows it, he sees its moral defects and its trivialities. In his quest for love, Marcel also passes through a series of tests and disillusionments. His love as a boy for the young girl Gilberte, his love as an adolescent for the older woman Oriane, duchesse de Guermantes, his infatuation for Mlle Stermaria, and finally his long painful suffering and jealousy over Albertine, represent initiatory degrees of love and passion. Here there is no real triumph for the initiate. The Proustian hero in love is either vanquished, or simply outlives his love, as in the case of Gilberte.

These tests, these initiations to the world and to love, are the great scenes in Proust's novel, and they continue until the moment, at the end of the work, when Marcel discovers the key to the one blessing in which he can believe. The title of the last volume, *Le Temps Retrouvé* (Time recaptured) is in reality the recapturing of a lost vocation. It is the writer's vocation we learned of in *Combray*, when Marcel's father discouraged his son from thinking of such a vocation, when Norpois, his father's dinner guest, encouraged him, and when Bergotte, encountered a bit later at Mme Swann's luncheon, incited him to reconsider the vocation.

Proust's original plan was to publish his novel in two volumes, the first to be called *Swann's Way* and the second, *Guermantes' Way*. These terms are carefully explained in the first volume, as designating the two walks the family could take in Combray, on leaving tante Léonie's house in order to reach the countryside beyond the town. Swann's way, or Méséglise, led through a field landscape past M. Swann's property. Guermantes' way led through a river landscape in the direction of the Guermantes' country house. But this was merely a topographical meaning, a clue to the geography of the book. Through the eyes of Marcel, and through the eyes of those interpreters of Proust who were curious about deeper meanings, the two landscapes designated two social worlds which seemed far apart at the beginning of the book. Swann belonged to the rich bourgeoisie, which was the social class of Marcel's own family. It was also the world of Mme Verdurin whom we meet because of Swann. The Guermantes are members of the aristocracy, one of the oldest families in the French nobility. To Marcel, the Guermantes appeared inaccessible, a world by themselves, living in a kind of fortress separated from the rest of the world. When Marcel grows up, this inaccessibility of the Guermantes dissolves, and he enters the world of the aristocracy with total ease.

Even if this theme of the two ways did not ultimately turn out to be the major subject of *A la recherche*, it was helpful in substantiating the theory that nothing in Proust's work is gratuitous. Everything counts. Each episode, each theme has its place and meaning in the whole. For many years, the episode of *Swann in Love* (*Un amour de Swann*) appeared detachable. But today, *Swann in Love* is an indispensable part of the entire work. There are multiple bonds between the character Swann and the rest of the novel. He participates in the two social worlds that Marcel is going to explore: thanks to Odette he is introduced to the Verdurin circle, and because of his intelligence, his culture, his charm, he is a close friend of la duchesse de Guermantes and of Charlus. He is instrumental in sending Marcel to Balbec where the young man meets members of the Guermantes family. Moreover Swann works intermittently on a study of the painter Vermeer, and this never-finished essay is a foreshadowing of Marcel's interest in writing.

The protagonist, Marcel, as a child first believes in the absolute of sentiments. But as he grows up, the sentiments he once believed in, change and become disloyal. They are not permanent but are submitted to laws of forgetfulness, of *oubli*, as Proust calls forgetfulness. And Marcel discovers in aesthetic contemplation what he had lost in the trials and adventures of life. The world is recreated in a work of art.

The social groups called *salons* are varied in Proust's novel, and depict most aspects of French society, of *le monde*, between

1890 and 1910, the twenty years during which most of the action of the novel takes place. Three salons, in particular, are described in the first part of the novel: those of Mme de Saint-Euverte, of Mme Swann, and of Mme Verdurin. Although these women come from different social classes—Mme de Saint-Euverte is a Guermantes, Mme Swann is a well-known *cocotte*, and Mme Verdurin a member of the wealthy bourgeoisie—the salon of each is characterized by a ruthless effort to mount in the social world, to reach a higher place in the social hierarchy. In order to bring about this change, the salon has to eliminate constantly elements which are not useful to it. It has to attract other elements which will replace those eliminated and which will indicate progress in the ascent. This is an avid form of snobbery, which in its worst manifestation leads the lady of the salon to practice cruelty in evicting those members of her group whom she no longer considers brilliant or useful. In this regard, Mme Verdurin is the most flagrant example of social cruelty, who will sacrifice anyone, even Swann himself, if she believes that in his absence she can invite a more important guest. She is totally tyrannical.

As one mounts the ladder of social eminence, there is less and less of this elimination and accretion. With the solidity of the highest ranks of the Guermantes, there is no need to change the ranks, there is no fear of rivalry from other salons. With the duchesse and the princesse de Guermantes there is complacency because there is no need to strive upward. They are quite literally the summit. To alter their status, a world war will be necessary and a huge social change. Mme Swann, who, as Odette de Crécy, frequented Mme Verdurin's salon, will create a similar kind of salon, based largely on a few people who seem to be in fashion, who are talked about, who are eminent for a day. The writer Bergotte is one of these. But as soon as his day is over, a Bergotte will have to be replaced by another figure who is attracting the attention of Paris society. Odette's snobbery is based upon fashion. Proust's depiction of Mme Verdurin and Mme Swann, in their role of tyrant, is always comic to some extent, because their avidity is apparent and because they can never be sure of how long they will attract the attractive or how long the attractive will remain attractive. They represent a curious amalgam of cruelty and silliness and insecurity. Their reign can only be temporary. Their snobbery is characterized by a humiliating form of greed.

The social ambition of Marcel, which is very real, has, however, no ingredients of avidity or cruelty. He is fascinated by society and drawn to the highest ranks by an overwhelming curiosity. The prestige of nobility is an enchantment for him. The customs of the world appear mysterious and he endows them with a poetic beauty. The achievements of the past and of civilization are in the very name Guermantes. In his own life, Marcel Proust was attracted by those friends who bore names famous in the history of France: d'Albuféra, for example, and Polignac, d'Haussonville, and Fénelon. In his novel, Marcel studies the unusual first names which the Guermantes bequeathed to their offspring, names that come from medieval folklore and that maintain in the twentieth century the charm of a distant poetic past: Basin, for the duc de Guermantes; Palamède, one of the many first names of the baron de Charlus; Oriane, duchesse de Guermantes, originally the name of a fairy.

Marcel enters the world of the Guermantes, not by flattery or by political maneuverings, but almost by chance encounters. At Balbec, his grandmother meets a childhood friend, who belongs to the Guermantes family, Mme de Villeparisis, and from then on, the introductions to all members of the proud family follow in the natural course of events. Marcel's desire to know the Guermantes is presented by Proust as a driving force totally different from Mme Verdurin's. To know the Guermantes is for Marcel equivalent to knowing the history of France, to understanding the lessons of the past and the achievements of his country. Near the end of the novel, this theme is recapitulated and deepened in a very poignant manner, when Marcel attends the funeral of his friend Robert de Saint-Loup, nephew of the duchesse de Guermantes, and he observes on the black funeral cloth hanging over the portals of the church of Saint-Hilaire in Combray, the letter G, sewn in red. Marcel's attraction to the Guermantes is an almost mystical attraction to greatness. Even after he has been disillusioned with all the members of the Guermantes family in whom he discovers serious moral defects, selfishness, frivolity, cruelty, both conscious and subconscious, he maintains an ardent belief in what they should represent. Even after the dramatic and cruel episode of the "red slippers of the duchesse," when Oriane refuses to give credence to Swann's mortal illness, an episode which illustrates for Marcel the profanation of friendship, he does not relinquish belief in the magical power of the name Guermantes. The longevity of their lineage protects them from the present when pettiness and vice distort their features.

The many defects, some serious and some not serious, which are forced upon the attention of Marcel as he encounters one after the other of the Guermantes, help to prepare the general picture of social transformation that Proust is very much concerned with presenting in his long epic story of time. Even during the twenty years of the novel's action, the Guermantes family is changed, by marriage and deaths and adoptions. The most ironic and spectacular social change in the novel is Mme Verdurin's entrance into the Guermantes world. This almost comic figure at the beginning of the novel, in *Du côté de chez Swann*, an overambitious despotic lady of the bourgeoisie, after two marriages, becomes herself the loftiest figure of the noble family, la princesse de Guermantes, in *Le Temps retrouvé*. Mme Verdurin as la princesse de Guermantes is a metamorphosis, explicable by the passing of time and by an infinite number of moral deficiencies in the make-up of man: greed, infidelity, egoism, sloth; by all the pettinesses of gossip and envy; by the mirage of grandeur; by the will to desecrate and ruin those reputations and those lives which stand in the way of the metamorphosis. Mme Verdurin is as relentless in vying with the Guermantes and ultimately conquering them, as Marcel is eager to know them and understand them.

Other disappointments in Marcel's experience are interpreted by him specifically as disillusionments: the church of Balbec, for example, the dramatic art of La Berma, Venice. The dream, when it becomes a reality is implacably a disillusionment for Marcel. The exception is the Guermantes milieu and his encounters with the various members of the noble family. He does not conceal or disguise the reality of this social climate. All the manifestations of Guermantes selfishness, indifference, vice, cruelty, ignorance, are described and analyzed by Marcel, and yet the prestige of the name, the glory of the past, the survival of power, manner, loftiness, aloofness invested at birth in these people, make of them, from the beginning to end of the novel, nothing less than an example of civilization which will never be completely understood or encompassed or assimilated. Time is both the principle of corrosion or change, and the preserver of values. Marcel, in his study of the Guermantes, is witness to minute and drastic changes, an admirer of a continuing force or example in the civilization of his country.

By the end of the novel, the social world in Paris is a network of lies, a vast caricature: la princesse de Guermantes is really Mme Verdurin, and the new marquise de Saint-Loup is really Gilberte, daughter of Charles Swann, son of a stockbroker. The novel slowly unfolds the multiple phases for this bewildering change. But we also know at the end of the novel, that the daughter of Gilberte, the young girl called Mlle de Saint-Loup, whom Marcel mistakes for her mother, is also the daughter of Robert de Saint-Loup, a representative of the noblest traits of the Guermantes family: intelligence, and even culture, generosity of spirit, thoughtfulness, beauty, suppleness of bodily movement. Robert de Saint-Loup, who in his first appearances at Balbec, was compared to a gold-crested bird, will live in his daughter. The evolution of a social group does not suppress the good traits of a family, even if it seems to exaggerate the bad traits.

The vast social changes studied by Proust, in which large segments of a population begin to think and act differently, are recapitulated in the novel's two major love stories and in the several secondary love stories. The episode of Swann in love is placed near the beginning of the work, and the longer episode of Marcel in love is placed near the end. The torment of the heart in love is the microcosmic study of the modification taking place in a single individual. This torment, more swift and intense than a social change, does however parallel the upheavals of history whereby entire social classes emerge with lessened power or with increased power.

Swann in love with Odette bears so many resemblances with Marcel in love with Albertine, that it is tempting to view the two loves as one story, one elaborate document on Proust's understanding of love. In the first, there is greater emphasis on the slow and almost naïve ways by which love grew in the heart of Swann. We see its forming almost in spite of Odette herself. At one point, Swann suddenly realizes it is there in him, as if it were a malady that has taken over all the organisms of his body. He has to acknowledge it. He has to submit to its torment. When it is over, he marries Odette and his exterior life changes. In Marcel's love for Albertine, the emphasis is on the prolonged phase following the acknowledgment of love. Marcel studies the spasms of jealousy as his experience spreads out toward its dissolution, toward its ending. The image of a malady, of a contagion applies equally well to Marcel's love. The organism of the lover is quite literally devoured by the suffering of love.

Love, for Proust, is an experience created by the imagination, and it transpires totally within the mind of the man who loves. (There is no example of a woman in love in Proust's novel. We never really learn what Odette thinks of Swann or what Albertine thinks of Marcel.) It is founded on uncertainty and grows because of jealousy. It seeks to know everything about the beloved, and it learns that nothing can be known with assurance. Nothing in the beloved's past can be ferretted out. No word or no act in the present can be believed in. Her future is unpredictable. The only thing real for the lover is his imagination and this becomes for him a cage of torment from which he cannot escape.

Despite these despairing insights into the experience of love, Proust unquestionably believes it to be the supreme experience for man, the one in which his entire being is involved, the one which provides him with the fullest sense of living. The implacable torment of never seizing any particle of truth concerning the beloved, the restlessness of the spirit which never comes to an end as long as the experience of love persists, the dimming of all other values in man's life during the span of his love—all this is accepted by the Proustian lover. He learns to live with a phantom who is constantly changing her form in his heart while his heart remains steadfastly the habitation of the phantom. The object of the lover's desires is a phantom unknowable, unseizable, ever present during the hours of his sleep as well as the hours of consciousness. Only the phantom is real, and yet Swann knows that she has nothing to do with the young woman whose name is Odette, and Marcel knows she has nothing to do with the young girl Albertine. No pleasure is derived from this love, not even a momentary pleasure. It persists precisely because there is no pleasure capable of being derived from the experience. It lives on the mysteriousness of obstacles which are generated daily and nightly by the mind of love.

The lover ends by believing himself a man condemned. He appears as an outcast from the society of men, a man who hides from everyone the only reality of his life, the one he loves who is no reality but a fictional being he continues to create and recreate as if this grim ritual were forced upon him by fate. A mere accidental meeting, an encounter that seems to have no significance, no reason, is at the genesis of a Proustian love. But once the suffering has begun, once the malady has taken hold, there is no way to escape. Swann and Marcel are condemned to love an intangible being. Odette and Albertine are always escaping, always advancing a pretext for not being where they should be, for maintaining somewhere a mysterious existence which the lover can never enter. His torment is the endlessness of his curiosity. It can never be satisfied. No matter how much Odette and Albertine share with their lover, he will discover moments, domains, episodes about which they reveal nothing, and on them the focus of his suffering will be fixed. The Proustian lover is the one who dispassionately invents reasons for suffering, who lies in order to uncover the lies of his mistress, who suspects every confidence freely offered, who is unable to imagine happiness in love because love is that total possession which the lover himself defines as not possible. The subjectivism of this love isolates the lover inexorably from everything else in the world, and hence prevents his knowing even mild forms of happiness during the time of his love. If his mistress does not come, he will be convinced that she is unfaithful. Presence and absence are both sources of suffering, then. And there is no other alternative to a way of life in the world: living in the presence of the beloved or living in her absence.

The very specific Proustian torment is the state of not knowing. It is the state of ignorance concerning some fact or some being. Marcel as a boy suffered from not knowing the Guermantes, and this kind of suffering is raised to a higher degree of suffering when, later in life, he is unable to discover the activities of Albertine. Again as a young boy, he suffers through not having seen La Berma act in the theatre. This ignorance concerning the art of La Berma tortures him endlessly and resembles the torture that Swann inflicts upon himself when he tries to imagine the mysterious life of his courtesan Odette with whom he is in love. Marcel Proust the writer, in his endless search for details, in his quest for knowledge of geneologies, of protocol in Paris society, of personal habits in the life of a cook or a baron or a violinist, prefigures Swann's attachment to the unknowable past of Odette, and Marcel's infatuation over the inaccessible duchesse de Guermantes. Ignorance is the torment of Proust the novelist, of Marcel the protagonist as he tries to learn the secrets of society, and of all lovers in the novel: Swann, Marcel, Charlus, Robert de Saint-Loup. Because love is nurtured on ignorance, it becomes, for Proust, the principal means to self-knowledge and even to knowledge of the world and the ways of men. Marcel learns how to watch himself as he suffers, and he extends to all of mankind the knowledge he acquires concerning himself, concerning the intermittences of desire, concerning his need of the presence of the beloved, concerning the climate of solitude in which he lives, even when Albertine is with him, or is sleeping in the adjoining room. Marcel learns that Paris can be a desert at those moments when he discovers new degrees of torment and hence new regions of his own self, new perceptions, new knowledge about man's fate.

Proust's novel is made up of countless borrowings from life and from countless metamorphoses to which he has subjected the borrowings. No law is easily deducible from the work and from what is known of Proust's life, which will explain the borrowings and their metamorphoses. What was once real for the novelist becomes for the narrator of the work fictional. The art is the use of the novelist's freedom. He chooses what he wishes and reinvents it with a new sense of order, a new skill of animation. The *snobisme* of Marcel Proust is never exactly that in his novel. The *snobisme* and the preciosity of Proust are clearly visible in his letters, but they are altered in the hero who says *je* in *A la recherche du temps perdu*. The biography of Proust seems insignificant when it is contrasted with the novel where Proust the writer adds to our knowledge of man in his analysis of society and of the human heart. The novel reveals an extraordinary truth about these subjects, whereas the facts concerning Proust's life are insecure, incomplete, contradictory. The novel does not present a biography of Marcel. The reader is always uncertain, for example, about his exact age in every episode. But the living part of the novel, the analysis of Marcel's sentiments, is so captivating in its detail, so revelatory, that the reader easily forgets the absence of traditional biography in order to follow the more significant developments of sociology and psychology.

In the careful choice he made of themes and episodes, Proust was able to construct an entire world, the world encompassed by the sentiments of Marcel. We are present at the genesis of a sentiment and then watch it rise up and develop, slowly diminish and finally die. The ego of Marcel is a series of successive egos: Marcel in love with Gilberte is one self; Marcel infatuated with the duchesse de Guermantes is another being. He is a son, a grandson, a friend of Bergotte, an admirer of Mme Swann, a friend of Elstir, a friend of Robert de Saint-Loup, a young friend of Charlus, an intimate friend of the duc and duchesse de Guermantes. He is especially described as the unhappy lover of Albertine. Time is consumed and lost as Marcel plays each of these roles. Through him we watch the disappearance of love and social intercourse and time. In Marcel's sentimental life we feel the uselessness of everything that time stamps with its death. A sentiment, by its very nature, cannot be fixed outside of time. It is characterized by an inexplicable beginning, by development and by dissolution. The universe of Proust is the analysis of these sentiments, of Marcel living through various states of being, of enacting a series of selves in which as hero he is despondent. He is unable to hold on to any sentiment or any being because of whom the sentiment has deepened. In this sense, Marcel is the victim of an abiding pessimism. But this pessimism about life in the deaths and resurrections of its metamorphoses, is contradicted by the optimism of Marcel the narrator and by Proust the writer. The narration of the book is a transfiguration. It is the immobilizing of what changes. Life, as described by Marcel, is proliferation, both continuous and mortal. But this proliferation, in the hands of an artist, has a second life.

Out of a life of oscillation and dreams, the mind of the artist creates order and richness of detail. In his creation of the two girls Marcel falls in love with—Gilberte and Albertine (whose names are so similar that they might be the same heroine)— Proust went far beyond his own experience. To deepen his own understanding of love, he had to reach a level of detachment from himself. Everything is recognizable in his universe, but also everything is new. The temperament of Proust is everywhere visible in his book: the man's intensity of feeling, his subjectivism, his own personal adventure on this earth. But Proust the writer was the technician who adapted all of that to the laws and the architecture of the work. His depiction of society and his analysis of the heart were revealed to him not as the man living in society and suffering from his sentiments, but as the writer who, alone in his room, filled the large *cahiers* with the writing which constituted his search for the absolute beyond time.

8. Gide: The Danger of Freedom

FOR SIXTY YEARS, between 1890 and 1950, André Gide was an attentive commentator on all the new developments of French literature, on the literary schools that flourished and died during that time, on the problems of war, philosophy, and social and political conflicts. His career as a writer began when symbolism resembled a movement, with a program and aesthetic principles. Mallarmé was the acknowledged master in 1890, and Gide attended the Tuesday evening gatherings in Mallarmé's apartment. Gide died at the beginning of 1951, at a moment when existentialism dominated literary expression and discussion, when Jean-Paul Sartre's influence on French youth was as strong as Gide's example had been in the late 1920's and early 1930's.

For a half century Gide was witness to many literary moods and quarrels and achievements: the flourishing of symbolism, the upheaval of the single performance of Jarry's *Ubu Roi* in 1896, the brief history of dadaism, and the group of young writers associated with *Littérature*, the formation of early surrealism organized and directed by André Breton and Aragon, the new Catholic orthodoxy of men like Maritain, Péguy, Claudel, the philosophy of Bergson with its new value placed on intuition and the subconscious, the proliferation of the novel destined to become the most varied and the most fertile literary genre of the century. The novel was not the possession of one school or one novelist. It served them all: the naturalism of Zola, the romantic confessional writing of Loti, the ideology of Barrès, the bourgeois-religious values of Bourget, the revolutionary Catholic ideal of Bernanos, the atheistic existentialism of Sartre, the humanism of Camus.

The miracle of Gide's position during these sixty years is the endless sympathy he showed all philosophies and all literatures, and yet maintaining at the same time his independence as a writer, his life-long concern with the problem of man's freedom which he considers in the earliest work *Les Nourritures Terrestres* of 1897, and in the last work *Thésée* of 1946. The lavishness, the steadiness of Gide's literary output are offset by the singleness of his theme. Freedom of the spirit, sincerity of the mind, availability—whatever term is used, the meaning is the same, the problem is identical in all the books: how can an individual man live, think, behave, in accord with his instincts, desires and convictions, and yet remain within a society, as a member of a social group whose laws demand subservience to a standardized behavior and morality? If survival in such a world is cherished by an individual, must he abdicate those values that are most deeply personal to him, and accept less authentic values? Must he play the roles forced upon him by his family, his school, his city, and his country, when these roles contradict his own personality, and when by dint of playing them they will form a new and false personality, so contrived that the original self is irretrievably lost?

Gide faced this problem differently in each book, trying to reveal its significance by means of all the literary devices: of farce, in *Les Caves du Vatican;* of tragedy in *La Porte Etroite;* of irony in *Paludes;* of lyric fervor in *Les Nourritures Terrestres;* of sophistry in *La Symphonie Pastorale;* of the short novel with two or three characters in *L'Immoraliste;* of the long complex novel with many characters in *Les Faux-Monnayeurs.* Each book is a different approach in style and form and tonality, to the one harassing problem of the self: the self's freedom and the compromises with this freedom.

Steadfastly Gide remained the moralist in all of his books, and he used as the principal genre for his writing, the novel, or some form of the novel. Even in the earliest, *André Walter*, there are traces of a novel although the book is primarily a confession in the form of a personal journal. The natural narcissism of Gide's nature is the subject of the early treatise *Narcisse*, after which he deliberately chose a modified form of novel, a *récit* or narrative, which was to become the necessary antidote to his narcissism. In *L'Immoraliste* of 1902, in addition to the principal character, who is Gide, or an aspect of Gide, there is a second character, the wife of Michel, Marceline, who exists outside of the narcissistically inclined narrator. *L'Immoraliste* has specifically the form of a novel, and Gide will continue, from that time on in his career, to exercise great freedom in the forms of the novel he elects to use. This constant experimentation with form, the freedom with which Gide moves from the simplest type of narrative with two characters to the complex novel of *Les Faux-Monnayeurs* with many characters, parallels the underlying theme of moral freedom.

This supple use of the novel as the most suitable form for the study of his theme, marked a separation between Gide and the symbolists, the literary figures to whom he was initially attracted, as well as others of his generation, such as Valéry, who, like him, were the descendents of the symbolists. On the whole, the symbolists, and the so-called "decadent" writers, looked upon the novel as an unworthy literary genre, as one in which psychological traits were arbitrarily assigned to imaginary beings. Gide's work was at all times to remain eminently personal, but in his development as a novelist, he grew in his power to depict human beings who were quite detached from himself. As the problems relating to man's freedom deepened for him, he sought ways to project his study of this freedom. In his most successful books, he created a literature that is both personal and closely attached to the needs and the preoccupations of his time. This relatedness of Gide to his age, at every point in his career, has not always been acknowledged. On the one hand, he listened to himself so fervently that his writing has an original freshness about it, and on the other hand, he listened judiciously to all the influences around him, and in these influences discovered ideas that he adapted to his own. *L'Immoraliste*, for example, is very close to autobiography, but it was written in a climate of Nietzscheism and today seems not only a novel but a document on one of the major intellectual struggles of the early part of the century. *Les Caves du Vatican*, of 1914, is a huge farce of characters and situations, a satire on the picaresque novel, but it is at the same time a presurrealist novel, a critique of the traditional novel, a study of a hero's liberation from constraint, of his attraction to the unusual.

Michel of *L'Immoraliste* and Lafcadio of *Les Caves du Vatican* are literary heroes closely resembling Gide himself in their emotional make-up and their intellectual curiosity, but they also stand by themselves, different one from the other, quite classifiable as heroes of fiction. Gide is in them, and the reader also is in them, or at least potential characteristics of the reader.

Gide gives to the word freedom meanings that are peculiar to him and that are not traditional. A man is not free to do as he wishes, but he is free to imitate such an exploration of himself that he may reach some understanding of his desires, some understanding of their genesis, of their development in him. Freedom is the freedom to understand, and such an understanding implies an absence of judgment in accordance with any fixed dogma. The writings of Gide are both confidential and confessional. Gide confides to his reader as he confides to himself, because the word confide is based upon the word faith. Faith is the basis of Gide's humanism: whatever instincts and whatever conflicts exist in a single human being belong to all of humanity. What a man is, is not as significant as the story of how he became what he is. The maturity of an individual is measured by the freedom he feels to understand himself, and the frankness, if he is a writer, with which he will describe his confidences. In the eyes of the world, all confidences, if they are frank, will be scandalous. A psychological anomaly, as well as a physical illness, has an explanation. Search for this explanation constitutes a man's freedom. It would be called an obligation for the writer. During the course of the search, what is habitually named illness, anomaly, mania, inferiority, can become in the make-up of a man, and especially of an artist, factors of progress, of an inner spiritual progress. A literary work is always the writer's understanding of himself, and it is secretly or blatantly a protest. This protest, first called by Gide *Les Nourritures Terrestres*, is a revision of norms and values. Man's chance for greatness is the expression he is able to give to his protest.

Even as a very young writer, Gide, with his strong Huguenot background, was conscious that the demands of rectitude were forcing him to express the truth about himself and that the memory of every artist tends to become a work of art. Both the Protestantism of Uzès and Normandy, and the vocation of the writer forced him to the creation of a self-portrait. In the early 1890's, Gide lived through in his own personal life the conflict of his entire age which was the realization that many of the conventions that had protected the moral life of man had collapsed. Many forms of social morality had been emptied of their meaning. A single man, as well as a society, had to learn how to govern himself without the usual directions, without the familiar dogmas. The solitude of this drama, lived by André Gide, explains much of his literary career.

The nervous tensions of Gide as a youth, his alternating fits of enthusiasm and depression, his highly emotional nature can be explained by his fundamental hatred of hypocrisy. The conflict between the morality of his family and his class, and his personal morality, which gradually evolved and demanded attention, is the conflict which Gide later recognized to be that kind out of which an artistic work comes into being. The anxiety of his nature cultivated in him that extreme form of attentiveness and scrupulosity and awareness indispensible to the make-up of an artist. The habit of self-examination which Gide acquired at an early age was the apprenticeship of sincerity whereby he judged any trace of hypocrisy in himself and was able to perceive and evaluate the moral perfection of the girl he fell in love with, his cousin, Madeleine Rondeaux.

In Gide's personal life, the first strong affirmation of freedom was the journey to Africa in 1893. The danger of this freedom can be measured by the young man's immediate reaction to it in the form of illness, diagnosed as tuberculosis, and later as an imaginary tuberculosis. But Gide's willed separation from his home and from the literary life of Paris, and his decision to live in Biskra was a significant moral experiment. The meaning of this experiment, during which Gide discovered the sincerity of desire as opposed to the formalism of morality, forms the basis of his two key books: *Les Nourritures Terrestres,* the dithyrambic account of his self-discovery, and *L'Immoraliste,* which is the same account, soberly recast in the form of a narrative. The first book is the vibrant exaltation over the discovery of sensuality, over the infinite varieties of sensation, and the second is the *récit*, deprived of almost all lyricism, wherein the hero Michel anaylzes the moral punishment that follows any indulgence in sensual freedom. Freedom of the senses is a lonely experience. Its reward is immediate and brief. Its intensity is such that a single life may be cut off from all other lives. Michel, in his will to know himself in the freedom of his desires, sacrifices his wife Marceline, not only in his neglect of her, but in the intensity of experiences by which all thoughts of her are obliterated. In order to become himself, Michel expels every other presence. In order to know his desires, he expels all responsibilities toward anyone else. Michel experiences the terrifying solitude of self-knowledge. In leaving Paris, he fled the dangers of authority of many kinds. His life in Biskra reveals to him the far more subtle perils of human freedom.

In one of the very few metaphors of *Les Nourritures Terrestres*, the narrator describes his soul as an opened inn at the crossroads: *mon âme une auberge ouverte au carrefour*. The book is Gide's most blatant revolt against all forms of pure intellectualism and all arbitrary moral dogmas. It only barely conceals an adolescent resentment against a puritanical training. Adolescent also is the barely concealed feeling that an artist's duty is to scandalize, to take his stand outside conventions and laws. The protest in Gide is far more ambiguous and subtle than the protest in Nietzsche. And the Dionysian element in *Les Nourritures Terrestres* is more subdued than in *Also sprach Zarathustra*.

In the character Ménalque, who appears in Book IV, and who represents an exaggeration of all the revolutionary tendencies in Gide, we have the clearest traits of the Dionysiac, of the hero who has separated himself from all moral duties. But there is a vast difference between the character Ménalque and what is known of the personality of André Gide. Ménalque is the strongest force of revolt in Gide, but he is constantly being offset by two other tendencies in Gide's make-up, by the Christian heritage and Gide's personal interpretation of the Gospels, and by the Apollonian or Goethian impulse of the artist, of the man who harmonizes in his work destructive tendencies in his life, who will reach the serenity of the creator. Even in his earliest books, as in *Les Nourritures Terrestres*, Gide is a virtuoso in the variations of his feelings. His work is the record of the contradictions of his nature and his mind. He was not as tormented as Dostoievsky, but he knew, as poignantly as Dostoievsky did, the cohabitation of contradictory feelings.

No sense of struggle characterizes *Les Nourritures Terrestres.* The unnamed hero is presented as a soul in love with its mobility. The body of the protagonist is never described, but his sensations are, and these sensations are multiple and ever changing. The book is the story of a soul's freedom and a body's freedom, but we never learn from what the body and the soul are being liberated. The lesson of the book is implicit on every page: the fundamental need of man to establish contact with the natural world, without any recourse to a symbolic understanding of the world. The book does not describe an action or a goal; the world of sensations is too inexhaustible for that. The emotions, and even the ideas of the narrator rise up gratuitously, and he is incapable of choosing. The central attitude is one of openness, of *disponibilité,* of fervor, and particularly the fervor of a young man who is experiencing fervor for the first time. After avoiding all forms of voluptuousness, the narrator welcomes them, but without attaching himself to any one. No preference, no choice is allowed in this new way of life. A choice would represent an immobilization and hence a limitation. Even the form of the sentences is sensual. Freedom is indulgence, provided one indulgence does not win over all others. By confiding in the reader, whom he calls Nathanaël, the narrator encourages himself in this endless quest for knowledge of the world by means of the senses. The cadence of the sentences, as well as what is actually described, indicate movement through landscapes, gardens, deserts, oases. The exaltation would diminish and die if this traveler stopped in order to know exhaustively any one sensation. Desire is what is never satisfied. *Les Nourritures Terrestres* is the canticle of desire, the greediness for desire.

This is Gide's first book against insincerity, against man's innate tendency to lie to others and to himself. It is his most exalted book in terms of style and in its emphasis on individualism. Gide's endless curiosity about every manifestation of life is visible throughout these *Nourritures Terrestres.* He claims his right to live as if he were a new prophet claiming a new way of life, a newly found sincerity. His voice of 1897 (*Ne souhaite pas, Nathanaël, trouver Dieu ailleurs que partout*) is not unlike Whitman's American voice of 1855 (*I take to the open road*), or Nietzsche's German voice of 1886 (*I teach you the Superman. Man is something to be surpassed.*). All three prophets, in their lyric intensity, denounce the intellectual, the bookish approach to life, and the sense of sin which Christianity has imposed on the world. They speak of life as being a source of joy, as being a Dionysian experience, where adventure is the expression of freedom, where the unknown is the excitement to be conquered.

It is a curious book because it is both Gide's denunciation of puritanism, of his own early training, of the arch-literary atmosphere of the symbolist salons, and, on the much bigger scale, it is Gide's expression of the anti-intellectual movement in Europe and America, his translation of desires that had been concealed and unavowed for some time in Europe. Gide's will to break with the past, with traditions and morality of the past, is a revindication of a new gospel of sincerity, of a new need in man to be astonished at everything, to enter into direct contact with things, to define a new duty of the artist, a new value in sensations of the present, to escape from human types that resemble him, to recreate the most primitive myths, to rediscover the mystique of the vagabond.

By comparison with the rich rhetoric and the ebullience of *Les Nourritures Terrestres*, Gide's novel *L'Immoraliste*, published five years later, in 1902, in its purity of tone and sobriety, seems the work of a different writer. In the earlier work, the experience of freedom is lived through with no reference, or with references that are immediately softened and obliterated, to the concept of evil. There is no reference to guilt, no fear of selfishness in the narrator's sensual quests. But in *L'Immoraliste* there is antagonism between Michel's new experiment with life and the moral structure of his background. The sentiment of guilt is never completely eradicated. He is never absolutely sure of his destiny, of the difference between an apparent value and a real value. Are the actions he perpetrates in accord with his intention? Do the words he utters translate literally his thoughts? Is there agreement between his sentiments and his convictions?

Michel's mind has the clarity and the logic of a scientifically trained Frenchman, and his nature has the bottled-up sensitivity of a privileged European bourgeois who has lived in harmony with traditional morality. The experience he wills to know after his marriage, his illness and his voyage in North Africa, is the discovery of a personal morality, of a personal code of behavior that will correspond to his deeply confined, deeply concealed life of the subconscious. The subconscious drives which intrigue him and captivate him are never fully described in the novel, because they are never totally clear to Michel. But he knows them to be in contradiction with the way of life that is expected of him. To see more clearly into the emotional drives that compel him, he will have to renounce the hypocrisy and the falseness of a self that has been formed through all the years of his life.

The autobiographical elements of *L'Immoraliste* are easily recognizable: Gide's first journey of liberation to North Africa in 1893, and his marriage trip to Algeria in 1895. Against this background, Gide constructed a story in which the hero, after believing himself imprisoned by archeological research and fixed patterns of moral behavior, discovers ecstatically, under the burning sun of Africa, the joys of anticonformity, a release in extroversion, an attachment to the world of nature, and to the young in Algeria, and later in Normandy, who live outside the law, in an ironic defiance of law.

Whereas the narrator of *Les Nourritures Terrestres* thirsted for the water of oases in the desert, for the juice of desert fruit, for the sustenance that will come to him from wild berries and plants, the protagonist of *L'Immoraliste* develops a thirst for the dark forces of nature that turn men toward the depraved and the disreputable. During his convalescence, as he recovers his health, thanks to the constant care and attention of his wife Marceline, he begins the study of the senses. He reeducates himself as he contrasts the moral values represented by his wife with the hedonistic values of the Arab boys and the Norman poachers. The contrast between the two sets of values is striking. As his body grows in strength, Michel's desire to understand and experience the perverse in nature, grows imperiously. This man of the north is bewitched by the sun and the sensuality of the south. He wills to uncover and know that part of his humanity which he had never even suspected prior to his marriage.

The thesis of the book is not merely a revolt against limitations, against the traditional sources of morality. It is not rebellion as much as it is the hero's will to explore the darker side of his own humanity, to learn the instincts of his own nature that join him with the demonic forces of nature. Michel's quest follows a mythological pattern which in its ultimate sense resembles the action of Lucifer or at least the boldness of Daedalus. The Gidian hero and Daedalus undertake a voyage to the sun to test their valor. Michel's exploration of himself and nature fails because he is unable to move outside of his purely human traits. He is unable to be alone, unable to rid himself totally of his love for Marceline and of all the bonds and restrictions that such a love implies. He does reach a kind of freedom, but then suffers from its uselessness. *Je me suis délivré, c'est possible; mais qu'importe? Je souffre de cette liberté sans emploi.*

Such a sentence records a failure, but this failure is felt in the aftermath of a self-testing. It is the disillusioned comment of the Gidian hero after his struggle to reach authenticity. This moment of failure is the substance of *Le Retour de l'Enfant Prodigue*. It is in Lafcadio's practice of piercing his flesh with a knife each time he abdicates his originality (*Caves du Vatican*). It is in Bernard's ultimate desire to return home (in *Les Faux-Monnayeurs*) and to reoccupy his place in the family after the many moments in his story when he reached an honesty of feeling and a response to this feeling. Each book of Gide is part of his search for the divine in the human make-up, for the original purity of his emotions.

Les Nourritures Terrestres is solely a lyrical confession, and *L'Immoraliste* is both a confession and a novel. The settings of Africa and Normandy were familiar to Gide and certain traits of the hero Michel are those of Gide, but the organization of the book, the narration of the hero's illness and of his recovery, the phases of his convalescence and his awakening to a life of the senses, all that is the work of a creative writer. The Gidian theme of freedom, after the rhapsody of its presentation in *Les Nourritures Terrestres*, is turned into the human drama of Michel and Marceline in *L'Immoraliste*. These books narrate the life of Gide, in the sense that they tell of the sacrifice of many of his beliefs, a sacrifice consumated in the name of a new freedom which he wants to know. The illusion of the identity between Gide and Michel is maintained by use of the first person pronoun, but the magnitude of the problem is such that Gide and his hero are surpassed. The mirage of freedom is eternal. Is there not another set of restrictions within freedom itself? The end of the book implies an affirmative answer to this question. The dark search

for the mysteries of man which Michel states in his own words
(*ma recherche ténébreuse*) is by its very nature endless and allied
with the original disobedience, with the original reason for morality. The immoralist tries to reach a climate where morality would
not exist and he actually moves toward the same expression of
pride which necessitated morality in the first place. The egotism
of *Les Nourritures Terrestres* where every page is an exercise in
the development of the self, turns into the egoism of *L'Immoraliste* where the hero is not alone and hence is never totally free
in the search of his own powers and the indulgences of his own
nature.

After the opulence of Normandy, where his life had always
unfolded passively within the accepted moral system, the strange
burning aridity of Africa, where he recovered his physical health
and found himself changed, led Michel to cultivate a taste for
cruelty, a desire to know what is forbidden in human conduct.
Willfully, and hence immorally, Michel cultivates a part of himself which he does not clearly understand but which intrigues
him and which he recognizes as being Satanic. He never becomes
abject or profligate, but he goes very far in his study of freedom
and the perilous consequences of freedom. As with all the others
of Gide, this book is the declaration of a problem of which the
solution is not written and which would be the kind of book
that would not have interested Gide. He always stops with the
work of art just before the moral system can be formulated.

The case history of Michel is the subject matter of *L'Immoraliste:* a young scientist intent upon knowing primitive basic and
dangerous drives in his nature, and who is at the same time a
young husband responsible for the death of his wife from whose
love he is never able to free himself completely. But more than
this, *L'Immoraliste* is the story of the earliest rebellion of man
against God, of that human will to grow in stature and independence so that man will rival his Maker. The moral fluctuations in
Michel's behavior form the exterior of the narrative, but they are
far less significant than the obscure change his nature undergoes
as he tests the dark powers of his being.

A quarter of a century after the publication of *L'Immoraliste*,
Gide released to a wide public, in 1926, three works that defined
his place in literature and justified all the promises made in

L'Immoraliste to a very small public at the turn of the century: his autobiography *Si le grain ne meurt*, his novel *Les Faux-Monnayeurs*, and the short treatise on the writing of his novel *Journal des Faux-Monnayeurs*.

The autobiography is an exercise in sincerity rather than one in self-justification. The novel is an exercise in experimental writing, one that will be applauded by the avant-garde, by the new surrealists. This mature work of Gide combines his familiar moral preoccupations still centering on the concept of freedom, with technical innovations in the art of the novel. The book is a novel about a novel, supplemented by the *Journal des Faux-Monnayeurs* which permitted Gide another perspective, another analysis or the story of a novelist trying to write a novel that bears the same title of *Les Faux-Monnayeurs*. This invention of technique is consistent with the solution of certain moral or spiritual problems. Yet not solutions in the full sense, but progress in the way of solution. The action of the novel turns into speech about the novel. The book is not solely the relationship between the hero and reality. It is persistently the problem of how this relationship can become the subject matter of a novel, of how life becomes art. The novelist Edouard in *Les Faux-Monnayeurs*, and the novelist André Gide in *Journal des Faux-Monnayeurs* are concerned with their limitless freedom in their choice of reality, in the decisions they have to make daily in the writing of a novel. The moral significance of choice derives from man's freedom when he faces all the possible choices he may make. Edouard's novel is a failure, and Gide wrote a novel about a novel's failure.

In *Les Faux-Monnayeurs* we see a novelist present in his own creation, and even if the theoretical criticism of the novel is introduced into the work, it is at the same time a novel of characters. The creation of such a novel demanded a total freedom, the acceptance of adventure and the quest for the unknown on the part of Bernard.

The possible parallels with Gide's own life are many, and have been pointed out by critics: Edouard who is Gide himself, Oliver who is possibly Marc Allégret, Passavant who may have been modeled after Cocteau (at least there is a play on words in the two names), Laura who bears resemblance to Madeleine Gide. In the final analysis, everything is confessional in literature. Edouard, Bernard, Olivier, Vincent are all possible developments of the temperament of André Gide who had read of this theory concerning the creatures of a novelist in Albert Thibaudet's *Réflexions sur le roman*.

Les Faux-Monnayeurs is a *summa*, an elaborate work demonstrating the multiple and at times contradictory impulses in Gide's nature. Despite the fictional form into which it is cast, it is the most personal, the most revealing journal of André Gide. The perpetual introspection of Edouard is Gide's life habit and Edouard's journal is quite comparable to the pool of still water needed by Narcissus. But this same narcissistic Edouard is also Proteus, the god capable of taking the form of whomever he loves, the restless spirit moving from one character to another, from one psychological dilemma to another. Laura makes this point about Edouard when she tries to describe him for Bernard. And the rich nature of Gide is hardly contained within these two mythological characters of Narcissus and Proteus.

The novel recapitulates and deepens the experiment with freedom, so clearly visible in *Les Nourritures Terrestres* and *L'Immoraliste*. This experiment could at this point in Gide's career be called the will to be faithful to oneself, the will to repudiate the false image of the self which is shown to others. Bernard makes the clearest statements in this regard concerning the kind of authenticity he wishes to reach in his behavior and in his human relationships. In speaking with Laura (part III, chap. 4), Bernard says: *Je voudrais, tout le long de ma vie, au moindre choc, rendre un son pur, probe, authentique.* The title itself of "counterfeiters" indicates the central motif of the book. Dogmatisms imprison the human spirit and bend it to a behavior not in keeping with itself. Pastor Vedel illustrates a counterfeit morality, Judge Profitendieu illustrates a counterfeit justice. Douviviers illustrates a counterfeit sentiment. Those characters in the book who strive for authenticity in their sentiments—Edouard, Laura, Olivier, Armand, and Bernard—are recognizably "Gidian." The expressions of their freedom represent threats to their human relationships. They want to be loved, and this need shows a greater human warmth than we read in *Les Nourritures Terrestres* and *L'Immoraliste*. They know that in order to be loved, they have to be esteemed, and in order to be esteemed, they expose themselves in confidences and confessions.

Ten years after the appearance of *Les Faux-Monnayeurs*, Gide published, in 1935, *Les Nouvelles Nourritures,* a work that he had been writing intermittently and sporadically during a period of nineteen years. The first reference to this book is a journal entry in early 1916, when Gide was going through a religious moral crisis. The conversion of his close friend Henri Ghéon, announced to him in January, 1916, had deeply upset him and forced him to reflect on his own religious convictions or lack of them. Seven passages of the book were published in the first issue of the Dadaist magazine *Littérature* of March, 1919. In a letter to Albert Thibaudet, in 1927, Gide refers to the work as representing his philosophy. In the early 1930's, at a moment when Gide believed communism offered the hope for a better world, some of the passages written at that time echo his brief but sincere adhesion to communism.

The writing of *Les Nouvelles Nourritures* is recognizably Gide's on every page, but the theme of joy found in the beauty of the physical world, and found in human relationships, and especially in his love for Marc Allégret, who is named in the text, is more sustained, more energetic, more optimistic than in any other work of Gide. All the familiar debates associated with Gide's writings are here—the debates between society and the individual, between Christian values and the individual—but they often reach a kind of grandeur that surpasses mere argumentation. Life is seen as a dazzling miracle (*ce miracle étourdissant qu'est la vie*), and this new Adam is in love with everything virginal he sees. Men habitually constrict life, but the author of *Les Nouvelles Nourritures* knows that life can be more beautiful than they can ever imagine it. *La vie peut être plus belle que ne la consentent les hommes.*

As in *Les Nourritures Terrestres,* thirty-eight years earlier, the name of God occurs frequently and appears synonymous with this man's joy, with the gratitude he feels toward life. *C'est la reconnaissance de mon coeur qui me fait inventer Dieu chaque jour.* Joy is spread over all the earth (*une éparse joie baigne la terre*) and whenever he is cut off from this joy, he knows it comes from the constrictions of his past. The Gospel theme of renunciation is repeated with greater insistence than in *Les Nourritures Terrestres.* Whatever a man is able to give up may become a force of affirmation. The real possession is that which is given away. This motif of asceticism brings with it the obligation to be happy, to enjoy the world not by possessing it, but by knowing it intimately as the source of life and beauty.

With greater subtlety than ever before, Gide, in *Les Nouvelles Nourritures*, joins his thoughts on the Divine with the exaltation he feels in a nonpossessive enjoyment of the world. To possess a creature would also be a failure, a restriction and a limitation. It would be equivalent to abandoning God and ceasing to live in eternity. Gide is trying to learn how to love without holding. His happiness, if he is to know it, will be the power to increase the happiness of others. The setting for such a spiritual experience has to be an impoverishment. He prefers a meal at an inn to an elaborate dinner lavishly served in a castle. He prefers the public garden of a city used by everyone, to a magnificently laid-out park enclosed by walls and reserved for very few.

The passages on sensuality, on the richness of the senses are more sober in *Les Nouvelles Nourritures* than in the early work. And yet he still claims that the awareness of being comes to him through the senses: *je sens donc je suis*. Of all basic assumptions, this is truest for him. Like his character Edouard in *Les Faux-Monnayeurs*, he wants to check his baggage at the station, and then willfully lose the baggage check. This liberation from material possessions is a bestowal of freedom on the life of the senses. His capacity to be astonished each day at the beauty of the world is religious. It is more natural for him to see God in a bud of a plant than in the ratiocinations of theology, and learn that God is more worthy of attention than the rest of the world, than himself, than all of humanity.

The entire movement of Gide's thought is to reach a state of oneness with the world and humanity that would free him from any need to depend on certainty. He uses the word *certitudes* to designate those dogmatisms or props that he wants to do without. How otherwise could he move toward the future, and follow the seasons, and allow today's joy to turn into tomorrow's?

Toward the end of *Les Nouvelles Nourritures*, he restores a word that had been sung of in *Les Nourritures Terrestres*, the word *volupté*, and again gives it a key place in the final passages. Voluptousness, or enjoyment of the senses, is more instructive than books. It is the experience in which a man becomes aware of his entire being. It makes possible all the admonitions that fill the last pages of the work: do not blame what differs from you; dare become who you are; understand your past and learn how to move far away from it.

Gide wrote *Les Nourritures Terrestres* for an imaginary reader Nathanaël, and in *Les Nouvelles Nourritures* the name seems too plaintive to him and he changes it to "comrade," but it is in this imaginary reader that Gide's youth will be prolonged. For the expression of human freedom, in both books, for its power and its peril, Gide created massive formulas, classical formulas, that have returned, only slightly modified in the writings of Sartre and Camus and René Char. The literary evolution, of which he was the greatest representative, has continued after him. His principal theme is the relationship between man and God. His family fortune and background permitted him the leisure and luxury of pursuing such a theme. His long life was one of self-examination, of courage in liberating himself, of testing himself in such experiences as Africa, communism, Catholicism. His attentiveness and the extraordinary freedom of his spirit kept him from accepting any one doctrine. Gide developed one need—that of doubting everything—and one obligation—that of never doubting himself.

9. Claudel: The Adventure of Love

Paul Claudel died in February, 1955, the last of a quartet of literary giants: Proust, Valéry, Gide. A few weeks before his death, he had been attending rehearsals of a new production of *L'Annonce faite à Marie*, at the Comédie-Française. His body was taken to Notre Dame. The procession passed before the very pillar against which Claudel had leaned on December 25, 1886, at vespers, while he listened to the singing of what he learned later was the "Magnificat." He has described that moment as a religious experience instrumental in his conversion. *Le Figaro Littéraire*, which appeared after his funeral, printed testimonials from three poets. Ungaretti, from Rome, wrote of the influence of Claudel's plays on Italian writers. W. H. Auden, from New York, spoke of the stylistic resemblance between Whitman and Claudel. T. S. Eliot, from London, recalled that Alain-Fournier, forty-five years earlier, had given him copies of *L'Arbre* and *Connaissance de l'Est*. While pointing out that the dramaturgy of Claudel is totally different from his own, Eliot hailed Claudel as the greatest poet-dramatist of the century.

These four important French writers, born about 1870, appear to us now as seekers of different goals and representative of a kind of secret. Proust, the first to die, was concerned with the secret of how to make eternity out of an instant, of how art can immobilize what passes with time. With Gide's work is associated the understanding of desire and longing, the need to understand change. Valéry pursued the understanding of ideas, or the structure of the mind, the way in which the mind formulates ideas. Claudel stands apart from all three in the secrecy of his quest.

Of the four, Claudel seems the least accessible, the least clear, or the most startling in terms of the entire tradition of French literature. The works of Gide, Valéry, and Proust prolong a well-established tradition of moralists, thinkers, memorialists. It is the central tradition of France, the one with which we associate a Montaigne, a Pascal, a La Rochefoucauld, a Stendhal, a Balzac. By comparison, Claudel seems unclassifiable. His mind is not essentially analytical. The French literary mind has been predominantly analytical in each century. Claudel's mind is more inclined toward the creation of a synthesis. His fundamental preoccupations are more metaphysical than is usual in French writers who on the whole tend to psychological and moralistic preoccupations. Moreover the seeming disorder of Claudel's style, its vehemence, its violence, its bluntness, separates his work from the central tradition of the French literary style.

Claudel's secret, the trait which marks him and keeps him apart in the contemporary tradition is the central place he gives to God in his work. He is the poet singing before God, and this may explain why Claudel seems disconcerting to so many French readers. By his strength, by the proportions of his work, by his attitude toward the Creation, Claudel differs from his contemporaries. Because he remained outside of all coteries, his work today is felt as an isolated and unique force. Every object in his writing is stated in terms of its meaning, of its role. The humblest things he can name are signs in much the same way that the characters of his dramas represent their salvation. When he speaks of divine joy as being the one reality, it is not difficult to believe that Claudel's fundamental approach to literature is different from others; different even from the methods of Rimbaud and Mallarmé to whom he owes so much.

By temperament, Claudel was hardly disposed to accept the rule and the model of other poets. His poetic practice may be reminiscent to some degree of Mallarmé and Rimbaud, but he forces and affirms his subject far more than they do. The desire to communicate the universal, the cosmically universal, forced him to cultivate his sense of discipline and hierarchy. Claudel revived and restated some of the oldest and noblest claims for the poetic genius. He implies that simply by listening to the voice of the poet, we are initiated into the mysteries of the universe. Before we necessarily understand the words themselves of the poet, we participate in their meaning. The work of the poet rises up from such profound sources that it is comparable to an element of nature. We follow first the ineffable part of poetry, because it is in harmony with the creation. We recognize it without understanding it, and we listen to it as we listen to the music of seas and rivers.

A poem is no more an "explanation" than a flower is, or a hillside or a sunset. It is that which means by its form, its beauty, its wholeness.

> *Tu n'expliques rien, ô poète, mais toutes*
> *choses par toi nous deviennent explicables.*

The poet is the man able to release the secret potentialities of a word which in ordinary speech is a purely conventional sign. The sound of the word, when it becomes audible in the poet's verse, restores a kind of existence to the object it names. The object is thus recreated, but not necessarily explained. The words, by their place and their sound in the poet's verse, find a new meaning simply in the order of their arrangement. The action of the poet seems, therefore, magical or supernatural. He calls words into being and finds for them a new life in the new complexity of their arrangement.

Claudel's visit to Notre Dame on Christmas Day, 1886, prefigured the important concept of his faith that man has to will to go to God and find his joy in that encounter. The creation of the poetic word is the poet's action. A poem is a testimonial, an apologetics consented to not merely by the reason of the poet, but by his sensibility and his entire being. The unity of the world is perceived by the experience of love which provides us with an imperfect and often tantalyzing *contrefaçon* of unity. Everything has its meaning in the world and everything can be sung of by the poet. At our birth we enter into a secret pact with all beings and all objects. The mission of the poet is that of pointing out our relationships with all the realities of the world.

Many of the most serious twentieth-century artists have been concerned with providing their works with an aesthetic justification. In the field of painting, for example, Braque has made theoretical pronouncements of considerable importance. Others, while not contributing any writing as massive as Delacriox' *Journal*, have spoken at times with conviction and acumen: Picasso, Matisse, Rouault, Masson, Severini. In literature, the achievements of Marcel Proust is the masterful way in which he combined his novel with the analysis of its origin and its meaning. Joyce, Mann, Gide, Valéry have all striven to propose a work and at the same time the aesthetics of the work. The five great odes of Claudel open with one entitled *Les Muses*, inspired by the frieze of the nine muses the poet had seen sculptured on a sarcophagus. The ode is a kind of poetics dealing with the poetic art, with its birth and its function.

On many points the theories of Claudel converge with those of Proust, and, behind him, with the tenets of impressionism and the theories of Ruskin. These artists and theorists believe that each time a new original artist arises, the world is recreated. He is able to confer immortality on what has no duration, a man's perception of the world. Aesthetic truth is not the same as scientific truth. It is not based on direct observation or exact notations. The reality of the world for the artist is his vision of the world. It is a particular universe not seen by other men until it is put in the form of art. The general public is ignorant about art or indifferent to new artistic creations. But each work will create its own posterity, and finally that work will reveal the temper and the soul of the period in which it was created.

Five years of the poet's life, between 1919 and 1924, were largely given over to the writing of *Le Soulier de Satin*. In every sense, this play marks a culmination in the long career of Claudel, a *summa*, or at least the conclusion of a cycle which had begun twenty years earlier with *Partage de Midi*. The giganticism of the work, its pure length and complexity, would not be sufficient to qualify it in this way if it did not, on examination, reveal the themes of the poet, his deepest preoccupations, and a mastery of his own style. Claudel himself has stated the importance of this work: *il résume tout mon art, toute ma pensée et toute ma vie.*

Such a work as *Le Soulier* testifies not only to the years during which it was being constructed, but to all the preceding years in the poet's life. Every man bears in himself all the events of his life before they occur, and the poet, by comparison with other men, is simply more intuitively aware of these events. The poet's life is intact within him at the start. If he is not ignorant of the future events, he is unknowing of the strength he will have with which to welcome or reject the events. For this poet, in particular, the teaching of Christian morality had extraordinary importance. Christian morality answers the needs and desires in us, and these are met with whatever strength we may have, in the physical and spiritual order. But it answers more than this, and *Le Soulier* is specifically concerned with this additional measure. It answers a strength which goes beyond ours. It turns a man into someone unknown to himself because he is the receptacle of a strength he can never exhaust.

The page-long poem *Ténèbres,* written in 1905, which was the year *Partage de Midi* was composed, is a text on the personal drama in Claudel's life, of which *Partage de Midi* is the first literary expression, and *Le Soulier de Satin,* twenty years later, the fuller and more resolved literary expression. The drama, therefore, in its biographical sense, lasted twenty years. But at its inception, in 1905, in this simple poem *Ténèbres,* the drama itself is formulated and its spiritual resolution as well, although actually the resolution was not to come until the passing of the intervening years. It might therefore be claimed that not only are events in a poet's life present in him at the start, but also the meaning of these events and the solutions which they are to reach.

The poet himself speaks in *Ténèbres* and says that he is here and the one he loves is in some other place, and the silence between them is awesome.

> *Je suis ici, l'autre est ailleurs, et le silence*
> *est terrible.*

The poem is about this absence and this separation. The symbol of darkness, of night, is this absence of communication, and the growing horror that fills the soul of the poet.

> *Je prête l'oreille, et je suis seul, et la terreur*
> *m'envahit.*

He speaks of hearing the resemblance of the beloved's voice and the sound of a cry. And the reader accepts the strange fact that this cry comes from a great distance, even from another continent. In his loneliness, the poet walks from one wall to the other wall of his room. He knows that the temptation that fills his heart is instigated by the Prince of the World, but he knows also that where sin abounds, there also the mercy of God abounds to an even richer degree.

> *Je suis que là où le péché abonde, là Votre miséri-*
> *corde surabonde.*
> *Il faut prier, car c'est l'heure du Prince du Monde.*

This poem of *Ténèbres* is a single cry, but so full and so swift that it carries the weight of *Le Soulier de Satin*. In a form even more radically reduced, are the two words of Saint Augustine that serve as an epigraph to the play: *Etiam peccata.* "Even the sins" are of some use in the indecipherable economy with which God orders the world. Everything is useful to the will of Providence. As the drama unfolds, in the multiple scenes that cover much of the globe and fill years of time, one follows it, if one follows it at all, with a spirit that gradually adjusts to God's patience. The salvation of a soul is a slow and seemingly devious process in which time and place and human character may be limitlessly drawn upon.

When *Le Soulier de Satin* was begun, Paul Claudel was a man who had reached the middle of his life. It is precisely that moment in a man's life when he is suddenly aware of the many coexisting currents and themes of his life, when wounds that have healed are still reminders of bitterness and pain. The playwright himself has said that *Le Soulier* represented for him the complete purging of his soul, the resolving of the very crisis in his own life of which *Partage de Midi* offers the explanation. *Le Soulier* is therefore a play of conclusion. It bears the mark of appeasement. From the prologue, spoken by the Jesuit priest as he is drowning, we have a sense of the breadth of this world, of its oceans and continents that are to be the site of the drama, and we have also a sense of a planetary universe, of a supernatural world where the meaning of a separation of a man and a woman will be different from the separation of Rodrigue and Prouhèze during the lifetime of their love, which is the subject matter of *Le Soulier de Satin*.

The prologue has the characteristics of a prologue. It introduces the play, but it is separate from the play's action. It is never completely forgotten throughout the unfolding of the drama. The prologue is a monologue, spoken by a priest who is tied to the high mast of a ship which is sinking into the ocean. The subject of his speech, which is a prayer, is the salvation of his brother Rodrigue. The priest prays that if his brother is attracted to evil, may it be so great as to be compatible with the good. He prays that if this evil be related to love, may it be so strong as to make of his brother a man wounded.

Faites de lui un homme blessé.

The boat sinks and the Jesuit father disappears. In a scene of the second day (the acts are called "days"), Rodrigue finds a piece of a broken mast with the partly decipherable name *Santiago* on it and knows that was the boat which had been shipwrecked when his brother the priest was on it. Rodrigue looks upon the piece of wood as a sign of salvation. It is the only specific reference to the priest whose prayer, however, controls and directs the action of the play.

From the initial scene we learn that the play is on the role of the supernatural, or the passage of the supernatural through the world and its intervention in the affairs of men. *Le Soulier* is a drama on communion and on the meaning of Providence. It is a reciprocal action taking place between heaven and earth. On the Atlantic Ocean, midway between two continents, on the equatorial line separating the two hemispheres, a pact is made by a Jesuit father. From this initial scene we realize that the unity of place in this drama is the universe. Correspondences are established between heaven and earth, between continents and the sea, between public affairs and personal dramas.

In this drowning of the priest, which we witness therefore at the very beginning, one of the major themes of the play is announced and enacted. It is the meaning of man, whom Claudel sees as the creature destined to pass. A human existence does not have the power to remain, to become fixed on any one place for any duration of time. The characters of *Le Soulier* are going to cover great distances of space and time. Each one lives simultaneously in an exile and in a public mission which is being carried out. The symbol of voyage is projected throughout the work as a bitter antagonism between man's desire to remain rooted in one place, to found his happiness under one sky, and the need to wander, to obey the will of a king, to placate the obsession of a conqueror.

The poet himself, Paul Claudel, had lived in its simplest terms, the action of his play before writing it. He had been the Frenchman deeply attached to his native province, to the beauty of his own landscape and the productive richness of his soil, and he had been also the diplomat who had spent most of his life outside of France, in the sometimes very distant missions to which his career of ambassador exiled him. The biographical meaning of displacement, of missions to distant lands that will test the heart of a man and separate him from his personal happiness, Claudel bequeathed to his characters: to Tête d'Or, to Mesa (in *Partage de Midi*), to Anne Vercors (in *L'Annonce faite à Marie*), to Rodrigue and Prouhèze.

In one sense, then, *Le Soulier* is the world's panorama. Claudel tells us that he began writing it when he was between Denmark and Japan. The poet's passage through the world is the play's itinerary. The many transformations are of little consequence. If what took place in Brazil for Claudel the traveler, takes place in Sicily for Claudel the poet in *Le Soulier de Satin*, the meaning of these distances covered is what finally counts in the work. This very sense of movement between cities and continents provides for the work a tone of jubilation and celebration. The sense of being free in movement, of being released in freedom is in itself joyous. The large number of characters encountered corresponds to the distance in space. But even more striking than these high dimensions in geography and population, is the impingement of the supernatural world on the natural world. Claudel reminds us of the intervention of the gods and goddesses in Homer, and claims that the supernatural world is for a Christian as real as our own world.

The love story of Rodrigue and Prouhèze is at the heart of *Le Soulier de Satin*, and this story is conceived of as unfolding throughout the total universe. It is an ensemble of time and space and action, a concert of forces which characterize and control every period in history: supernatural, historical, intellectual, and passionate. The personal drama of this man and this woman, of Rodrigue and Prouhèze, cannot be dissociated from the drama of the world. Their love is vulnerable to all these forces. No one episode can be isolated from the world. You can take nothing from the universe unless you take it all. The world involves the good and the wicked. Even each crime has its reason and its necessity. The epigraph placed by Claudel at the beginning of the play in its first version, and therefore corresponding to the ideal of the play, in the mind of the poet, is two famous words of Saint Augustine: *Etiam peccata*. The sins also of the world have their function in the scheme of the whole.

The geographical symbolism of *Le Soulier*—Spain, Naples, a French province, England, Africa, America, the islands of Japan —indicates clearly that the poet is concerned with the life of a conqueror, of a *conquistador*. The character of Rodrigue reminds us of Tête d'Or in the early play, and the situations in which he finds himself remind us of Mesa in *Partage de Midi*. The vastness and the complexity of the Renaissance form the backdrop of the play: the revival of Plato, the activity of the explorers Vasco da Gama and Columbus, the work of the scientist Copernicus, the art of Michelangelo, the founders of religious orders, Francis Xavier, Saint John of the Cross, Saint Teresa of Avila. The spirit of the conqueror, of the empire builder is not unrelated to the spirit of the poet, creator of such a work as *Le Soulier de Satin*, who refuses to relinquish any scene of this cosmic action.

Such a word as cosmic applies to the poet's greed in putting all the richness of a century and a world into one work, and yet the drama's action is one of total simplicity. It is the story of two lovers, of Rodrique and Prouhèze, who are together in a spiritual sense, but who are separated by continents and oceans. They form with the traditional pair of lovers an extraordinary counterpoint. This love is the drama of separation, of incommunicability, of the impossibility of reuniting. From the spectacular largeness of the setting, in time and place, we move to one point deep within a single heart.

In all the plays of Claudel, love is the principal element and cause of the dramatic action. In *Le Soulier* it is still preeminently at the center of the play's action, but in a manner far more mysterious, far more concealed than in the other works. Rodrigue's love for Prouhèze and her love for him are an intense form of passionate love. It is the form of love which in the tradition of the French theatre is Racinian. The great lovers of

Racine—Hermione, Bérénice, and Phèdre—suffer from the drama of passion in its absolutism. This absolute of passion is the same in Racine and Claudel, but the impossibility of its realization, that is, the reason for its being forbidden and the suffering that comes from it, are radically different.

The love felt by Hermione, Bérénice, and Phèdre is in each case a passion that cannot be satisfied because of the human destiny of the character, of the role she must play in the world. Her fate is to love what is forbidden because of her position in the world of men. In Racine's dramaturgy, the sentiment of love is a force in conflict with the world, a force which separates the character from the world to which he belongs. In the Racinian tragedy we follow this thwarted power of love during a few hours only in the life of the heroine or the hero. The unity of time, observed by Racine, demonstrates this love at its highest point of frenzy when it makes the lover a victim. The unity of place turns the palace room into a cell out of which there is no escape. And the unity of action turns the suffering into the ceremony of death.

In Claudel's conception of tragedy, the focus is not so much on the human destiny of the characters as on their eternal destiny. This is the radically different perspective which helps to explain the opening out of time and space in *Le Soulier de Satin*, the aggrandizement of scenes and the multiplying of personages. Human passion, which is the immediate problem in the hearts of Rodrigue and Prouhèze, is not forbidden solely because of the human and social destiny of these two characters, but because of their eternal destiny. The clash between such a commonplace experience as human passion and the incomprehensible concept of eternity is the dominant struggle, the agony of this play, prefigured in the prologue, where a dying priest speaks to eternity. The play's action never relinquishes this tension between the immediate and the eternal, between the human and the divine.

This fundamental difference between Racinian and Claudelian tragedy, between *Bérénice* and *Le Soulier de Satin*, both of which are concerned with the inevitable separation of two people who love one another, is supported by a corollary difference which is elusive and difficult to define, and which has to do with the problem of human happiness. The realization of love, in *Bérénice*, would be the goal of happiness. This is the goal that both the queen Bérénice and the emperor Titus have in their hearts when they anguish over the impossibility of their love, an impossibility caused by the claims of the throne. It would be difficult, and even false, to define for Rodrigue and Prouhèze happiness as the goal of life. It might possibly be for them a by-product. They would subscribe to the harsh thesis that by looking for happiness, man does not find it. It comes, when it does, in other ways.

And yet, love, for Claudel, is the essential means by which man can know himself. And since love, in this case, is love for someone else, the real significance of a man's life is in someone else. Love is an experience of joy in one of the characters of *Le Soulier*, in Dona Musique. And love is an experience in suffering for Dona Prouhèze. These are extreme roles played by love in the human drama. We are close here to the famous definition of love by Lacordaire that has had such meaning for Claudel, and for Mauriac in the twentieth century, namely, there is only one love. All the degrees and all the varieties of what the world calls love, are definitions devised by the world to designate the sole experience of Divine Love.

The love existing between Prouhèze and Rodrigue bears all the familiar traits of human passion and worldly love, but it also bears the characteristics and demands of a higher love. Love is that experience which, according to a much used physiological image, creates in a man or a woman a vacancy, a void, a hollowed out center that provokes a call or a need for the one loved. It is felt both as a physical need, a desire for closeness and fulfillment, and as a spiritual need for self-realization and completion. Claudel does not look upon these as contradictory loves. One is used as the instrument for the other.

The physical dying of the priest in the prologue is offset by the prayer he makes that the greatness of his brother Rodrigue be tested by love. This scene in its mystical meaning is paralleled in the early scene of the play where Prouhèze offers one of her satin slippers to the Virgin:

Vierge mère, je vous donne mon soulier
Vierge mère, gardez dans votre main mon malheureux petit pied!

She explains her prayer by saying that if ever she rushes toward evil, it will be with a limping foot:

Mais quand j'essayerai de m'élancer vers le mal,
que ce soit avec un pied boiteux!

This woman, whose name is Prouhèze, meaning *prouesse*, or prowess, is a French woman from the northern province of La Franche Comté, who will ably demonstrate and justify such a name. (Claudel told Louis Gillet that he found the name Prouhèze on the sign of a cobbler, *un savetier*, in the rue Cassette, in Paris.)

In this scene of prayer where Prouhèze offers her slipper to the Virgin in a gesture reminiscent of the feudal ceremony of the glove homage, we have the impression that a pact is being drawn up between a creature and the Creator not unlike the prologue pact between the Jesuit priest and the Almighty. We have the impression that Prouhèze has already been chosen, that she is already in the realm of grace, that whatever happens to her will happen in accordance with love and grace. On the one hand, she seems made for combat, for great human enterprises and trials, and on the other hand she demonstrates the most disarming traits of the feminine soul, of submission and tenderness. She is obviously the kind of woman who will be able to bear the long separation from the man she loves, and also the kind of woman whose love will not diminish in its intensity.

Rodrigue is sent with a letter to Prouhèze by the king of Spain. He comes into the presence of his rival Camille in Mogador. He knows that Prouhèze is beyond the curtain where the two men are talking. This is the strange impossible meeting between Prouhèze and Rodrigue at the end of the second day. She returns the letter with a few words written on the envelope, *"Je reste. Partez."* That is all. He calls to her and knows that she hears his voice. But there is no answer. The entire dramatic scene is one of shadows. Camille and Rodrigue themselves are shadows cast against the curtain, and Prouhèze is invisible. This is the scene of meeting between Rodrigue and Prouhèze, and yet they do not meet. Rodrigue speaks of the great law written on stone that separates them. He accepts the order to leave.

This scene is followed by a very brief scene, in the acting version of the play, which is an ingenious device of the playwright to explain the meaning of this love and this separation, and to project dramatically for the spectators the mystical joining of the two characters. It is the scene of the Double Shadow. Against the backdrop can be seen the shadows of a man and woman, and the two voices can be heard joined in the recitative.

Rodrigue and Prouhèze are separated, but in one sense they are joined. This scene of *l'Ombre-double* is their joining in another realm. We see and hear the one being which they make. At one moment in their existence they were joined and this can never be, as the poet says, subtracted from the page of eternity. Their love, which was a joining, albeit brief, can never be effaced from the archives of eternity. So this play of Claudel that shows principally scenes of great separation when Rodrigue and Prouhèze are at two ends of the world, shows, by means of the double shadow cast on a screen, their eternal life together, as they exist in their minds, when their bodies occupy two widely separated points of geography.

The final scenes of the Second Day are among the most difficult of the play to stage and to understand. In them Claudel tells us that each of these two people, Rodrigue and Prouhèze, has lived in the other. Each has lived in the thought of the other. This thought is represented on the stage by the Shadow, by the Double Shadow. Even more significantly, Claudel is telling us that the lover, by his desire to possess another creature, is separated, detached from everything else in the world. But precisely because of this extraordinary detachment which love operates, the lover proves himself capable of an even more perfect detachment that promises him the absolute and the fullness of Joy. Joy in the highest theological sense, which is the love of God.

In speaking of his drama, Claudel once made the claim that for the spectator to follow and comprehend it, to participate in it, there is no precise need for his being a Christian. In those specific aspects of the play thus far discussed—the prologue, the world setting, and the theme of love—the action concerns a man and woman who love one another and desire one another, but who are kept apart, who are kept separated in great distances and in long periods of time, by a power that might be called metaphorically the hand of God. The lovers accept this plight or this separation because of their love of this power. This acceptance of God's love in the life of man, and the two key scenes of mystical action—the prayer of the dying priest and the slipper scene of Prouhèze—make it impossible to interpret the play in purely human or traditional terms. God is the invisible actor, the impresario who uses human passion, all degrees and all kinds of human passion, for the realization of His own goal.

In several of the letters Claudel wrote to André Gide, especially those of 1909, he emphasizes the specific Christian drama of man as opposed, for example, to the drama of man in antiquity. During the life of the Christian, his salvation is never assured once and for all. The Christian has to strive for a daily salvation. Day after day for the believer, the struggle that goes on between the visible and the invisible has all the characteristics for Claudel of tragedy. Man is in danger of tragedy at every moment. He does not know what the sage in antiquity knew, a balance or an equilibrium in his life. The Christian life, for Claudel, is a constant state of conflict. *Le chrétien vit à l'état de conflit.*

The adventure of Rodrigue and the adventure of Prouhèze testify to the conviction that a Christian life is always in the process of being constructed or formed or composed. It can never be seen as a whole or as a pattern of life that is terminated. The consequences of our acts are never over. They continue to be felt unexpectedly, intermittently. In a single life, the major events of marriage and death have little significance when compared with the goal of a Christian life, which is eternal life or eternal death. Claudel attempts to see the lives of Prouhèze and Rodrigue from this dizzying height of Catholic theology. In a sense, the story of Rodrigue and Prouhèze is not their own. It is a representative story of the perpetual drama of humanity as expounded in Christian theology.

Claudel often said, with the seeming arbitrariness and rigor for which he has been castigated, that only the Christian knows the full experience of desire. In such a statement, he implies that the Christian, when he is fully aware of the metaphysics of his faith, knows in the experience of desire what he really desires. For such a man, what is often called human tragedy can never be thus limited. It inevitably moves into the dimensions of a cosmic tragedy when centuries form the setting and all of humanity the actors.

This conception of tragedy is implicit in some of the most mysterious or mystical scenes in *Le Soulier*. The scene between the Angel and Prouhèze, which takes place toward the end of the third day, is one of pedagogy when the personal dilemma of Prouhèze is raised to a lofty generality. The Angel is trying to explain to her the technique of salvation and compares a sin to a bait thrown out by God and which, catching in the entrails of a man, serves in the action of his being pulled out of the state of disgrace into a state of grace. The art of fishing is an analogy for God's use of sin in a human life.

In the earlier play, *Partage de Midi*, a meeting takes place between a man and a woman, between Mesa and Ysé. This is followed by an experience and an explanation of love. And at the end of the play's action, the form of appeasement in human terms is reached. The mark of this appeasement in human terms is everywhere in *Le Soulier de Satin*, but it is raised to an exceptional level of explanation. *Le Soulier* is a fuller, more absolute explanation of the earlier play.

Tête d'Or, written when Claudel was twenty, *Partage de Midi*, written immediately after a personal crisis in the poet's life when he was thirty-seven, and *Le Soulier de Satin*, written when Claudel was in his fifties, represent a chronological development and at the same time the deepening in comprehension of a persistent theme. Jean-Louis Barrault defined the three plays, in a conversation he had with Claudel in 1939, as the sap, the trial, and the synthesis *(la sève, l'épreuve, la synthèse)* of the dramatic works of the poet.

In its language and structure, *Tête d'Or* has the boldness and the vitality and the defects of a twenty-year-old playwright. It can easily be interpreted as the poet's farewell to his youth. Tête d'Or is a serious young man who, like Rimbaud, believes he has seen all countries and experienced all forms of passion. He suffers from an anxiety to which later, in his successors, Catholicism will bring an answer and a remedy.

The passionate love in *Partage de Midi* is insatiable. Many of the speeches of Mesa and Ysé are cries against death, refusals to consider the inevitability of death. Passion is equated with the violent love for life, for all things earthy: rivers, trees, and landscapes.

Le Soulier de Satin offers a picture of a superabundant life which is constantly transcending daily life without ever destroying or underestimating the daily life we know. Rodrigue and Prouhèze, and their predecessors, Violaine, Pierre de Craon, Ysé, and Mesa, never exhaust their human love because it constantly grows greater and more abundant. Prefigured in the earlier plays and fully exemplified in *Le Soulier*, human love in Claudel inevitably grows into the drama of love between the creatures and the Creator. The same temperament and the same traits dominate Tête d'Or, Mesa, and Rodrigue. They are proud men of action who venerate God. In each case, love wounds their pride and makes an opening in their stalwart self-assurance. It is this very wound, this opening which will be used by Divine Love for entrance into a human being. The Claudelian hero is always able to effect a reconciliation with his destiny. Human life, in spite of all its complexities and trials, is never looked upon as an impasse, but rather as a road that mounts toward the final vision of serenity and love.

The play is fundamentally about the sacrament of marriage. Prouhèze and Ysé in the earlier play, and their famous predecessor Yseut of the *Tristan* story, all signed a contract before God. Pélage, the husband of Prouhèze, expresses the thought of Claudel, when he says: "It is not love which makes marriage, but consent." (*Ce n'est pas l'amour qui fait le mariage, mais le consentment.*) The marriage pact in *Le Soulier de Satin* is not unlike the pact which Claudel made with the universe and which permitted him to compose such a text of euphoria and victory.

The work is a spiritual testament of multiple intentions in which Claudel bequeathed, to whoever would listen, the secrets of a joy he believed definitive. Access to this joy is allowed only after the harshest trials, after doubts and suffering. This is certainly one of the major themes in the text: joy comes at the end of separations and distress and passion. These are moments in a life story during which the protagonist is helped mysteriously. Love between man and woman is a drama of a hundred aspects whose setting is the universe. It is a quest leading across oceans and through deserts, the quest of a spiritual adventure, carried out with purely human means, and which, in *Le Soulier de Satin*, involves moments of burlesque and satire and buffoonery. The letter, for example, which travels around the world and reaches its destination when it is far too late, comes from one of the oldest traditions of comedy. But this comedy is "divine" because it reveals to its hero and heroine the meaning of eternal life.

PART IV

Picasso's Paris at the Turn of the Century

10. Painters and Poets

THE EARLY YEARS of the century, when Picasso lived in Paris for the first time, seem to us today in many ways the dawn of an age whose twilight or ending we are living at the present. Artistic and literary movements are usually characterized in their early years by an ambitious program, by a delirious youthful ambition to impose theories on the world, and even to change and modify the world by means of a particular vision. In almost every instance, the immediate effect of an artistic movement on the world is very slight. Its strength, its power of influence, what the French call its *rayonnement*, are more easily measurable in the years that follow its most active period of expression, when the lesser figures of the movement, who perhaps were the most articulate and the most ambitious in the early years, are somewhat forgotten, and when the really profound aspect of the debate is maintained by two or three strong personalities.

Picasso inherited in his formative years in Barcelona and his first years in Paris, not the entire romantic movement, but the qualities and the order given to French romanticism by Nerval and Baudelaire. He inherited, not the complicated and prolix school of symbolism, but the very specific contributions and the particularized art of Rimbaud, Lautréamont, and Mallarmé. In the early Paris years, and even in the earlier Barcelona years, Pablo Picasso lived in the center of a world of picturesque gifted painters and writers who were concerned with tracing a new way to very precious goals. Those that have been named the most often are: a new kind of happiness in the world, a new release of the human spirit, and a new understanding of freedom. These are the three French words, *bonheur, esprit, liberté,* that return constantly in the writings of the poets who surrounded Picasso.

Now, sixty years later, when the frenzied and histrionic activities are over, when exhibitions, banquets, conversations, manifestoes and manifestations have been carefully recorded in histories and memoirs, two or three figures seem best to represent the age and its new movement in art. Picasso and Apollinaire, in particular, as the painter and the poet; Max Jacob and André Salmon, who were perhaps the closest friends of Picasso and Apollinaire, and who understood better than others Picasso's ambitions, his anxieties, and his genius. Two other figures of the same age should be named, one a poet and the other a man of the theatre. Saint-John Perse and Antonin Artaud, who, although quite removed from Picasso and not participators in his immediate circle, helped to trace the way to this new understanding of man's happiness, spirit, and freedom at the beginning of a century which, at least by its midway mark, will appear to most of the living as an age of tragedy.

These figures have not been chosen too arbitrarily. Their work for us today justifies this designation as those artists who in the early 1900's promised themselves and promised one another to found a new city. A city within the city of Paris consecrated to art.

One of the most privileged and prosperous eras in the history of Paris extended from approximately 1895 to the beginning of World War I in 1914. Wagner was sung at the Opéra; Debussy's one opera *Pelléas et Mélisande* was sung at the Opéra-Comique; Sarah Bernhardt was the great actress of the moment; Bergson in his public course at the Collège de France was adding new prestige to French philosophy and indicating a possibly new approach to art; Anatole France was the popular writer of the day; Cézanne and Monet had revealed a new visual world; Mallarmé, who died in 1898, had left two long poems, *L'Après-Midi d'un Faune* and *Hérodiade*, which, even if they were not always understood or read, were already looked upon as two landmarks in the history of French poetry. The national budget and the budgets of individual citizens were balanced. The Third Republic had finally brought prosperity and contentment to France.

The spectacle of elegance and beauty that could be seen in the Bois de Boulogne was the symbol of this national prosperity and happiness. The long line of horses and carriages, the silk dresses of the ladies indolently reclining in their carriages were visible aspects of a world of great wealth and refinement. Marcel Proust, at the end of the first part of his novel, *Du côté de chez Swann*, has left the permanent picture of that spectacle when he describes Odette de Crécy or Mme Swann passing in her carriage along the Avenue des Acacias and acknowledging the bows of the gentlemen on foot, all members of the Jockey Club. Proust was writing *Swann's Way* when Picasso was engaged in his cubist period, around 1907, but during Picasso's first years in Paris, Proust was composing the first draft of his novel, *Jean Santeuil*, which did not come to light until 1952. However, Proust's world of the Avenue des Acacias and the salons of the Faubourg Saint-Germain was not Picasso's world in Paris.

His world was closer to a famous apartment at 18, rue Cassette, near Saint-Sulpice. There lived Alfred Jarry, called "le Père Ubu" because of his play *Ubu Roi*. This was a representative bohemian center for Picasso and his friends. They called it "La Grande Chasublerie" because in the same building was the atelier of a maker of religious vestments (of *chasubles*). Many have written of the disorder of this apartment on the rue Cassette, of Jarry's life-sized portrait done by the douanier Rousseau, of a porcelain owl, and of the friendly silhouette of the writer.

The most important café for painters and poets around 1900 was unquestionably La Closerie des Lilas, in Montparnasse, almost in the Latin Quarter. Picasso came often from Montmartre with his friends. They usually crossed Paris on foot for those visits to Montparnasse, which was just beginning to serve as a center for painters. Picasso especially enjoyed the company of Paul Fort who was one of the faithful habitués and readers of poetry at the Closerie. The poet Jean Moréas held court there. On one occasion,

Moréas spoke to Picasso about the relative simplicity of being a poet. He said, "What bothers me in painting is the paraphernalia you need: easels, tubes of paint, brushes, a studio! I compose my poems walking in the rain." And then he added, "And you even need models!" Picasso did not answer and his intimate friends did not remind Moréas that Picasso usually did without models. Before his invention of the art movement *il futurismo*, Marinetti used to come to La Closerie. Once he arrived from Milano in a long white automobile for the marriage of Gino Sévérini and the very young daughter of Paul Fort.

But Picasso's Paris had as its center his studio on the rue Ravignan in Montmartre. Especially between 1903 and 1907, his small studio was the meeting place of his friends, where they watched him testing illusions and hopes. So many artists came to the rue Ravignan that the new art has been called the Ecole Ravignan. A list of just the most famous would sound like a list of comparable artists and writers who attended Mallarmé's salon on the rue de Rome ten years earlier: Apollinaire was a frequent visitor; Marie Laurencin; Matisse who seemed always more solemn and serious than the others; Derain; and Braque who was a Norman, born in Argenteuil, more suspicious and hesitating in his opinions.

During the first three years of the century, Picasso moved back and forth several times between Barcelona and Paris. These were the famous years of the so-called "blue period" when the influences of the art circles in Barcelona and Picasso's Spanish background were fused with his first impressions of Paris and his first friendships with French painters and writers. It is quite true that Picasso became in Paris the universal artist we know today, but his fundamental attitude toward the world and toward modern art was formed in Barcelona during the years immediately preceding his first trip to Paris in 1900, and during the two or three return trips before he settled in France. In Barcelona he had already taken his stand against all forms of *snobisme* in art, and he had felt there the strong attraction of French culture. He had learned to feel horror for the type of philistine who was closed to all innovations and new movements in art. The example of Flaubert, and perhaps especially of Baudelaire, had instilled in Picasso and in the Catalan painters of Barcelona a strong dislike for the bourgeois philistine. A sense of opposition and even destruction was present in the earliest Picasso. Much later, in 1934, he confessed to Christian Zervos that his works are summas of destruction. (*Mes oeuvres sont des sommes de destruction.*)

There were doubtless many reasons for Picasso's choice of Paris. Most of the Catalan painters felt attracted to the city, those in particular who felt a need to indulge in fantasies and experimentations. The so-called Bohemian life in Paris, the free life of the artist, exerted a strong appeal throughout the world at that time. There were linguistic and economic reasons also for Picasso. Catalan speech is not too unlike French, and it was reputedly easier to sell paintings in Paris than anywhere else in the world.

And so, at the age of nineteen, Picasso came to Paris for the first time, in September, 1900. He stayed until early December when he returned to Barcelona for the Christmas holidays. There were not many sales during those first months, but some of the young Paris painters were enthusiastic about Picasso and called him *le petit Goya*. He was consciously cultivating at this time a return to innocence, a Rousseauistic primitivism. He was obsessed with the painting of Millet and Maurice Denis and Gauguin. In 1901, the book of Mecislas Goldberg, *Lazare le Ressuscité*, was widely read in Barcelona. It is a text largely on the art of Puvis de Chavannes. Picasso's use of the guitar may have been suggested by an article of Nicolas Maria Lopez, on *La Psychologie de la Guitare*, which analyzed the guitar as the symbol of sentiment and the instinctive feelings of the people. That is why, according to this article, the guitar has the form of a woman's body.

In 1901, during Picasso's second visit to Paris, the Galerie Vollard on the rue Laffitte presented his first Paris exhibit. Seventy-five pictures were shown. There were many subjects: horse-racing (a theme closely associated with Degas), bull-fights, nudes, other subjects drawn from his wanderings through Spain, which touched on various forms of vice and which were reminiscent of Toulouse-Lautrec. In a practical sense, it put him into contact with the dealers. It was chez Vollard that he met Max Jacob, who was the first real enthusiast for Picasso's work and who became his closest friend during the early Paris years. The entire second sojourn put Picasso into closer contact with certain aspects of French culture he was to cherish, with the poetry, for example, of Rimbaud and Mallarmé and especially of Verlaine who became for him one of his *magots sublimes*, "magot" signifying a sage and even an ugly figure, but one who understood the meaning of freedom and art.

By the end of 1901—Picasso was now twenty—he was back in Barcelona. Both the color blue and the spirit of this color were gradually penetrating all the work of the painter. Jung has offered a very striking psychoanalytical explanation for the dominance of this color blue. He sees it as representative of the first stage of schizophrenia, the color of the submerged and even infernal world of the subconscious. The very sensitive art critic and historian Christian Zervos offers a more purely aesthetic explanation. He has attempted to demonstrate that the blue of Picasso is Cézanne's blue magnified. When Jung explained Picasso's treatment of prostitutes and impoverished wretches set in an atmosphere of decrepitude and decadence as indicative of the painter's inner torment and depression, Zervos replied that such themes were currently in vogue in Barcelona.

Aspects of these two diametrically opposed explanations of the blue period may be incorporated by contemporary students of Picasso. It is true that blue was the infernal color for the Egyptians and an obvious symbol of evil, or shame, or darkness, or even of the feminine passivity of night. The psychoanalysis of blue could easily designate the descent into the lower more obscure regions of the self and hence designate the dissolution of a man's being as he withdraws from the upper world of his consciousness. It is also true that the use of blue as a dominant color was no invention of Picasso and that it corresponded to an aesthetic atmosphere and even an intellectual ambiency in Barcelona at the beginning of the century.

The visual and the thematic effect of the blue paintings of Picasso is an extreme form of pathos and suffering. But ever since Diderot's famous paradox on the art of the actor, we know that in order to move spectators very deeply, as Picasso does in these paintings, it is not necessary for the actor or the painter or the poet to be comparably moved himself. This was the first world that Picasso revealed to his new friends and to his new public in Paris. They were disconcerting haunting apparitions. The French used the word "saturnine" in describing them, and one thinks instinctively of Verlaine's first volume of poems, of 1866, *Poèmes Saturniens*, where the poet, in the music of speech, evokes a world comparable to the pictorial world of the painter of 1901 and 1902. One of the first French critics to write about Picasso was Apollinaire, who saw in those early paintings the announcement of a new kind of painting transformed into an art as completely detached from the concrete world of objects as music is.

The meeting of two or three poets in the Montmartre studio of Picasso was the genesis of the new movement in art. The innermost circle of the "school" was composed of members who seemed to come from every direction: Pablo Picasso from Spain, Guillaume Apollinaire from Rome and Monaco, Max Jacob from Brittany, André Salmon from Russia. This was the group that was to help found the new French art. The city itself of Paris, Montmartre and the rue Ravignan, was the force able to fuse such disparate talents and races.

Max Jacob was the first new friend and admirer of Picasso. He had attended the first exhibit at Vollard's in 1901. Max called on Picasso the next day in his studio, then on the Boulevard de Clichy, under the pretext of writing an article on his painting. Picasso, twenty at the time, was a small slender fellow with strange eyes and an expression on his face of great solemnity. He felt immediately the goodness and generosity of Max Jacob who was to help him and support him through many difficult moments, particularly during the years 1903–12, when Picasso lived and worked at No. 13, rue Ravignan.

This address was a large uncomfortable wooden house, called "Le Bateau-Lavoir." Painters lived there, and sculptors, writers, actors, laundresses, dressmakers, vegetable hawkers. It was a cold house in the winter, and a furnace in the summer. Picasso settled there in 1902, on a return trip from Spain. He became a familiar figure in the neighborhood. He knew all the tradesmen on the small Place Ravignan, which is today the Place Emile-Goudeau. He wore principally the blue costume of the French workman: a blue jacket opened on a white shirt, pulled tight around his waist by a fringed flannel sash. He painted largely at night. Through the daytime there was a fairly continuous procession of Spanish friends, coming and going. A box spring on four legs was in one corner. There was a small rusty stove, a yellow wash basin, a small black trunk, a cane chair, easels, canvases of all sizes, tubes of paint scattered on the floor, brushes, and in a drawer of the table a white mouse cared for by Picasso.

In 1903 two young fellows met just outside Picasso's studio. They shook hands, introduced themselves. One was Max Jacob and the other was André Salmon. Jacob came from the Boulevard Barbès where he lived with one of his brothers, *mon frère le tailleur*, and Salmon came from the left bank, from the rue Saint Jacques. The night before, André Salmon had been introduced to Picasso and the Bateau-Lavoir by the Catalan sculptor Manuel Hugué, known as Manolo. Picasso was working on one of his blue paintings and using the light of a candle. Salmon has called this meeting his introduction to a new universe of painting and pathos. He saw in the middle of the studio a tub resembling the tub Bonnard put in his paintings, and in the tub he noticed a copy of a book by Claudel. Picasso had said to Salmon: "Come to lunch tomorrow. You will see Max Jacob. I want you to know him." And in the morning Picasso had alerted Max Jacob: "Come to lunch today. You will see André Salmon. I want you to know him." A week earlier Picasso had been introduced to Apollinaire in a bar near the Gare Saint-Lazare. Apollinaire, who was a bank clerk at that time, was unable to attend this first luncheon, but he joined the three men at the end of the day. Picasso himself called this meeting the opening of an era when painters and poets influenced one another.

Perhaps the one who was the most convinced of his mission in this meeting of poets and painters at the Bateau-Lavoir was Picasso's old friend from Barcelona, Manolo, the sculptor, who was the earliest friend to look upon Picasso as a very great artist. He remembered that Pascal at the age of twelve had reinvented geometry and he liked to think of Picasso, who was still very young, as inventing a new geometry destined to dazzle mankind. Manolo had led a picaresque life. He was the illegitimate son of a Spanish general and a young lady from Barcelona. He spent most of his youth in the company of thieves and rogues in Barcelona. But he became a sculptor and a designer. In Paris he even wanted to become a French poet and used to recite his French verse at the Closerie des Lilas before Jean Moréas. Manolo, by his wit and story-telling skill, was one of the best loved members of Picasso's group. The others were always amused by the strong Catalan accent of his French and heartened by his gaiety. He was undoubtedly the most picturesque of them all.

If Manolo had perhaps the deepest conviction about Picasso's future, Max Jacob had the deepest conviction concerning the entire group, *la bande à Picasso*, as it was to be called. He was the earliest historian or the earliest theorist for the "Ecole de la rue Ravignan," the one the most anxious to teach that the new art, painting and poetry both, must comply with no authority, must follow no one leader.

Max was more ceremonious than the others. He was a short man, quite bald, whose face had Semitic features of great beauty. He was famous for his wit and brilliance, for his stories, and he had more personal charm, more personal seductiveness than the others. He soon came to live on the rue Ravignan, at No. 7, where he occupied a single room. He received, in a more formal way than Picasso did at No. 13, on Mondays only. He was curious about the gossip and the stories of the neighborhood. He collected anecdotes of the rue des Abbesses, of the rue Lepic, and added them to the anecdotes he had brought from Quimper, his native Breton home. Many years later, during the German Occupation, long after Max had been converted to Catholicism and when he had received recognition as an important poet and a talented painter of gouaches, he died in a concentration camp. In February, 1944, he was taken from his room at Saint-Benoît-sur-Loire to Drancy. Picasso was alerted and used all the influence he had to have his friend released. But it was to no avail.

In the days of the Bateau-Lavoir, no one knew exactly how Max lived, how he survived, how he was able mysteriously to help Picasso in a practical sense more than the others. His friendship and loyalty counted tremendously for the painter. Most of what is known today about Max Jacob during the early years of the century, we owe to Picasso. Max was modest about his own work and spent much of his time praising and promoting the work of his friends. He showed his prose poems only to Picasso because he was able to count on the painter's discretion. Around 1904, Jacob concealed both his pastels and his poems. In a group he delighted and amazed everyone by his knowledge and wit. Picasso always spoke much less and preferred to enjoy the improvisations of his friend.

In terms of the future of the artists who assembled around Picasso, Max Jacob was the most discerning. Once he said to André Salmon, "They used to talk to you about Racine, La Fontaine and Boileau. Well, now we have their place." (*On a dû te parler de Racine, La Fontaine et Boileau. Eh bien, maintenant, c'est nous.*)

Guillaume Apollinaire was the prodigious walker of the group. He organized meetings at bistrots and cafés in various sections of the city. On the Boulevard Saint Michel, in the Latin Quarter, right at the river, was Le Caveau du Soleil d'Or, one of the favorite meeting places. Apollinaire celebrated it for the first marriage of André Salmon, on July 13, 1909. This was the *caveau*, he writes, where they met when they were young and where they waited for dawn, drunk on the words whose meaning will have to be changed.

> *Nous nous sommes rencontrés dans un caveau maudit*
> *Au temps de notre jeunesse*
> *Fumant tous deux et mal vêtus attendant l'aube*
> *Epris, épris des mêmes paroles dont il faudra changer*
> *le sens.*

Sometimes the occasion for the meeting was a banquet. Apollinaire seized every opportunity for a celebration. Those held at the Odéon, on the rue de Seine, were rather slight meals, but they were symbolic festivities where the poets and artists made plans for a triumphant future. They exchanged poems, discussed doctrines, judged one another with a terrifying lucidity. They played jokes and uttered monstrosities because every extreme counts when a new poetic universe is to be constructed.

Apollinaire probably benefited more than the others from these meetings. He became the most intoxicated with his speech and his ideas. He decided that the two literary magazines of Paris, the traditional *Mercure de France* and the symbolist *La Plume* were no longer sufficient, and drew up plans in a brasserie of the rue Christine for the founding of a new magazine *Le Festin d'Esope*. Nine issues were printed, every one of which has important documents for the history of the first decade. Apollinaire was an antiquarian, a lover of archives, an expert on erotic literature. He led the brawls and was responsible for the more violent aspects of the group. In this he was seconded by Picasso who owned a Browning revolver and enjoyed shooting it in the streets on his return late at night to the rue Ravignan. Apollinaire was perhaps the most paradoxical of a very paradoxical group. He was both theatrically bombastic as well as naïvely simple. His heavy coarse laughter was famous in Paris. His gestures had the ceremoniousness of a prelate and they confirmed the legend, started by Picasso (and proved erroneous today) that Apollinaire was the illegitimate son of a cardinal or a pope of Rome. Apollinaire, as his fame increased, became the leader of the group. Under his direction they passed from one hilltop to another in Paris: from the Montagne Sainte-Genevière in the Latin Quarter, to Montparnasse which was becoming an important center for painters, back to Montmartre and the Bateau-Lavoir.

The noisiest and most crowded reunions of painters and poets were those held every Tuesday at the Closerie des Lilas. They were presided over by Paul Fort. André Salmon served as secretary. The most eminent and the most loquacious were Moréas, Jarry, Stuart Merrill, Gustave Kahn, Georges Duhamel, Apollinaire, Braque. Picasso was the least talkative. Moréas often instigated the discussion. Once he greeted Picasso with the question: "Tell me, Picasso, was Velasquez talented?" (*Dites-moi, Picasso, est-ce que Velasquez avait du talent?*)

Picasso's immediate group were more at home at their own Montmartre restaurant *Le Lapin Agile*. The history of this famous restaurant has been recorded in books by Carco, Dorgelès, MacOrlan, André Warnod. The name itself *Le Lapin Agile* is an error. It was originally *Le Lapin à Gill*, the rabbit belonging to Gill, the name of the caricaturist who had painted the sign showing a rabbit jumping out of a casserole. The owner of the restaurant, le patron Frédé, liked the company of painters and poets. He easily extended credit to his friends or magnanimously bestowed meals "on the house." *Le Lapin Agile* was an important center of gastronomy and poetry for *la bande à Picasso* around 1903 when Montmartre was an unclassifiable village.

On the whole, life in France around 1900 did seem easy and agreeable and refined. Proust's picture of the Bois de Boulogne and the Faubourg Saint-Germain is ample proof. But there was also distress, not only economic but psychic as well. The best depiction of this distress is in the paintings of Pablo Picasso, in the poems of Max Jacob and Apollinaire, and in the memoirs of André Salmon. These friends never forgot that in 1896, just a few years before their meetings at the Bateau-Lavoir, Verlaine had died in a hovel, on the rue Descartes, in abject poverty and desertion. For all of these friends Verlaine was a very great poet.

Picasso was not yet famous. He was just emerging from the blue period and beginning to paint clowns and circus performers. It was the beginning of *l'époque des saltimbanques*, when a rose-pink was the dominant color. He still accepted odd jobs, such as a commission to paint for *Le Grand Guignol* (the horror theatre in Paris) the poster for *La Sainte Roulette*. One could still see in his studio the blue painting of a crippled man leaning on one crutch and carrying strapped on his back a large basket of flowers. This pale emaciated figure was only one of a countless number of men, women, and children who were painted almost contemporaneously with the expansive warm friendships that Picasso had in his first Paris years. There was an exceptional communion of spirit among these men, an interchange of ideas and theories, a kind of comradeship that was both affectionate and practical.

As the blue period was gradually turning into the rose period, Picasso was being more and more frequently visited by art dealers. His regime began changing. He had to stay at home more. He had to be up during the morning. With the new theme of the *saltimbanques*, he began painting during the day when daylight fell directly on his canvases. Vollard was going to purchase *en bloc* all the paintings of this new period. As for Max Jacob and Apollinaire, work was for Picasso a deeply felt need. It excited his mind and stimulated him to explore as far as possible all of his fantasies.

During 1903, Picasso's studio on the rue Ravignan was constantly invaded. On the easels the universes were side by side, the blue and the rose, and they both seemed limitless. The newer universes of the circus and the fair reduced life to a spectacle. It was not yet the universe of the many-sided (polyedrous) cubes, nor the universe of the Dinard monsters. The atelier of the rue Ravignan was not comparable to what the other Paris studios of Picasso were to be: on the rue La Boétie, or the rue des Grands-Augustins, or the studio in the south, at Vallauris, or the castle at Mougins where he lives today. It was such a small room that his friends used to call it the maid's room (*la chambre de la bonne*). But it was in that small room that the surreal world of blue anguish was painted: the starving, the crippled, the emaciated mothers. In 1905 André Salmon published his first volume of verse for which Picasso engraved a picture of two small clowns. The blue period was over.

The Paris of the poets has never been the Paris of elegance and fashion. It is not the Place Vendôme or the rue Matignon. It would be, first, the Paris of Villon, of the rue Saint-Jacques and Cluny. It would be, next, the Paris of Baudelaire whom his creditors forced to move so often that it is difficult to assign him one address. It would be especially for Picasso and his friends the Paris of Verlaine. The left bank Verlaine, who had been imprisoned, best represented the Paris of dreams and illusions, of excitement over creative work, of early successes and recognition.

The immediate Paris inherited by Picasso and his group had been pictorially transcribed by Toulouse-Lautrec (who had died in the south, far from Paris, in 1901.) It was the Paris of bistrots and music-halls, of famous singers and dancers: Le Casque d'Or, Jane Avril, Victorine, and perhaps especially La Goulue who had been celebrated both by Lautrec and Manet. Picasso was to feel something of the same curiosity and anxiety and even concupiscence that had forced Lautrec to paint such subjects.

Paris has always been a city of theorists and critics. At the turn of the century the best aestheticians and the best critics were precisely the poets and the painters. When Max Jacob was alone in his small room on the rue Ravignan, he wrote his poems and he painted. But in public, with his friends, he was unstintingly critic and stimulator. He theorized on every subject: the theatre, orphism, cubism, hamletism. His other roles of dandy, of wit and punster, were always subordinated to his penetrating critical sense. Apollinaire, even more than Jacob, was critic and theorist and impresario for the painters. His article, published in *La Plume*, of December, 1905, was one of the first important critical pieces on the art of Picasso. Apollinaire, and to a lesser degree, Salmon and Jacob, and then a bit later, Jean Cocteau, fulfilled the same function for Picasso that Baudelaire had fulfilled a half-century previously for Daumier, Delacroix, and Constantin Guys. Particularly in the early 1900's, poets and painters helped one another and shared the same fraternal distress and enthusiasms.

Together they lived through the paradox of extremes, of humor and disenchantment. They knew the name which Verlaine had given to the new artists: *les poètes maudits*, those artists born under a curse. Absinth was both a symbol and a reality. This mysterious unity called Paris seemed to provoke among the artists a need for expansiveness, for confession, for public confession in art and in poetry, for regrets especially. From Villon to Verlaine there is a theme of grief in the poet over having wasted his life and his youth.

> *Qu'as-tu fait, ô toi que voilà*
> *Pleurant sans cesse,*
> *Dis, qu'as-tu fait, toi que voilà*
> *De ta jeunesse?*

Picasso and his friends, walking along the dark streets of Paris at night, could evoke an earlier kind of bohemianism, an earlier but familiar litany of poets: Musset, Nerval, Corbière. The long martyrdom of Baudelaire, especially, was significant for them. They remembered Laforgue wearing his tall hat. They had almost no wealthy friends. Few heeded their distress signals. From time to time, a brother of Max Jacob would return from the colonies, wealthy, and he would generously give them a new start.

They used to call the new century Apollinaire's because he told them they ought to love their century, that it was far more stimulating than the nineteenth. (*Il faut aimer son époque. Notre 20e siècle est bien plus passionnant que le 19e.*) The new spirit in poetry and art was more free, more abrupt, more spontaneous. The perceptiveness of the new artist seemed open to an inexhaustible world of impressions. Poetry was everywhere. It was no longer restricted to a classical canon. The boundaries between prose and poetry seemed to be breaking down. An everyday world with its commonplaces entered the pages of the poets and appeared on the canvases of the painters: posters, newspapers, le pont Mirabeau, trains and particularly *trains de luxe*. It was an exceptional moment of cosmopolitanism for France.

Apollinaire's first volume of poems, *Alcools*, did not appear until 1913, which was also the year of publication of *Swann's Way*, but he had been in possession of the themes and the forms of his poetry by 1903, the first full year of Picasso's Bateau-Lavoir. In 1903, he met Derain and Vlaminck, and, in accordance with his custom, went on long walks with these painters. From their conversations and from his close friendship with Picasso and Max Jacob, emerged the theories of a new aesthetics: *l'esprit nouveau*. These were the principal actors in a revolution of literature and art. A casual visitor at No. 13, rue Ravignan was always struck by the prevailing tone of paradox of *Picasso et sa bande*. They spoke in a kind of ubuesque manner, in honor of Jarry's *Ubu Roi*, as if they were initiates to a special cult. They were united in their desire to upset the old order and to create a new art, but each one was ferociously independent. Painters joined with the poets, especially around a restaurant table. At one of their favorites in Montmartre, called *Aux enfants de la Butte*, it was not unusual to see gathered together Utrillo, Modigliani, Derain, Braque, and Vlaminck. They had two things in common: genius for painting and poverty.

For us today who are readers of the poems written in the first decade of the century and admirers of the paintings which are already in many of the great museums of the world, the most important study is an understanding of what was meant by these artists when they spoke of *L'Esprit Nouveau* and *L'Ordre Nouveau*. They had deep convictions that the age in which they were living belonged to them. It was their age and their art was the art of their age. This statement may not be the commonplace it seems, if one remembers that these artists looked upon themselves as champions of the 1900's. Four of these painters, still in their twenties, were just beginning to attract some attention to their work: Picasso, Matisse, Derain, and the douanier Rousseau.

In his manners and behavior, Picasso was perhaps the most reserved, the most unassuming. It is well known that throughout his now very long career Picasso has made no important formal critical statement about his work. He has been questioned a great deal about the intentions and the meanings of his work, but he has almost always replied curtly in aphorisms or refusals or jokes. And yet it is because of Picasso especially that all the leading questions on aesthetics have been raised once again. He would seem to be the leading exponent of *L'Ordre Nouveau*, the leading representative of the generation which, believing in art, dared to lay waste to what they called "artistic life," *la vie artistique*. Picasso, more perhaps than Matisse or Derain, forced a large number of artists and amateurs to a new examination of the principles of art.

Picasso was first recognized as a master, as a great painter, by the poets. What is impossible for us to measure is the degree to which Picasso himself was influenced and changed by the example he saw constantly around him of the poetic discipline. There was unquestionably a new freedom, a new emancipation in the discipline of the poets whom Picasso knew. And it was a discipline of a lofty nature. What another age would have called moral themes or moral curiosity was so skillfully fused with the purely formal aspect of the poems, that it existed without altering the pure art. Purity in art has been defined in many varying ways. For Picasso, and for *L'Ordre Nouveau* as proclaimed by Guillaume Apollinaire, it would seem to be the deliberate repudiation of anything picturesque or artificially literary. Poets and painters both, largely inspired perhaps by a famous line of Verlaine, grew to despise the word literature and its connotations of arbitrariness and canonical tyranny. (*Et tout le reste est littérature.*) The work of the painter in the new order must become associated with the purest works of the human spirit. The three terms—happiness, spirit, and freedom—are almost synonyms in designating the characteristics of the art in the first decade of the century.

11. Apollinaire: Violence of the Surreal

THE VAST AMOUNT of documentation available on Apollinaire is largely due to his colorful enigmatic personality. Many of those who knew him in Paris have tried to explain his character and have left in their memoirs or monographs portraits and anecdotes and interpretations of the anecdotes. Placed side by side, these documents would offer the portrait of a monstrous, complex, and unpredictable personage. The truth is probably more simple.

This very pure French poet had a Polish mother, of Slavic ancestry, and an Italian father. After a Mediterranean childhood (he was born in Rome), when he studied in Monaco and Nice, he came to Paris where, after a brief Rhineland voyage of great importance to his personal life and poetry, he gradually assumed the role of impresario of the arts, especially of poetry and painting. But Apollinaire was far more cosmopolitan than most of the Paris poets. The persistent curiosity that stimulated his mind led him to cultivate his taste for the unusual book in literature and the exceptional kind of human being whom he chose as friend and companion. He espoused and then helped direct the intellectual and artistic bohemianism of Montmartre and Montparnasse. His knowledge, a curious kind of erudition, and the exuberance of his character, made him quickly into the leader of his group of friends. In an extreme sense, he was a performer for whatever circle of friends he was with. But in a private and personal sense, he was an attentive friend, generous and sympathetic to a wide variety of friends. It is obvious today that no one friend was acquainted with all of Apollinaire's life. There were many compartments in this man's nature, many friendships and interests that were maintained concurrently. He was strongly attracted to women, both erotically and sentimentally. Apollinaire probably demanded too much from his relationships with women: both carnal excitement and deep tenderness. He forged for himself and the future of his name: *le mal aimé*, the one who was badly loved. But he himself corrected this and said he was probably *le mal aimant*, the man who did not know how to love well.

More than anyone else, Apollinaire dominated and illustrated the new art of his age—the first decade and a half of the twentieth century—not in reality by inventing the new art forms, but by adopting them instantly, by using them in his own work, and by interpreting them to others. He was both assimilator and stimulator. Every conversation, every encounter, every aesthetic experience became for him an intellectual adventure. His mind and his heart were always open to what was new and unpredictable. André Breton, some time after Apollinaire's death, in attempting to assess the place of the poet and his contribution, said that to the highest degree, Apollinaire incarnated the "intellectual adventure." This judgment, on the whole, was accepted by the other surrealists who were the first to understand and acknowledge the importance of Apollinaire. The religious problem did not exist for him. In late childhood he seems to have lost his Catholic faith. Without metaphysical worries, he was a far different poet from Baudelaire, for example, in his indifference to religious faith and the philosophical anguish of many of the European writers.

During the First World War and the years that immediately followed it, Baudelaire's influence was strong on two generations of writers: on Proust and Valéry, and on the Catholic writers,

Claudel, Bernanos, Mauriac, and Maritain. Not until World War II and the years following it, did Apollinaire reach a comparable position in his effect upon writers and the life of literature. Since those years, all of his work has been examined and is being examined by scholars in France (Durry and Décaudin), in Australia (Lawler) and America (Shattuck, Breunig, Greet)—his two major collections of poems, *Alcools* and *Calligrammes,* and three briefer posthumous volumes, *Ombre de mon amour* (for Louise de Coligny), *Tendre comme le souvenir* (for Madeleine Pagès) and *Le Guetteur mélancolique.* His critical writings are also the object of considerable study.

Today Apollinaire speaks directly to the young poet and the young student of literature. They see in him the authentically modern poet. They approve of the importance he gave to the word modern. They are fascinated by the relationship they sense between his poems and the art of Braque, Picasso, Derain, Matisse. They are struck by the efforts Apollinaire and the painters made to reach beyond the *real* to the *surreal.* It is true that much of the serious poetry being written today in the 1960's in France, such as that of Yves Bonnefoy, owes more to Mallarmé than to Apollinaire. But the example of Apollinaire for poets of the 1930's and 1940's, for Eluard, Aragon, Cocteau, is obvious. The recent Sorbonne course on Apollinaire by Mme Durry, which has now been published in three volumes, significantly marks a new era when the once seemingly rebellious poet becomes the object of scholarly investigation. Mme Durry's own accomplishments as poet, in addition to her scholarly competence, has made her one of the ideal interpreters of Apollinaire. American scholars have made significant contributions. Professor Breunig, of Barnard College, has studied the sources and structure of *La Chanson du Mal-Aimé.* Roger Shattuck, of the University of Texas, and Anne Greet, of the University of California, further illustrate the attraction that Apollinaire still exerts on the new kind of teacher who is both practicing poet and scholar.

Apollinaire came midway between the two great generations of the symbolists and the surrealists. But he does not appear overshadowed by either one: he inherited many of the traits of symbolism and announced the new traits to come, of surrealism. The case of Rimbaud had somewhat fixed the portrait of the youthful poet as a vindictive, sullen, and even persecuted adolescent, hostile to family and state and religion. The case of Apollinaire changed this portrait to that of a young man without family and country, and without a sentiment of vindictiveness. His attitude was one of gratitude to France for receiving him (an attitude similar to that of many artists—Picasso, Picabia, Chagall, Giacometti), of constant gratitude to his family of friends. Breton called him a *jobard* ("easy mark") by temperament. And yet the major poems of Apollinaire (which are among some of the most mysterious and beautiful poems in the French language) were the result of a secret solitary life. The poems perfectly preserve the ambiguity of his character and the secrecy of his inner life.

The famous lecture, given by Apollinaire shortly before his death, and published a month after his death, in December, 1918, in *Le Mercure de France*, is the synthesis of his major theories on poetry and the modern spirit in art. It helps to explain even his earliest poems, written at a time when he was trying to formulate his theories and experiment with them.

A sense of exuberance or exaltation must preside over the source of the new spirit: a desire to explore everything, to explore regions of the world and regions of the mind; to bring to every experience that critical sense and that common sense which the Frenchman believes he inherits at birth. An artistic form can never be static. The artist is the searcher of new forms, of new combinations. He must never neglect the new popular form of art (Apollinaire would say "pop art" today): the movies, for example, for which Apollinaire was a prophet. With his mind open, with an indefatigable curiosity, the modern artist will acquire an encyclopedic knowledge, information on everything, so easily found in newspapers and on the radio. The machine age, with its telephones, aviation, magazines, records, art collections, puts the world within every man's grasp. The age of vague sentimental dreaming and isolation for the artist is over. Apollinaire uses the word *wagnérisme* to designate the artist's romantic revery and he uses it in a deprecatory sense. A new sense of order and duty demands that we pay attention to everything that is happening in the world. As the world itself is constantly reordering itself, recomposing itself, so the poet has to follow the same principle of searching for new combinations of words and images. There is no end to possible new combinations. And each combination, if it is struck off with genius, will be a surprise. The new spirit, according to Apollinaire, is in the power of surprise. The era of the airplane has invalidated the flight of Icarus. His story is no longer a fable. It is the poet's duty to imagine and create new fables. The art of poetry and the creativeness of man are identical. It is therefore possible to be a poet in every domain of human activity. What is indispensable for the new poet is the spirit of adventure, the spirit of rediscovery. The point of departure for this kind of adventure may well be a trivial circumstance, a thoroughly innocuous event. Apollinaire imagines the example of a handkerchief falling: this could be, he insists, the genesis of a new universe, the beginning of a vast synthesis. As other examples, he gives the striking of a match, the cry of an animal, the odors of a garden after rainfall. These examples of trivia may bring about the element of surprise, which he calls the mechanics of the new poetry. (*La surprise, l'inattendu est un des principaux ressorts de la poésie d'aujourd'hui.*)

The passage on dreams, in *L'Esprit Nouveau*, on the closed night world of dreams, will be a valuable guide for the surrealists. The life of dreams exemplifies for Apollinaire man's perpetual renewal of himself, the endless creation of himself, so comparable to poetry, a force that is always being reborn and by which man lives. Apollinaire looks upon France as a seminary of poets and artists, a land where the modern poets are creators and inventors and prophets, and in that sense, they are opposed to aestheticism, to formulas in art, to cultism and snobbishness. The new poet will thus work differently from poets in other periods, in his struggle to understand clearly his own age, to open up a new understanding of the exterior world around him and the inner world of his spirit and his dreams. He will be, in fact, the first to understand his age, because he will be the poet of the truth of his age. Truth is constantly being renewed and reassessed with the change of time and customs.

Alcools of 1913 was the first collection of poems published by Guillaume Apollinaire, but almost all the poems (written between 1898 and 1913) had previously appeared in magazines. They are not arranged chronologically in the collection. *Zone*, for example, opens the series and was one of the last to be written. Slight changes had been made in several since their first appearance in magazines, and all punctuation had been suppressed.

The year 1913–14 was a remarkable one in the annals of French poetry and art, the *annus mirabilis*. Apollinaire published both *Alcools* and his book on the new painters, *Les Peintres Cubistes;* Proust, *Du côté de chez Swann;* Alain-Fournier, *Le Grand Meaulnes;* Gide, *Les Caves du Vatican.* Jacques Copeau opened his theatre of *Le Vieux Colombier.* Stravinsky directed the first performance of *Le Sacre du Printemps.* Cubism, as a new school in painting, had been founded in 1908, with the first cubist paintings of Braque and Picasso. By 1913, it was a fully established school, sometimes called "orphic cubism," when the paintings would be made up of elements created by the artist and not necessarily copied from reality, but elements endowed by the artist with a surprising sense of reality.

These visions of the painters, which Apollinaire had contemplated during the period when he was composing his poems of *Alcools,* reflected for the poet a universe of phantoms juxtaposed with the real universe of humanity. The diversity of cubism is in the diversity of *Alcools,* with its symbolism (as in *Ermite*), its elegiac tones (as in *Le Pont Mirabeau*), its program of modernism (as in *Zone*), its theme of nostalgia, reminiscent of Verlaine (as in *A la Santé*), its obscure poetry (as in *Le Brasier.*)

Apollinaire avoids all rhetorical bombast, all pointed melodramatic effects. There is no overt perversion in his eroticism, no maudlin quality in his tenderness. There is no direct imitation of nature when he speaks of a river, of a city landscape, of the memory of a distant country, of the stars, of a woman's body. When he evokes a theme close to the occult and the mysterious, he avoids any direct mysticism. As he avoids, at the other extreme, any rationalistic approach to a theme. There is no concept of sin in the poems, but Apollinaire is a moving poet when he speaks of the heart's distress. He is able to describe simultaneously the tenderness of a love experience and its ruin. He is a magician when he uses a commonplace, a worn-out poetic theme and transfigures it. There is no such thing as poetic language for Apollinaire, and with this belief and practice he did institute an important change in poetry, almost as significant a change as that brought about first by Baudelaire, and then by Rimbaud. In deflating the traditional concepts concerning poetic language, he established his new code of shock and surprise. Somewhat in the tradition of Rimbaud, but especially in that of Alfred Jarry, Apollinaire at times used coarseness or comic or absurd traits in his effort to hold his reader by an effect of surprise.

Two poems in particular from *Alcools* will hold our attention in an attempt to analyze Apollinaire's reaction to experiences of violence. He has said that each of his poems is a commemoration of an event in his life. This is luminously clear in the first of these poems, *La Chanson du Mal-Aimé*, his most famous and one of his longest. The second poem, *Le Brasier*, is perhaps less clearly autobiographical. The two poems amply illustrate the degree of seriousness with which Apollinaire considered existence. In his role of jovial companion that has been so often related in books, he refused to take himself seriously. But in his art of poet, in the most profound instances of this art, he underscored the tragedy of man's solitude. *La Chanson du Mal-Aimé* and *Le Brasier* are two exercises, two experiments on this solitude, seen not from a purely personal egotistical viewpoint, but in a wider context of mythological man, and man in his specific dilemmas of today's history.

In the epigraph preceding *La Chanson du Mal-Aimé*, Apollinaire tells us that this love poem, *cette romance*, was written in 1903, when he knew his love affair with Annie Pleyden was over, when he was still suffering from her rejection, or at least her refusal to marry him, and before he realized that his love, like the phoenix of mythology, would rise up again. This is doubtless an allusion to his love for Marie Laurencin, which began in 1908. The long poem of 295 lines is in six fairly distinct parts. Professor Leroy L. Breunig has convincingly demonstrated that the various parts were written at different times, and then placed together, in a fairly flexible sequence (cf. *La Table Ronde*, September, 1952). There are moments in the poem of tenderness, moments of recall when the poet's heart had been full of hope for the realization of his love. But *La Chanson du Mal-Aimé* is primarily a poem on the violence of suffering, of that special kind of suffering that comes from unreciprocated love. Everything that occurs to the lover, every encounter, every memory, brings back his love to him, and the knowledge that his life is, at least momentarily, emptied of every reason for living. This agony is extreme because the lover is alone and humiliated.

In a literal sense, the action begins in a London street, in the fall of 1903 (lines 1-25), just after Annie has told Apollinaire she will not marry him and is going to America; and it ends in Paris, in June, 1904 (lines 271-295), when the failure of his love is definitive and when his *romance du mal-aimé* takes its place beside other tragic love songs of the past.

The opening line resembles the beginning of a tale,

Un soir de demi-brume à Londres,

but the rest of the stanza (lines 2-5) is a picture of startling violence in the street scene of London fog. A boy coming up to him and looking at him suggestively embarrasses the poet, but such is the power of his love that the boy (*voyou*) personifies Annie, and the poet follows him. The boy, his hands in his pockets, whistles and leads the way to what he obviously believes a facile conquest. But the boy disappears immediately from the poem as the violence of the poet's torment grows. The image that describes this torment is as sudden and spectacular as the unpredictable identification of Annie with a youthful male prostitute. The sinister walk in the London street suddenly becomes the flight of the Hebrews in Egypt. The space between the two rows of houses becomes the Red Sea. The waves have parted as in the Bible story. The poet's love, in the guise of a boy, is the Hebrews, and the poet himself is Pharaoh. The red bricks of the houses and the evening gas light in the fog permitted the tortured mind of the poet to make this transformation. The reality of a street scene in 1903 is converted into the *Exodus* story of a flight from slavery.

So the Israelites went through the midst of the sea dry-shod, with its waters towering up like a wall to right and left. (Exodus 14:22)

And we know the end of the story. We know that the Hebrews (the boy) escaped and the pursuer (Pharaoh) was destroyed when the waves crashed over him. This ending is not given in the poem, because it is not necessary. Only the violence and degradation are related.

The poet first gives an intimation of his fate by the anaolgy he establishes with Pharaoh: complete annihilation. And then, he wants, in one sustained cry (stanza 3), to declare the power of his love. The story of *Exodus* will still serve him. The reality of his feelings (of his suffering) is such that he calls upon the brick waves on either side of him to collapse if his love for Annie is not true. If she is not his one love, then he is the sovereign lord of Egypt,

Je suis le souverain d'Egypte,

and moreover, to make the comparison more hyperbolic, he is his own sister-bride, his own army. He needs to utter an oath to testify to the truth of his love. An event in biblical history, the crossing of the Red Sea, is used to describe the face of reality.

In contrast with the examples of two faithful wives—Penelope waiting for the return of Ulysses and Sakontala waiting for the return of Dushmanta—the modern poet denounces the infidelity and cruelty of his love. In the eighth stanza, which terminates the initial scene in the London street, he thinks of those kings who had been happy in love,

J'ai pensé à ces rois heureux,

and contrasts that happiness with the falseness of his own love: *le faux amour*. He has confused his love with the shadowy figures, first of a boy and then of a woman coming out of a pub. These strange encounters and the inevitable identification with Annie had distressed him, because his love is still strong.

The struggle is now clear. It is the effort of the poet to get beyond his suffering, to move beyond the memory of his life, and the persistence of this memory, the tenacity of his love. Sadness and anger alternate, because he calls Annie's infidelity a betrayal.

As this initial passage reaches its conclusion, the poet says farewell to this betrayal:

Adieu, faux amour . . .

He has lost the woman he loved, and he knows he will not see her again. He raises his eyes from the street scene, and he forces his thoughts to move beyond the cases of history he has just evoked. He looks up at the sky in order to question the stars, as men have done since the earliest times when they are curious to know what their fate is to be.

In one of the most beautiful stanzas, which Apollinaire will repeat as a refrain near the end of the poem, he speaks to the Milky Way: *Voie lactée*. From the minuteness of the London street scene, he looks up at the vast accumulation of stars and sees it as a whitish wave over the night sky. The stanza is both an intense meditation on how the suffering poet can move beyond his suffering and transcend it and an example of an extraordinary mingling of images. The Milky Way is called the luminous sister of the white rivers of Chanaan.

> *Voie lactée ô soeur lumineuse*
> *Des blancs ruisseaux de Chanaan.*

The whiteness of milk in *lactée* must have suggested to the poet the description of the Promised Land that God had given his people: "a land flowing with milk and honey." It is another allusion to the book of *Exodus* (chapter 3). In Greek mythology, the whiteness of the Milky Way was accounted for by the drops of milk that had fallen from the breast of Juno as she nursed Hercules.

The third line of the stanza is more surprising still. The Milky Way is also the sister of the white bodies of women in love:

> *Et des corps blancs des amoureuses.*

The poet is imagining his love as belonging, in time, to all other lovers, elevated to the heavens. He wonders whether he and other men, with great effort, swimming in death, will continue to follow the ones loved, like a river, rising toward other accumulations of stars in the heavens.

> *Nageurs morts suivrons-nous d'ahan*
> *Ton cours vers d'autres nébuleuses.*

The entire stanza is based upon the first word *Voie*, "way." Here, this word designates the ultimate way to be taken by lovers, in order to transcend momentary betrayals and disappointments. In France, the Milky Way (*voie lactée*) was once called *le chemin de Saint Jacques*, in honor of the famous medieval pilgrimage to Saint James of Compostella, in Spain. The stanza is a question, with its key verb: *suivrons-nous*—"shall we follow?" Will the poet's fate change after the failure of his love? With the word *ahan*, one senses the great effort necessary to bring about the change of fate, and once the change is made, the continuing effort afterward to reach some mysterious redemption. An answer is not given to the question.

Midway in the poem (vss. 166-170), a poignant stanza speaks

of the double suffering of the poet in his spirit and in his flesh. The spirit is evoked by the unicorn (*la licorne*), associated with virginity, and the flesh, by the goat (*le capricorne*) or capricorn, associated with carnal desire.

> *Douleur qui doubles les destins*
> *La licorne et le capricorne.*

In the first line, the poet addresses his suffering and uses the unusual verb *doubler*. Suffering is so close to destiny, that it resembles a lining. It accompanies destiny as closely as a lining accompanies a coat. The body and its suffering, like a coat and its lining, like the duality of unicorn and capricorn, are called, in the third line, spirit and flesh:

> *Mon âme et mon corps incertain*
> *Te fuient ô bûcher divin qu'ornent*
> *Des astres des fleurs du matin.*

The adjective *incertain* is used to modify the body (*mon corps*) because of the body's double vocation of sanctification and sensuality. Suffering is here conceived of as a part of destiny, willed by the gods. And the poet's impulse is to avoid this sacrifice, this sacrificial fire. Suffering is designated as a strange ornamentation for the body, and the poet here is in revolt against it, and against the romantic cult of self-sacrifice.

The final stanza of the poem, used once previously in lines 91-95, is an important motif for the entire piece and a solution to the harassing problem of the suffering from love. It is not a conclusion, in a literal sense, but it is a statement about poetry and man's need to write poetry. It is perhaps the best answer that Apollinaire offers to the kind of violence from which he is suffering. The art of poetry is a science that has accompanied the entire history of man. Lyricism is a remedy, a magical incantation, a charm that permits man to live and to understand or at least to accept his fate.

In this refrain stanza, which is the last one heard in *La Chanson du Mal-Aimé*, nothing is concluded and everything begins again. This, after all, is the characteristic of a "song," and indeed of all of poetry, because the poet's ego, his particular dramas and sufferings and aspirations, are repeated in each reader. Already, in the *Voie lactée* stanza, Apollinaire had identified himself with his reader, and with all lovers living and dead: *Nageurs morts suivrons-nous*.

Auspiciously the stanza opens with the personal pronoun *moi*, but immediately the poet's personality is submerged in a series of names designating forms of poetry. Each of the five lines has one form of the poetic art: *lais, complaintes, hymnes, romance, chansons*. And each genre is succinctly defined:

1. *Moi qui sais des lais pour les reines*. The medieval *lays* were narrative poems of tragic love. The queen Marie de France herself wrote some of the most celebrated.

2. *Les complaintes de mes années*. A *complaint* is a personal poem, a chronicle of the poet's own life and usually of his own self-pity. The term today is often associated with Jules Laforgue.

3. *Des hymnes d'esclave aux murènes*. For the term *hymn*, Apollinaire makes a learned allusion to the Roman gastronome Vadius Pollion who, to punish a slave, had him thrown into a pool where he kept carnivorous fish called *murènes* (muraena or moray). A hymn is traditionally an entreaty, and in this verse doubtless stands for the prayer of the slave as he is being thrown to the sea monsters. It is a line of extreme violence in an otherwise subdued stanza.

4. *La romance du mal-aimé* is Apollinaire's own poem by means of which he places himself in the center of a long tradition and calls himself the man badly loved. This role he ascribes to himself is in each of the terms used to designate the poem—lay, complaint, hymn, romance, and, of course the word in the last line:

5. *Et des chansons pour le sirènes*. The fable of the Greek mythology and the Lorelei, of the seductresses leading the mariners to their death, has its significance in Apollinaire's poem. The stanza is composed of all degrees of suffering from love, from the lover's complaint to the slave's useless exhortation for pardon before his violent death. In each case, the male is the sufferer, and the woman who is loved is reported as cruel and oblivious to her lover's torment.

The poet's fate is unjust, but it is a reduplication of a recognized fate. Lyricism has a sovereign power to alleviate suffering, not only for the composer himself, for the poet who writes, but for the reader of the poem, who listens and assimilates his own with the poet's fate.

Before its appearance in *Alcools*, the poem *Le Brasier*, initially entitled *Le Pyrée*, had been published twice. Apollinaire had a predilection for this poem which he considered one of his most successful. It is a difficult piece, one of the richest in metaphor, one in which lines of regular versification are followed by free verse, and in which visions of fire and destruction are allied with theories of poetry. *Le Brasier* is a poem of violence and an *ars poetica* at the same time. It is an experiment in lyricism and also a commentary on a new type of humanism. Reality often seems to us discontinuous, an upsetting series of contrasts and contradictions, without an even motivation, without a unified functioning and a visible goal. Poetry, according to Apollinaire, may reproduce this effect of discontinuity, of violent contrasts, of experiences so different one from the other, that any meaning of experience seems impossible to ascertain. *Le Brasier*, of 1908, written at a time when Apollinaire was in love with the painter Marie Laurencin, is an example of the poet's art that tries to reproduce the convulsions of living, the destructions and the rebirths that figure in the reality of living.

The title itself, *Le Brasier*, evokes a funeral pyre, a burning brand, a sacrificial or purificatory ceremony. All the allusions are in the poem: the sorcerer's death and the heretic's, the phoenix rising up from its ashes, the concept of hell and eternal suffering, the heroism of suffering, the fire of love, both mystical love and passionate love. This poem, more directly than any other of Apollinaire, brings to mind *Les Illuminations* of Rimbaud, in the difficult intense passages of fire imagery where a human experience is metamorphosed into the experience of language.

The first part of the poem (vss. 1-25) is written in five-line stanzas, of octosyllabic lines. They are strong vigorous lines, a deliberately bold beginning, where the poet tells us he is casting into the fire the Past (a word he capitalizes and personifies.) The Past is a being, and the poet is obeying the will of the flame, the will of the "noble fire," in hurling into it the skulls representing what is dead in his past. Thus the poem opens with the destruction of the past, and the fire, the means of destruction, is worshiped by the poet. He dedicates the past to the power of the flames.

And immediately the entire cosmos is involved in this act. The stars are heard galloping across the skies, and this sound is mingled with the neighing of the male centaurs in their breeding grounds. All growing things, plants and trees, utter plaintive sounds. The fire ceremony of the first stanza is accompanied by a vision of cosmic sexuality, in the second, where the forces of copulation are audible.

> *Le galop soudain des étoiles*
>
> . . . .
>
> *Se mêle au hennissement mâle*
> *Des centaures dans leurs haras*
> *Et des grandes plaintes végétales.*

And then just as suddenly as the gallop of the astral bodies was heard, the poet turns inwardly, in the third stanza, in lines obviously reminiscent of Villon (with whom Apollinaire has so much in common) and the personal lament replaces the cosmic act of reproduction. He asks: Where are the lives he once lived?

> *Où sont ces têtes que j'avais?*

Where is the god of his youth?

> *Où est le Dieu de ma jeunesse?*

This god referred to is love, and he is named in the third line:

> *L'amour est donc mauvais.*

Love is no longer that force celebrated in *La Chanson du Mal-Aimé*. It is bad. It has become a force of evil that has kept him from self-realization. The word *brasier* is now used, when the poet hopes to see flames reborn, as his soul is stripped and bared before the sun. The fire is indeed purificatory.

> *Qu'au brasier les flammes renaissent*
> *Mon âme au soleil se dévêt.*

The fourth stanza seems to justify this harsh interpretation of the third. The heads of the dead, which had designated the poet's past in the opening stanza,

> *Ce passé ces têtes de morts,*

are now called heads of women, or heads of his former loves, and they are the stars that have bled. The image of heads and stars is transported to the land (*Dans la plaine*) where the poet's heart, in its various incarnations, hangs like fruit on lemon trees. The entire stanza is startlingly similar to a surrealist picture by Tanguy or Magritte.

In the final stanza of this opening section, the poet seems at a great distance from the earth. He sees the river as if it were a ribbon pinned on the city:

> *Le fleuve épinglé sur la ville.*

The fire brings about this visual effect. The fire is comparable to a creator, to Orpheus who made the animals obey him, and to Amphion who, by playing on the lyre, made the stones of Thebes take their place on the ramparts.

> *Partant à l'amphion docile.*

This is a difficult line which means "at your departure, you obeyed Amphion." This peacefulness, this docility, where the flames take on all colors and invest the very stones with agility, is the creation of the poem.

> *Tu subis tous les tons charmants*
> *Qui rendent les pierres agiles.*

The fire (*le brasier*) is the force of rejuvenation, which begins by destruction. The poet has to be stripped and burned, as in a holocaust. He is, first, victim of the flames, and then he is his own metamorphosis, a new being, alone and separated. Everything seems, at first, in the poem, hermetic. But that is because the poet, in his propitiatory act, described in the five opening stanzas, is renewed and revived, and is facing the unknown. His death in the flames is cosmic. He is not alone there because he dies with and to the universe. But he is alone, afterward, in the rebirth, in the aesthetic rebirth of the poem.

12. Max Jacob: Violence of
the Supernatural

E ARLY IN LIFE, in Quimper, where he was born in 1876, Max Jacob wrote poems and sketched. He lived very much by himself, in a world of his own creation. This apartness he maintained in his family, in school, and with his schoolmates, where he played a sociable, animated role, a mixture of martyr and clown, a performer that was the protective covering of his life. Later, in Montmartre, in the center of poets and painters, he continued to lead the dual existence of writer-artist working in total solitude and that of exhilarating central figure in the lusty groups that congregated around Picasso and Apollinaire. At the end of the life, at Saint-Benoît-sur-Loire, a similar duality continued. In his devotional life of pious Christian he was alone, far more alone than a monk would be in his monastery. But in his role of adviser to the young, in his role of friend to so many poets and seekers, Jacob maintained his wit and whimsicality, his skill at endowing the commonplace with freshness, and converting the routines of life into unpredictable joys.

After a few weeks of military service, Max was released on

general grounds of incapacity and weakness, and it was at that point in his life, in 1896, that he went to Paris as a candidate for a full bohemian existence. Poverty plagued him all his life but especially in the early years in Paris, from 1896 to 1911, when he tried all manner of occupations, from art critic to baby-sitter. One event above all, and as mysterious as it was important, changed or reorientated his life. The apparition of Christ in his room at No. 7, rue Ravignan, on September 22, 1909, was as significant for Jacob's life as the famous night of November 23, 1654, was for Pascal. *Le Mémorial* is Pascal's account of his experience, and *La Défense de Tartuffe*, first published in 1919, is Jacob's personal account.

On the day after the apparition, Henri Kahnweiler, a picture dealer and art publisher, called on Jacob to ask him permission to publish a book of his with illustrations by Picasso. This book, *Saint Matorel*, did appear in 1911, and from that time on, the intense problems of poverty ceased. Between 1909 and 1914 Max lived as both penitent and sinner, and the extremes were so obvious that his close friends refused to take seriously his desire to become a Christian and to be baptized.

A second apparition occurred to Max Jacob in a movie house, on December 17, 1914. He renewed his request to become a Catholic. He received instruction from a priest and was baptized on February 18, 1915, and took the baptismal name of Cyprien. Picasso was his godfather. From that year until the end of the decade, Jacob wrote an extensive number of prose poems and led a life of piety characterized by drastic penance because of his sexual sins. In 1912, he had moved from the rue Ravignan to No. 17, rue Gabrielle, and it was from that address that he published at his own expense in 1917 *Le Cornet à dés*, a collection of prose poems which is one of the important sources of modern poetry. A year after Apollinaire's death, in 1919, Jacob published his principal book on his conversion and his religious experiences: *La Défense de Tartuffe*. He was thinking at this time of leaving Paris and living somewhere in the provinces, in a quiet place where the temptations to sin would be reduced.

By 1920, just prior to his first visit to Saint-Benoît-sur-Loire, where he was to find some degree of peace for a few years, Max Jacob had become a well-known figure in the avant-garde circles. He already belonged to the somewhat older group that included

Apollinaire and Reverdy. The younger poets who embraced the freshness and originality of Apollinaire and Jacob, and who profited from them, were Breton, Soupault, Eluard, and Aragon, all destined to play major roles in the surrealist movement; Cocteau and Radiguet, who remained independent from any school; Tristan Tzara, with his Dada movement, a veritable enterprise of demolition. The most revered figures in French literature about 1920, whose work seemed the most certain of survival, were Gide, Claudel, Valéry, Léon-Paul Fargue, and Proust. In music, Cocteau was promoting the work of Erik Satie and patronizing the group of new composers he called *Les Six*. In painting, the school of cubism had taken over first place with the work of such painters as Picasso, Braque, Roger de la Fresnaye, Juan Gris, and André Lhôte.

For all the arts, the period was exuberant and fertile. Max Jacob had not only announced the period, he incarnated its characteristics: its love of parody and humor, its nonconformity, its manner of considering philosophical and aesthetic problems. Breton's *Manifeste du surréalisme* of 1922 did not include the name of Max Jacob, and yet most of the practices of surrealism were familiar to the poet who was living at that time at Saint-Benoît-sur-Loire. He was hurt by this official negligence, but he continued to approve of the work of Breton and Aragon and Reverdy. When he returned to Paris, in 1928, to live at No. 55, rue Nollet, he knew he was returning to a life of dereliction. Homosexuality was always a torment for him. He looked upon it as a fatal accident and rarely spoke of it to his friends, or he spoke in general terms, as in his confession to his friend Andreu: *ma vie est un enfer.*

His return to Saint-Benoît in 1936 was definitive. From that time until his death, in 1944, he succeeded, according to all available evidence, in living a life of humility and obscurity, a life of constant prayer. He received visits from his most devoted friends, many of whom are poets today: Béalu, Michel Manoll, Jean Rousselot, the painter Roger Toulouse, Alain Messiaien, Doctor Szigeti. The war years were difficult for him when his friends were almost unable to get to Saint-Benoît. He served the six-thirty mass each morning. From 1942 on, he was obliged to wear the yellow star of Israel. He was arrested by the Gestapo in February, 1944, and interned in Drancy on February 28. His last two letters were written to his parish priest at Saint-Benoît and to Jean Cocteau. Max Jacob died in a concentration camp on March 5, 1944.

From his writings, from his letters, and from testimonials of his friends, his religious faith would seem to have been simple and efficacious. It had the power to destroy the passions that made a man cruel and hostile. It served as the basis for all his meditations on Paradise and Hell, on the blessings of God, on death and the Last Judgment. In his letters to friends, he often emphasized their need to practice their faith even if momentarily they had lost their faith. (*Si tu ne crois pas, pratique. C'est la théorie de Pascal.*) Being a Christian for Jacob, did not necessarily mean being virtuous. It meant primarily having faith and being baptized. The life of a Christian is a long struggle with oneself. Jacob was an avid student of the symbolism of religions. Like Pascal he placed great importance on the prophecies and miracles of the Old Testament. In the history of the Chosen People, everything is symbolic for him.

His religious spirit penetrated everything, even his most burlesque writings. His nature was one of great expansiveness. He needed to confess his acts and thoughts, the best and the worst. André Blanchet, in his admirable critical edition of *La Défense de Tartuffe*, justifies his belief that Jacob remained always very close to Jewish tradition in his life of a Christian. The apparition of 1909 which changed his life, was Judaic in its form and intimacy. He studied Judaic theosophy, both orthodox and nonorthodox. The apparition of Christ on the wall of his room on that day in 1909, when he returned from the Bibliothèque Nationale, never ceased to count in his life, and never lost its mysteriousness of an enigmatical sign. Both as a poet and as a believer, Max Jacob waited for signs, expected signs, remained in a state of availability.

The exact books he studied are not known, but he referred to the *Zohar* and the *Kabbala*. He expected a dramatic inner change, a spiritual revolution which would make him into a new being. The visible and invisible worlds form one universe for Jacob. Men inhabit circles that are close to God or far away from Him. All the circles are in relationship with God, and it is therefore impossible to escape from Him. In this Dantesque conception, a life of sin can precipitate a man from one circle to another, and a spiritual revelation can dramatically transform him. *Ma chair est tombée!* Jacob wrote thus in his account of the apparition. The key word in Max Jacob's aesthetics is *situation,* and it has the same importance in his theology. A man's "situation" with respect to God is the definition of his character. Since there is only one universe, Max believed he cohabited with angels as well as with demons. He believed himself pursued by Satan as well as by God's angels. The extremes of Montmartre and Saint-Benoît-sur-Loire illustrate the two opposing climates in which this poet lived. His visions were decidedly apocalyptic; they described either the extreme drabness of reality or they transcended reality in a sumptuous flash of supernatural beauty.

On the day following the apparition, in 1909, Max Jacob called on a priest and asked to be baptized. This was denied him. For five years he led a tormented life, puzzled by the Church's refusal to receive him, apprehensive about asking help from a priest, but quite fully engaged in religious readings and study, determined to understand the experience that had so drastically modified his life. The first version of his accounts are in *Saint Matorel* and *Oeuvres Burlesques,* which are journals where Max tries to understand not only occurences in his own life, but the meaning of the Gospels. He was an autodidact in this research and eagerly accepted the medieval fourfold symbolic interpretation of the Bible as opposed to the currently entrenched historical school of literal interpretation. Later Paul Claudel also will oppose the school of historicism in his volumes of biblical exegesis.

These years were difficult in every day, because Max was still very much involved with his friends in the two groups around Picasso and Apollinaire. But before his baptism and after it, he fervently believed that his life would find some semblance of order and meaning in the sacraments of the Roman Catholic Church.

In 1917, Jacques Doucet asked to buy Jacob's manuscripts. This proposition resulted in the publishing of two books: *Le Cornet à dés,* of 1917, a collection of prose poems, and *La Défense de Tartuffe,* in 1919, a far more complex book whose various kinds of writings are related to the religious conversion. The title first chosen was *Le Christ à Montparnasse.* This was rejected in favor of *Monsieur Tartuffe.* The third choice became the definitive title. It would indicate that Max Jacob looked upon himself as guilty. Every Christian is a dual personality. Every Christian is a Tartuffe, a religious hypocrite, to some extent.

From *Saint Matorel* to *La Défense de Tartuffe*, the five poems on Jacob's conversion underwent several changes, as André Blanchet points out in great detail in his edition. In *La Révélation*, the mysteriousness of the apparition is restored by a suppression of passages of explanation. The action moves swiftly, from the moment of the poet's return from the Bibliothèque Nationale to the apparition on the red tapestry of the wall. In a second (*Oh! impérissable seconde!*) he was stripped by lightning. In the brief dialogue with the angel which follows, the poet is treated as the innocent. He has been transported and he understands:

> *Ravissement! Seigneur! Je comprends, ah! je comprends.*

The text of the second piece, *Visitation*, was especially abridged and tightened. Here the casualness and familiarity of Christ's apparition to Max Jacob is stressed. *Ma chambre est au fond d'une cour.* Even the address is given: *le No 7 de la rue Ravignan*, and the significant detail that the zinc roof had been opened to admit more light. The dialogue between the Lord and the poet is totally simple. The Cross must come into the room. It is there for the poet to look upon.

> *Regarde la croix!—Oh! Seigneur! toute ma vie.*

The other three poems are less narrative in form. They combine the elements in the life of *Saint Matorel*, burlesque and mystical elements. They are far more typical *poèmes en prose* of Max Jacob than the first two poems.

Entrevue describes a vision: a golden ray forming a crown over the poet's bed. The elements of the vision are apocalyptic (the horse dominating the sea) and familiar (a poet at the piano). It is a picture that is drawn, a Marc Chagall assemblage of objects that do not usually go together and that appear in unusual places. There is a reminiscence of Rimbaud in the phrase: *Des incendies s'allument au loin.* And at the bottom of the picture, in miniature, the poet: a slave on his knees, whose expression is so changed that he does not recognize his own face.

In *Significations*, the poet is a terrified monk praying before a stained-glass window of St. Eustache. The poet explains his belief in symbolism. The picture of Christ on his knees or on the cross explains the meaning of the Body of Christ. The wound in the side of the body explains the Heart of God. When there is no direct contact with God (as there had been in the first two poems), he speaks by signs and objects and events. This *moine peureux* wonders whether he should try to understand or simply try to pray.

The problem of understanding the incomprehensible is the theme of the fifth poem: *Exhortations*. Here the poet is the naïve Breton seated in the midst of the flags of the world. He is in the act of studying, but he must interrupt his reading if he wishes to receive another visit from God. On the angel's sleeve he sees three Hebrew letters he cannot read, and he wonders whether the Holy Spirit will give him the gift of language. The poem ends abruptly with the angel impatient at seeing him so stupid:

> *L'ange est furieux de me voir si bête.*

The unusual religious experience of the poet is thus related in five poems where he plays five slightly different roles. He is first the occupant of the Montmartre room, No. 7 rue Ravignan, who returns from the library and sees, without preparation, without solicitation, the figure of Christ on the wall. He is the one chosen by God for a revelation, and he is stunned and shocked by this occurrence. The revelation becomes a visit in the second poem where Max is sleeping on a mattress supported by four bricks. The Lord knocks at his door. His cross has to be brought in through the window, because it is too large for the door. The poet promises his visitor to contemplate the cross for the rest of his life. Again from his bed, the poet, in the third poem, has not a visit but a vision: a horse, a woman haloed, a poet at the piano, and distant fires. Here the protagonist is a slave on his knees, straining for some understanding of this vision, for some understanding of who he is. The question of prayer and study is central in the fourth piece which is on "meanings" (*significations*). Without the immediacy of revelation and visitation, what is the poet's conduct to be? How can he understand the symbolism of objects and events? The final poem, an "exhortation," is an answer to this problem. Man is, in his natural state, ignorant and closed off from the ultimate mysteries, but promise is made to him that progress can come about, that the Holy Spirit can infuse understanding. The gift of tongues once came to the Apostles.

These poems transcribe a very personal experience, and announce a poetic method. Max Jacob felt in his room the supernatural presence of God. As a poet, he will have to project this experience by means of color and form and reminiscences. After being invaded by a Presence, he will become the prey of images. He will never dissociate poetic creation from divine revelation. The passivity he knew at the moment of revelation, he will continue to know at the moment of poetic creation. In the choice he has between the head and the heart, he chooses the heart. The apparitions of God to Abraham, to Moses, and to other Old Testament figures, often took place in familiar casual settings. The apparitions of Max Jacob in a Montmartre cinéma and in his room on the rue Ravignan could be interpreted as belonging to a Judaic tradition.

But there were bewildering contradictions in Jacob's life which continued until a few years before his martyr's death on March 5, 1944, in the concentration camp of Drancy. And it was often difficult, even for those who knew him the best, to comprehend the phenomena he spoke of, to know how subjective and hallucinatory they were, or to know whether they were of a divine origin. Some of Jacob's earliest friends, and notably Picasso who called him the only poet of the period (*tu es le seul poète de l'époque*), looked upon his work as a major expression of modern poetry and art, but they refused to take seriously the religious turn: the *extases* and *remords* of the converted Jew, words which appeared as subtitle to *La Défense de Tartuffe*. This was for them a joke, a disguised *clownerie* of their friend who was famous for his mystifications. Before the definitive departure from Paris in 1936, during the years 1928–36, when the varied and often dangerous life of the capital absorbed him, Max Jacob was the dandy who wore a monacle and who had once been the close friend of Apollinaire and Picasso, the inventor of the real *poème en prose*, a man famous for his tireless wit, for the unusual strangeness of his clothes, one who told fortunes by horoscope, who was an active member of the *Société des Amis de Fantômas* (SAF). He was a medley of characterizations: novelist, essayist, pamphleteer, painter, designer, caricaturist, and above all, a poet. It was known that at Saint-Benoît, he had played the role of the good thief and pious parishioner. After his return to Saint-Benoît, Paris, that is, those Parisians interested in art and poetry began to forget him. In the 1960's, long after his death, Max Jacob was called by Charles Le Quintrec, a young poet, also a devout Breton, "our last picturesque poet" (*notre dernier poète pittoresque*). In his art, Jacob is probably closer to Raymond Queneau today than he ever was to Guillaume Apollinaire. His biography will be a most difficult book to write, because the sources are scattered and because the testimonials are so varied and often contradictory. His close admirers tended to beatify him too quickly. And his detractors have tended to see in him only the caricaturist, the fop, the eccentric. Max allowed the legends about him to grow, and rather than rectifying them, added to them.

In the diversity of Max Jacob's writings, which reflect the burlesque and the mystical, the parody and the very serious, he created a form, a genre, which he called *le poème en prose*. Baudelaire composed his *poèmes en prose* with a very specific subject matter, but avoided all poetic effects, all picturesqueness. Mallarmé reduced in his *poèmes en prose* the subject matter and emphasized picturesqueness. Jacob, in his *poèmes en prose*, reduced both subject matter and picturesqueness. His use of parody was almost a discipline for him, and he chose one of the most hallowed of literary passages, the opening of Baudelaire's *Invitation au Voyage*,

> *Mon enfant, ma soeur, tu pleures aujourd'hui*
> *tu regrettes la foire de Quimper,*

where the lovers' ideal country becomes the Quimper market; and the fifth canto of the *inferno* where Dante's Paolo and Francesca stopped reading because of their mounting passion,

> *Ils ne lurent pas plus avant*
> *Et la belle a fait un enfant.*

At any cost, the traditionally lyric and mythological must be avoided. Mercury therefore will be called a postman:

> *Mercure est un divin facteur.*

The serious study of Max Jacob's art has barely begun. It will include, as time goes on, a study of the way he presents a word in different meanings, from different angles, a method very close to cubism. It will also study the ways by which he destroys emotion by means of irony and parody, his art of transposing traditional themes. When he decomposes the elements of a city scene or a landscape, in order to recombine the elements in a new way and reach a new total effect, he was practicing the aesthetics of cubism, and he was combining in the same poem ideas that do not ordinarily cohabit one with the other. The universe is one, for Jacob, and therefore everything can cohabit with everything else: judgments, emotions, memories, sensations, philosophical concepts, literary allusions. The subconscious dictates to the poet. Long before the surrealists defined this practice as orthodox, Max Jacob practiced it. His poems often appear to be fortuitous inventions, devoid of any visible relationship with the real world. The final poem could therefore be a total surprise to the poet. Something monstrous or diabolical would be perpetrated without the creator being fully aware of how it had appeared and from what sources.

The art of Max Jacob was a series of efforts to write a poem that had no subject, or one that would have only the slightest trace of a subject. The four lines of the poem *Pour ne rien dire* (*Le Cornet à dés*) begins with a cart of thunder ending in Spain in a rainbow ball:

> *La brouette du tonnerre se termine en Espagne par*
> *une boule d'arc-en-ciel.*

The second and last sentence speaks of a country whose churches are surrounded with multi-colored geraniums, and where on the tail of a horse, the poet saw the rainbow fall.

> *Dans un pays où les églises sont entourées de géra-*
> *niums de toutes couleurs je l'ai vue sur la queue*
> *d'un cheval.*

We move easily from such commonplace objects as a cart and a geranium to the full expanse of the heavens: a rainbow, and a horse, who might well be Pegasus, in flight across the sky. The title claims the poem says nothing, and in truth all lyric effects are absent and all coherent narrative. But nevertheless the reader is transported from the finite to the infinite and back again to the finite on a horse's tail that would seem to have magical propensities surpassing the commonplace.

Pour ne rien dire is typical of this art that is ceaseless metamorphosis, an art that refuses to be fixed in a rhetorical pattern, that refuses to adopt one specific form. One thinks of a clown's improvisations before a public amused by grimaces and gestures that accentuate the clowning and disguise all human attributes. Max Jacob's public remained at such a distance from his performances that they could not see that the eyes of this bouffoon were those of a desperate man. His conversion for them was simply one more acrobatic farce. And since the clown's performances continued, the public never reflected that a religious conversion does not modify the character or the fundamental nature of a man. The new source of purity in him remained concealed. The histrionics of the public appearances continued.

The source of the poem for Jacob was an experience, and more often than not, a spiritual experience, but the poem itself was an experiment. And since the daily life of a Christian is a constant struggle, Jacob's laboratory of experiments on poetry was always open. His faith added a great richness of details to the experiments, but all forms of experimentation are disguises, and ways of approaching a problem from a great variety of possibilities.

About 1910 a major battle for modern art was being waged by Apollinaire and Picasso. Certain texts of Max Jacob define the theories and aims of this new art, as lucidly as some of his prose poems illustrate it. By far, the principal text is the six-page preface to *Le Cornet à dés* (1916). But important concepts are discussed in *Lettres à Jacques Doucet* of 1917, in the short *Art Poétique* of 1922, in *Conseils à un jeune poète* of 1941, and in the general correspondence which Max carried on with countless young poets during the last fifteen years of his life. He was, in his own way, a theorist, a teacher. *La pédagogie est l'oeuvre de ma vie*, he wrote in a letter to Béalu.

In the earliest texts he speaks of the "situation" of a work of art, of the atmosphere in which it is placed, and of the necessary distance from the reader it must occupy. In later texts he seems to emphasize the importance of emotion and of the perfecting of an artist's inner life. He repeats many times that emotion is the true sentiment of the heart and that the first gift of the poet is the power of articulation, the actual volume of his voice, the will to exteriorize his feelings by specific means. (*L'art c'est l'extériorisation*.) The public is attracted if the writer's heart reveals its violence, because the public is anthropophagic. It devours the

writer's ego. Art must therefore effect a union between words
(*mots*), if the artist is poet, and the disastrous experiences of the
heart, evils (*maux*), which Jacob calls them in a letter to Emié,
in order to repeat the same sound: *mots–maux*.

Jacob claims that the writer has the choice of two possibilities:
that of writing (*écrire*) and that of moving his reader (*émou-
voir*). If he chooses the second, there is a chance that he will
become an artist, a man able to describe and measure his sentiments, to make their mobility felt by means of syntax, to demonstrate their power by means of a well-composed sentence.

Max Jacob believed that he was the inventor of the true *poème
en prose*, that before him the genre had been impure. The poems
included in *Le Cornet à dés* were written during the years when
he lived on the rue Ravignan, and his friends—Picasso, André Salmon, MacOrlan—often called on him in the morning to ask to read
the poem they were sure he had written the night before. In a
lecture given at *Le Salon des Indépendants* in 1907, Apollinaire
called attention to his friend Max Jacob. This was the first public
acknowledgment of Jacob's work, but he had already for some
time been composing poetry in accordance with principles that
would eventually be taken over by the surrealists. These principles centered on the subconscious, on the poet's effort to apprehend in every way possible the activity of the subconscious
(*les données de l'inconscient*), to grant freedom to words as they
enter the poet's consciousness, to welcome free associations of
ideas, to draw upon the stories and situations of dreams, to transcribe hallucinations and obsessions. These principles, referred to
by Jacob himself in a brief historical notice written in 1943 for an
edition of *Le Cornet à dés*, are identical to many of the precepts
of surrealism. He believed that most surrealist poetry illustrated
simply a freedom of words and did not reflect the power of the
emotions. On this point he believed his art was different from
theirs.

The opening sentence of the 1916 preface is the basis of Jacob's
aesthetics: *Tout ce qui existe est situé*. A poem, as well as a
human being, has a situation in the world, and this situation is
determined both by the mind of the poet and by the way in
which he writes, by all the artifices of his craft. In other words,
the poet's sensibility is exteriorized by language. He restates a
famous belief of Poe and Baudelaire that beauty is so intense that

it cannot last long, that there is no such thing as a long poem. He contrasts the long poem of *Eve* by Péguy to a letter of Mme de Sévigné, and a novel to a prose poem. Art, in terms of the artist, answers for Jacob a need of his nature. For the reader, art is a magnetic force attracting him, absorbing his vitality. A marriage takes place between the poet and the reader, in which the poet is the male and the reader is the female, who has to be subjugated, whose will has to be forced. A work of art is "situated" far from its subject matter, far from the initial emotion which brought it into existence. But this very distance, this "situation" stimulates another kind of emotion in the reader, an artistic emotion. In the prose poem that Jacob offers to his public, he always tries to avoid the kind of story or parable used by Baudelaire and Mallarmé in their prose poems. Jacob seems to approve more of the prose poems of Aloysius Bertrand (*Gaspard de la nuit*), but criticizes them for their romanticism in the style of Collot, that is, for their indulgence in too much lurid color.

Poetry would seem to be for Max Jacob the control of violence, the control of remorse. In reading the finished poem which is "situated," the reader finds himself situated in another universe from which he can see many things: reflections, irruptions, dreams, enthusiasms undermined by irony, incoherences of man that are parodied, examples of the universal stupidity of man (as in the portraits of *Cinématoma*).

The prose poems of *Le Cornet à dés* cannot be summarized or paraphrased because they are themselves the paraphrase of some dream, of some intuition, of some memory, which is copied down in its initial incoherences, with its unusual juxtapositions. In *Nuit Infernale*, for example, a voice from heaven calls out the word monster, and the poet cannot decide whether it is himself or his vices that are apostrophized, or whether the cold visquous sensation on his neck and shoulders is a being attached to him and who is being called *monstre!* There are six lines of horror, close to the kind of horror Baudelaire reaches in some of his poems, when he tries to describe the inescapable, the irremediable. Rimbaud had tried to measure the weight of *mes vices*, and Sartre will use the word *visqueux* to describe an awareness of self in the world.

The poem *La rue Ravignan*, which follows *Nuit Infernale*, is more representative of Jacob's art, where the real experience, which may well be one close to horror, is muted and transposed into an arresting comment. It is a stanza of fifteen lines bulging with proper names. At the beginning a sermon text from Heraclitus reminds of us of the constant change to everything brought by time. But those ordinary individuals whom Jacob sees every day passing along his rue Ravignan have been given names by him drawn from the annals of history and mythology: Agamemnon and Mme Hanska, among others. An old ragpicker, *vieux chiffonnier*, is given the role of election, the name of Dostoievsky. Again, one thinks of the transposition in Baudelaire's poems on Paris, on the power of metamorphosis, by which the real world is changed into a spiritual world. Poetry is this unifying of two worlds, of the drab rue Ravignan with the worlds that continue to live in the mind of the poet and with which he invents the present. Man's adventure is the same from age to age. The name of Dostoievsky, which ends the poem, is the major recall of that phenomenon of vice and virtue inhabiting the same character and giving to every life its color, its animation, its reality.

Le Soldat de Marathon is literally a poem about a party in a sanatarium for the mentally ill:

C'est fête à l'Asile des Aliénistes.

A few of the inmates are performing a play for the somewhat uneasy public of friends and relatives, and one of the actors stepped out of his part so often by dropping to the ground and shouting, "I am the Marathon soldier," that the guards had to intervene to bring him back to the present, to the presence of those around him and to a sense of hierarchy. This phrase in French is underscored by a comedy of sounds, *présent, présences, préséances,* which is repeated at the end when the poet says the guards could not use a club because of the *présent, présences, préséances.* The poem is on the problem of alienation in a far deeper sense than insanity. It is a poignant picture of the one against the many, of a Gérard Labrunie who called himself Gérard de Nerval, *prince d'Aquitaine,* of Max Jacob, *converti juif,* of that violence of an inner life which is masked by a name, by a title, by a profession, by a role played in society.

The poem with the almost clinical title of *Métempsychose* recalls the violence of murder and bloodshed. Pools of blood have the shape of clouds, in the foreground of the picture. But the seven wives of Bluebeard are not in the closet.

> *Les sept femmes de Barbe-Bleue ne sont plus dans le placard.*

A surrealist art transforms the picture into the art of a Magritte. In the place of the bodies there is an organdy coif (*il ne reste que cette cornette en organdi*). But far off, filling the top of the picture, seven galley ships appear, as if by some ominous transformation. They must be the bodies of the seven wives because heavy ropes (*cordages*) hang down from the topsails (*huniers*) into the water, like braids of hair on the backs of the women. The poem ends swiftly with the sensation that the ships are coming close, that they are here beside the spectator:

> *Elles approchent! elles approchent! elles sont là.*

The "metempsychosis" described takes its start from the darkness and silence of the poet's mind. The sight of pools easily suggests blood, and the story of the seven wives of Bluebeard flashes through the poet's mind to account for the blood. But the bodies have vanished, and the water, transformed into the ocean, has lost the signs of murder and the bodies are reconstituted in the seven galley ships whose ropes recall the braided hair.

All worlds are juxtaposed in these poems of *Le Cornet à dés*. The title is appropriate, because from a dice box fall the dice, and each time with a different result, with a different sum. A surreal picture, such as that of seven galley ships can be traced back to its origin in the mind's memory, to the seven murdered wives of Bluebeard; a Marathon soldier, back to a man who has lost his reason; Dostoievsky, back to a ragpicker; a convert, back to the poet Max Jacob living on the rue Ravignan, in Montmartre, in the first decade of the twentieth century.

PART V

The Postwar Climate

13. Existentialism

Existentialism, in its profound meaning, constituted an important aspect of modern philosophy before Jean-Paul Sartre began writing. It is unjust to apply the word merely to his books and his thought. However, he is responsible for the popularity of the word, for its widespread use today, and for the interest it has aroused. Sartrian existentialism is one form of a wider movement including several philosophies of existence.

Sartre and the German philosopher Heidegger see in the meaning they give to the term existentialism a reaction against a philosophy of ideas. Man's existence is for them the foremost preoccupation of the philosopher. Socrates, with his famous maxim "know thyself," is an existentialist. Pascal, in his opposition to Descartes' emphasis on science, is an existentialist when he analyzes the character and the problems of man. The Danish philosopher Sören Kierkegaard is one of the earliest existentialists in the modern world. His writings were translated into German at the beginning of the century and were first read in French translation in the 1930's, in the years that immediately preceded the advent of Sartre.

Before the writings of Sartre, existentialism had long been looked upon as a Christian philosophy. In fact, writers like Pascal and Kierkegaard would look upon the word "existentialism" as almost a synonym of Christianity. Jaspers, a German phenomenologist closely associated with existentialism, carried on his investigation within a Christian context. The Russian branch is represented by Chestov and Berdiaev. The Jewish branch by Buber. In France, the philosopher Henri Bergson has existentialist traits and today the French Catholic writers Emmanuel Mounier and Gabriel Marcel are looked upon as existentialists. The background of Sartrian existentialism, and of its Christian interpretation in Marcel and Maritain, forms much of the movement of modern philosophy.

As an inquiry into the meaning of existence, this contemporary movement has reached a wider audience than philosophy usually does, because it is clearly related to the problems of all humanity created by the wars of the twentieth century and by the extraordinary development of science and technology during the past fifty years. In every effort to give meaning and value to human existence, the ominous question is raised: Should human existence be continued? We are now a community possessing the atom bomb, possessing scientific powers capable of destroying all of humanity. More than ever before in its history, human life needs justification today. Teilhard de Chardin has pointed out how, because of the advance of science, each one of us today is present everywhere, at all moments, on the sea, on the land, and far above the sea and the land.

The three leading philosophies of man today, Christian existentialism, Sartrian existentialism, and Marxism, are all seeking ways of measuring the value of man. The cosmos has ceased to be for us something beyond our imagination and our intelligence, because events taking place at a great distance from us affect us almost immediately. A Parisian and a New Yorker may be seriously affected by events taking place in Tokyo or Africa or India or . . . on the moon.

French philosophy, as it is expressed directly or indirectly in existentialism, has evolved very much in relationship with recent historical events: first, with the Spanish Civil War, with Munich, with the war of 1940 and the defeat of the French, with the German Occupation of Paris and the Resistance movement, with the serious and justified demands of the working class, with the demands that today are being made by the aroused populations of Asia and Africa. And in this sense, existentialism is the expression of a world anguished and torn by gigantic problems and threats. Merleau-Ponty and Sartre believe that existentialism, in accordance with their explanation, can cure the world. Both atheistic and Christian existentialists study the actions of man, the concrete dramatic existence of man, and there they discover some meaning they can give to his responsibility, to his freedom, and to his anxiety.

The phenomenology of the German philosopher Husserl is an important aspect of Sartrian existentialism. It developed largely from a critical moment in the history of science, when faith in science had lost some of its strength. In his book, *Crise des sciences européennes*, Husserl ascribes to the word crisis the meaning of that moment when scientists and theorists seemed to abdicate their belief in an authentic humanity, in human existence responsible for itself. In his study of the development of science, Husserl goes back to the sixteenth century and concludes that today science tends to exclude the problems of meaning and value.

Phenomenology, as defined by both Husserl and Sartre, is a reawakening of responsibility in man, an effort of man to understand himself as being responsible for his acts. Each man is alone responsible for his acts and for the way of life he chooses, whether it is a life of heroism, or a life of drunkenness, or a life of cowardice. This would mean that a man is not necessarily or naturally any one thing. His self-awareness, man's consciousness of himself (*sa conscience* is the French word) is a freedom. He is free to become what he wishes to become. This theory would be diametrically opposed to any scientific objectivism or determinism. Man's freedom of consciousness is subjective. It is the source of his affirmation about existence which will give to existence a meaning and a value.

The words themselves existential and existentialism (*existentiel* and *existentialisme* in French) are neologisms based on *existence*. Ontology, the philosophical study of being, distinguishes essence from existence. Essence is what a being is. "John is a man," for example. And existence makes essence real. "John is" designates existence; and "a man" designates the essence. In Plato, and in classical philosophy in general, essence precedes existence. But in Sartre's philosophy, existence is primary. Existence precedes essence. Existentialists show little interest in essences and abstractions. They are phenomenologists who study phenomena as they occur in immediate experience. They have always shown a marked predilection for the writings of novels and plays and personal journals.

Such forms of writing are best able to reproduce the fluctuations of a man's inner life, the constant restlessness of a man's thought, the moving back and forth of his mind before the intellect imposes logic on his spirit, an ordering of his thoughts which comes from the outside. Novels and plays allow a recording of the original flow and contradictions of existence. Whereas classical literature tends to describe man in a general sense, to describe his essence, existentialist literature, that of Sartre and Simone de Beauvoir, as well as that of Bernanos and Julien Green, represents a return to the concrete, to the existence of things in the world, and to the astonishment that man feels with the simple fact of existing. When Pascal recorded his amazement at living in one particular moment in time and in one particular place, he was translating a sentiment which Sartre will use three hundred years later, in *La Nausée*.

Existence is the privilege of man, but how many men do not make a choice concerning their existence. According to existentialist philosophy only those who make a free choice of what they are to be exist in an authentic sense. An authentic existence has been defined in this way by Jaspers and Heidegger, as well as by Sartre. Existence therefore is not a state of being, it is a constant becoming, a transcendence, a surpassing of oneself.

In accordance with the fundamental thesis that existence precedes essence, man chooses his essence, and this power of choice derives from his existence. All other beings are predetermined. A flower, for example, is predetermined by its seed. Of course, a man does not choose to be ugly, but he chooses his attitude toward his ugliness. Man's consciousness depends on the world. He is in the world, and without the world he would cease to exist. But what the world is for him, he will make it so. Some existentialists go so far as to say that man creates the world by being conscious of it, and at the same time he creates himself.

For the existentialist there is no ideal type of man. No civilization in the history of man, no religion, no philosophy has fixed a norm for the human species. This belief is equivalent to saying that what a man is to be is not determined by religion or culture or morality. Man has to invent himself.

The word "commitment" (*engagement*), used so often by the French existentialist thinkers, has both a passive and an active meaning. There is a passive form of commitment in the sense that every man born into the world is committed to the world. The active form is apparent in the belief that each man is free to choose the commitment of his life. He may commit himself by becoming a soldier or a student or a bank clerk. The active form of commitment, to a cause, for example, is limitless, because one can never estimate how far such a commitment will lead. This kind of commitment is comparable to existence itself in its limit-lessness and unpredictable future. Both existence and commit-ment are mystical experiences.

Pascal speaks of the freedom we have to choose a belief in God or its opposite. But whichever choice we make, we are committed. For the classical philosopher, belief in God leads quite easily to a moral system of behavior. But for the atheistic existentialist, who does not believe in a world of ideas, his choice is made without any guiding principle. This is the foundation of his anguish. There is no sense, no justification for his choice.

With the word existentialism today, the name of Jean-Paul Sartre comes first to mind, rather than the religious existentialism that preceded Sartre, largely because he has systematized his phi-losophy and demonstrated his principal theses as corresponding to contemporary currents of opinion. To distinguish it from other forms, Sartre's philosophy is often called atheistic existentialism. Sartre looks upon himself as a philosopher of freedom. This free-dom of man is demonstrated not only in his willed actions, but also in his emotions and passions. They are also free because they depend on the being that man is. In a now famous sentence, Sartre writes that his fear is free, that he chose his fear. (*Ma peur est libre et manifeste ma liberté . . . je me suis choisi peureux.*)

And yet Sartre argues that the free actions of men are absurd; they are not controlled by reason. With the exercise of freedom, the two sentiments of anguish and responsibility are experienced. The sense of responsibility extends far beyond what has been chosen freely by a man. He is responsible for everything, for a war even, as if he had declared it. His responsibility is in his attitude toward the war. Sartre establishes extraordinary equivalences: to choose is to live; to be distressed by war is to choose it.

Sartre is one of the foremost witnesses of our age when he speaks of its chaos. The first principle of his philosophy has become a belief of the twentieth century: man is what he wishes to be and what he plans to be in the future. He is nothing else save what he makes himself to be. His freedom is his power to negate everything his personal history claims he should be, everything the society surrounding him claims he should be. This concept of freedom, so basic in Sartre's philosophy, is therefore the opposite of self-sufficiency and complacency and satisfaction with self. It rises up from a man's will to deny the strictures imposed on him by his world. It is a man's refusal to be formed by the demands and the limitations of the world.

Man is free to commit himself to some cause. The character Matthieu in *L'Age de raison* argues over this problem when he says: What is the point of freedom if it cannot be used for a commitment? (*A quoi ça sert-il, la liberté, si ce n'est pas pour s'engager?*) Sartre elevates the function of a project which is an awareness of the possibility of another kind of life for man. A project (Sartre uses the word *un projet*) is both the denial of what the world is demanding and the affirmation of a man's free choice of something else.

Man himself then is free. He has limitless power to change. But Sartre has studied in many of his writings the degree to which each man is determined and immobilized by others, by those who see and know him and who have decided what his character is. Others define us in terms of what they believe they know concerning our habits, our vices, and our virtues. Sartre has often pointed out, as in his play *Huis Clos*, that we tend to resemble what others have decided we are. We abdicate our real character for a fictional character created by others. This is, for Sartre, an alienation of our freedom. Whenever we rely on others to understand ourselves, we lose the freedom of our being.

In his analysis of man's behavior, and especially of man's moral behavior, Sartre calls the objects surrounding us "utensils." Roads, railroads, tools, instruments, keep us in constant communication with those who designed and built them. They are parts of our social world and our institutions that create, or help create, our behavior. Sartre calls this never-ending communication between a man and his world "an ontological solidarity." It exists for the exploitation of the world. From society, first, and then from history, in a more opulent way, the world derives its form and its meaning. However, Sartre, in his final analysis of this "solidarity," of this situation for man's moral behavior, argues that the meaning of the world is not in itself. The meaning of the world is in each individual man. This meaning depends on the project of a man. History therefore has no meaning in itself. Its meaning is given to history by men.

Marxism is not merely a philosophy for Sartre, it is a climate of thought, an atmosphere in which French intellectuals have developed their ideas. He believes that intellectuals today have to define their position with respect especially to marxism. Socialism would be a broader word, a term designating for Sartre the contemporary movement by which, in the existentialist sense, man is in the process of changing and constructing himself. Existentialism, since it became an accepted philosophy in France, has lived through momentous trials and problems: the German Occupation, the Resistance, the Liberation, the cold war, organized activities of the working class, organized activities of Algerians in their effort to reach independence. And on many occasions, Sartre has explained his philosophy in terms of the conflicts of his day. Revolution is the supreme example of man's freedom. It testifies, more clearly than any other act, to man's right to invent his own laws.

There is no doubt that Sartrian existentialism has neglected religious values in the twentieth century and has often appeared as a destructive force in terms of Christian philosophy. And yet—the paradox is omnipresent—the existentialist attitude is favorable to religious philosophy. Kierkegaard predicted this when he stated that an ever deepening understanding of human existence would inevitably make men more attentive to the values of Christianity.

At the beginning of the twentieth century, an indifference to Christianity was fairly prevalent. Henri de Lubac has analyzed this state of affairs in his book, *Le drame de l'humanisme athée.*

The discovery of the novels of Dostoievsky, perhaps especially *The Possessed*, contributed to a change of attitude toward Christianity. His study of the anguish of the inner life of man, of his psychic conflicts, made him into a prophet of existentialism. At the same time, Etienne Gilson was describing Thomas Aquinas as a forerunner of existentialism. Thomism was being considered by Gilson as a philosophy of existence as opposed to the Platonic doctrine of essentialism (of essences).

The writings of Gabriel Marcel, in particular, justify the use of the word existentialism to describe Catholic philosophy today. He refuses to look upon Christianity as a "system" that brings comfort to the problems of existence, that does away with doubt and struggle and contradiction. He does not look upon God as the perfect Being of the philosophers, but as that Being with whom man as a sinner has a direct experience. Man is as fully committed to the reality of God as he is to the reality of the world. It can rise up before man like a lost Atlantis, a transcendental world of Being. Marcel often compares his experience with the Platonic myth of the cave and man's emergence from the cave.

The world itself, if that is all there is, is constantly dehumanizing man and his social relationships. The world can become a series of objects, an abstraction at the end of which is death and the voiding of human effort. Within the experience of despair, Marcel finds a sentiment of apprehension, a suspicion that the world is merely one section of an invisible reality that contains it and that is able to provide man with the experience of hope. With such a theory, discussed in his *Journal métaphysique*, Marcel fuses the Christian dogma of the Fall with Plato's myth of the cave. Whereas Sartre speaks of man's "freedom," Marcel emphasizes man's "participation." Man is a being in a situation. Everything existing in the world or in history is situated in relation to man's body. The most complete form of man's participation is called by Marcel an experience of love. In his being he is changed by the presence of someone else. The rigor of Sartre's philosophy makes it almost impossible to establish man's relationship with other people. For Marcel, man does achieve communication with others and hence participation with being.

Love implies the presence of a being whose appeal is able to transform a man's life. Love, in the sense of *caritas*, is love for the being of an individual, and not for all that is said by others about that individual. Marcel sees in the experience of love a conjunction between incarnation and transcendence, because love for a human being is also love for God. The infinite is reflected in the intimate relationship between two human beings.

Faith is defined as a commitment (*engagement*) of the entire being of man. Thereby he participates in the totality of being, because participation in the fullest sense for Gabriel Marcel, is man's relationship with himself, with the world, with other human beings, and with God.

If Gabriel Marcel is doubtless the leading philosopher of Christian existentialism, Emmanuel Mounier was until his recent death, the principal exponent of personalism (*le personnalisme*). This word designates not a separate philosophical movement, but one closely associated with Christian existentialism. It is an effort to define man's responsibility and his position in the world and in history. Between 1930, when it was organized, and today, it has opposed the marxist view on man's position in the world, and on human responsibility, as expounded by atheist existentialism. It would be fairly accurate to define personalism as an attempt to reconcile Karl Marx and Kierkegaard.

The economic depression of 1929 was the immediate reason for Mounier's activities in urging a combined economic and spiritual revolution. The magazine of the movement, *Esprit*, was founded by Mounier in 1932, and the leading editorial of the first issue was entitled "Refaire la Renaissance." It was clear from the start that Mounier was opposed to that form of individualism created by the French Revolution. He saw in that individual a man without attachment, without a sense of community, a man whose freedom has no direction and who has grown into a being who is calculating, distrustful, vindictive.

Mounier does not analyze the society of his day, as Sartre does, but he defines the ideal community, one quite obviously fashioned on St. Augustine's *City of God*, and reminiscent of the dogma of the communion of saints. In emphasizing the primacy of the spirit, he opposes marxism, and borrows from Gabriel Marcel theories on man's participation or "communication," as he calls it. From Péguy, he borrows theories on the degradation of man's spirit in the twentieth century. The human person (*la personne*) is immersed in nature, but also transcends nature. Mounier exalts matter almost as fervently as Teilhard de Chardin does (*la sainte matière*), but he also sees in matter, in the material universe, an obstacle to man's spirituality.

Personalism presents an entire program of action, which is a series of reforms: an economic reform involving a more efficacious use of technology; a moral reform aiming at a greater authenticity in human behavior; a religious reform which would bring about a more perfect, a more universal relationship between man and God; and finally a social reform which would be a perfecting of human relationships. In presenting such an elaborate program, Mounier was constantly aware of the danger that such purity of action involves and that had been clearly analyzed by Charles Péguy at the beginning of the century. He knew that a fresh motivation, a fresh impulse for reform can easily be degraded into mere habit. He knew that a reform which at its beginnings is mystical in nature, can be degraded into politics. And he knew that every revolution tends to be transformed into diplomacy.

During the past twenty years in France, ever since the publication of the first books of Sartre, the writing of Catholic thinkers has been largely concerned with the meaning of existentialism and their relationship with existentialism. Among the most recent is a man whose work may in time become the most significant. He is the Jesuit priest, Père Teilhard de Chardin, who died in 1955. A paleontologist, Teilhard de Chardin was a student of the phenomenology of nature. His research in geology and prehistory was an effort to discover the meaning of evolution. The title of one of his books, *Le Phénomène humain*, could serve as the central motif of all his works.

The world, the universe itself, is an evolution for this scientist-priest. It is a genesis. Universal history comprises the history of matter, of life and of man. When Teilhard de Chardin claims that everything is part of the natural history of the world, he recapitulates an important theme in Karl Marx who called the science of history the only science. Teilhard gives to the word evolution its broadest meaning because it comprises inorganic matter, life and the development of man. His philosophy involves so many disciplines simultaneously that the specialists have looked upon him as an adversary: scientists, phenomenologists, and theologians.

For Teilhard de Chardin, man is the summation of the entire movement of the universe. The history of nature is achieved in man and continues to develop in him. But in man alone this evolution becomes conscious of itself. On the last pages of *Le Phénomène humain*, this priest describes the possibility of a world tragedy: man has today the power to destroy his own universe.

Man has to choose between two all-encompassing forms of belief: either the world has no meaning and we are moving in the direction of a cosmic suicide, or we find in the world and in history a meaning which gives us reasons for living and hoping and procreating. Today's enemy for Teilhard is the doctrine of the absurd, when, in the language of the paleontologist, he reverts to the neolithic age. He finds the present moment in history important for the history of the earth. The development of industry, the emergence of totalitarianism, revolutions, wars, and strikes, have made men conscious of their collective strength. Although Teilhard never defined his political position, he was obviously against all secular and religious forms of pessimism. His conception of the world is a combative optimism. His confidence in man and man's future is as strong as the confidence of the Encyclopedists in the eighteenth century and as the belief of Karl Marx in the nineteenth. For this paleontologist, man, in the joy he feels in his development and evolution, is the supreme result of matter.

The problem of the compatibility between traditional Christian philosophy and the newest form of existentialism is the most persistent philosophical problem in contemporary France. This problem is not merely philosophical, because it involves the related domains of social action, politics, history, literature, science. The word itself is all-encompassing. And whatever meaning is given to it, whatever belief is granted to it, affect our understanding of all these related fields.

The moral problem of the writer's "sincerity," raised by Gide and Bernanos in the 1920's and 1930's, was replaced in the 1940's and 1950's by the metaphysical problem of existentialism. Many thinkers claim the word and claim to be exponents of the philosophy. A student once asked the Russian writer Berdiaev what his

relationship was with existentialism, and he replied: "I am existentialism." (*L'existentialisme? mais c'est moi!* This is related by
Roger Troisfontaines in *Existentialisme et pensée chrétienne*.)
Jaspers, Heidegger, Marcel, and Sartre have all revindicated the
word in their writings and their particular application of the word.

All of the writers associated with existentialism in the twentieth century are subjective thinkers. They are concerned with
their own human qualities and traits, with lessons derived from
their own existences. Their books are personal experiences, testimonials that substantiate their vision of the world. One of
Sartre's most recent books, *Les Mots*, is an excellent example of
this conviction that what is learned from an emotional experience
is stronger than what is learned from any imposed system of
belief. Existentialist writers tend to elevate St. Augustine over St.
Thomas Aquinas, and Pascal over Descartes. They are sensitive to
the drama of a man's conscience and to the discoveries of a man's
consciousness.

This impressive focus on subjectivity in existentialist thought is
explained by its moment in history when the world was threatened, as it still is today. At such moments, everything is drama-
tized, even philosophy, and those doctrines that are related to the
meaning of life are the most heeded. Two world wars and the
imminence of an ending to all civilization account for entire populations living quite literally a form of anguish. Heidegger, in the
trenches of World War I, experienced the absurdity of existence,
and Sartre, in a concentration camp in World War II, experienced something of the anguish he was to describe in his philosophy.

Existentialism is the philosophical experience of a historical
period. And yet very different kinds of thinkers have acknowledged allegiance to it: Jean-Paul Sartre and Marcel, Kierkegaard,
Heidegger, Jaspers, Berdiaev. Philosophical reactions to the same
kind of human experience have been very different. The one
term that seems to apply to all of these writers is "subjectivity."
Kierkegaard wrote that "truth is subjective." By this, he seems to
be saying that what is true has to be lived by him personally. It
can never be anything objective.

Each of the major figures in the history of existentialism represents certain emphases, religious and nonreligious. Their agree-
ments and disagreements, their use of one another's theories, their

search as individuals for the meaning of existence have formed, not one coherent school, but a prolonged moment of philosophical inquiry.

By almost everyone, Kierkegaard (1813–55) is acknowledged as the immediate forerunner. A religious man, a Protestant, an individualistic thinker, he has recorded in his *Journal* the account of his anguish and his hesitations. In his book *Fear and Trembling*, Kierkegaard has used the Bible story of Abraham's sacrifice of Isaac in order to analyze the believer's anguish. In the *Genesis* account, Abraham's anguish over his obligation to his son is omitted. The believer chooses in the night. He chooses in fear and trembling because he does not know whether he is one of the elect of God or the victim of a demonic illusion.

In Heidegger's (1889-) philosophy, human existence is being-in-the-world, *Dasein*. Existence is being related to a world of objects. The prefix *ex*, of *existence*, indicates that a man is outside of himself in his practical relationship with things. To be is to be cast into the world without choosing it and without wanting it. He experiences *anguish* when he recognizes the absolute *nonsense* of things. He exists authentically when he throws himself (*projet*), projects himself into the world. A *project* is his meaning; but it is for no reason. Heidegger believes that most men take refuge in an unauthentic kind of existence where they fabricate idols for themselves, such as God and science.

By comparison with the theories of Heidegger, Karl Jaspers (1883-) emphasizes a religious philosophy. He claims that man's empirical being (his social relations, his past, his temperament) should not be confused with his existence. Man's relationship with the world is a failure, but it may lead him to a transcendence, to a meeting with God where he will be authentically himself.

In many ways, Gabriel Marcel (1889-) is close to Jaspers in his philosophy. Since his conversion to Catholicism in 1929, his meditations have centered on the themes of fidelity and freedom. He believes in a transcendent presence and acknowledges faith in an absolute beyond human understanding. His plays describe the obstacles to man's union with God.

Jean-Paul Sartre (1905-) is, of course, closer to the philosophy of Heidegger. His celebrated sentence in *L'Etre et le Néant*,

"Man is a useless passion" (*l'homme est une passion inutile*), is the conclusion of Sartre's argument that our actions are impossible desires to become divine. Our bad faith (*la mauvaise foi*) disguises truth for us. We are nothing save our own actions, our own projects of the moment.

For Albert Camus (1913–60), man is the outsider (*l'étranger*). He describes in man a schizophrenic consciousness that has lost all affective contacts. Camus says that man has to choose God or time, the eternal or history. Camus chose history because he prefers evidence (*parce que j'aime les certitudes*). Since we cannot make over the world and man, we must act as if we could. (*Il faut imaginer Sisyphe heureux.*)

Is there a common definition of the existentialist in the writings of so many diverse and independent thinkers? At least it is possible to say that the existentialist is the individual aware of himself, passionately aware of his life that he knows he will have only once. This awareness is his freedom and the origin of his values. In his actions and experiences he will discover some significance for his existence.

There is no one philosophy of existentialism. There are several developments of existentialist thought. In 1945, Sartre had attracted so much attention to his writings that the word, quite justifiably, is more closely associated with him than with any other single name. After the word was firmly fixed to his name in the minds of the public, it was then found to be applicable to St. Augustine and Pascal, to Baudelaire and to Kierkegaard.

Sartre's philosophy is that of an atheist thinker who finds the world absurd, but in which all is not lost. Each man has to invent the meaning of *his* life, by carrying out *his* action. These actions will liberate him from society, from God and from himself. Such philosophical reflection as this comes from a dizziness similar to that nausea provoked in man by the sight of the world's absurdity. It is the moment when the cosmos seems to be chaos, and when man finds himself an outsider to everything in the world, and deserted by everyone. Existentialism is therefore the reflection of a man on a unique experience that human anguish gives him.

14. Antitheatre

CHRONOLOGICALLY the antitheatre in France preceded the anti-novel by a few years. The first play of Ionesco, *La Cant-atrice Chauve*, was performed in 1950, and in this work he appeared as the playright refusing one of the principal conventions of the theatre: a coherent dialogue carried on between human beings. A few years later, in the novels of Robbe-Grillet, Butor, and Sarraute, the writer refuses to narrate a story in accordance with the usual rules of story-telling. Ionesco, in his first play, wanted to demonstrate not the technique of a traditional play, but the banality of man's daily conversation, the repetitions he uses, the stupid inane thoughts to which he gives expression, the conventions of dialogue that keep him from saying anything of significance, and even anything that has meaning.

Ionesco was questioning the very subject matter of the theatre, which is human speech, and the new novelists have been questioning the validity of telling a story in a so-called logical manner. Ionesco has revealed that the idea of his first plays came to him from a textbook for conversation destined to teach a Frenchman how to speak English! The senseless repetitive verbiage of this type of book seemed to the writer the caricature of our life when we so often continue speaking long after we have ceased having anything to say.

The same intention is apparent in the plays of Adamov, plays highly esteemed by many critics, although they have not reached the popularity of Ionesco's. In *Ping-Pong*, for example, Adamov denounces the tendency in man to act as a puppet, to act in a mechanical way, as he leads a stereotyped existence. The principal theme of the play seems to be a study of human solitude, or the absence of communication between human beings.

In a more terrifying and absolute way than in the plays of Ionesco and Adamov, this theme of solitude is used by Samuel Beckett as he gives it a metaphysical dimension reminiscent of Kafka. In his most famous play, *En attendant Godot*, two men stammer bits of confused exasperated dialogue without our ever learning who they are or whom they are waiting for. Although the play was first performed only thirteen years ago, in 1953, there are already countless books and articles telling us who Beckett's tramps are and whom they are waiting for. The critics, however, do not agree, and Beckett has offered no very sound clues in his text and in the very infrequent interviews he has given.

These examples of antitheatre tend to be incoherent and even shocking because they deliberately ridicule what their authors denounce as the false clarity with which man habitually analyzes any problem, or the false logic he brings to bear on the conundrums of daily life. Both the new dramatists and the new novelists seem to be proposing an art that is a parody or a caricature. But they have found, particularly the dramatists, a public, an international public, that approves their art. The serious part of this public agrees with the dramatists that our world in its moral and social aspects grows more and more standardized. The major forces of communication—popular magazines, movies, television, radio—exercise on the whole debilitating influences. The satiric spirit in the new plays and new novels, when it is flagrant, is directed against mediocrity in human life.

During the first fifty years of the century, the major French writers were primarily concerned with man's moral adventure. They were keenly aware of what André Malraux called "man's fate" (*la condition humaine*) as it was related to the moral issues of their day. This statement would apply to such differing but equally important writers as Gide, Malraux, Bernanos, and Albert Camus. This focus, this emphasis seems to change by 1950, with the first plays of Ionesco and Beckett, and the first novels of Alain Robbe-Grillet. These new authors are defiant of the usual moral issues in the style of their writing and in the themes of their work. They have imposed a new vision of man's existence by avoiding any comment on it, by avoiding any rationalization about it. By comparison with the literature of the two preceding decades, the new literature of the 1950's, and especially the theatre, is characterized by an absence of moral problems, of moral interrogations.

In one of his books, André Malraux defined art in a way easily acceptable before 1950, when he wrote that art rectifies and humanizes chaos. Art imposes form on what is unformed. Today's art seems to move in the opposite direction, toward an absence of form, or toward something that seems to be stylistically without form. A new science of incoherence presides over the change that traditional art is undergoing. The new art rivals existence itself in its multiplicity and in its gratuitousness. Unquestionably this new art is a symptom of something more important than art itself, of a change that has taken place in man's own opinion of himself. Traditionally, in keeping with the humanistic ideals of the Renaissance, man looked upon himself as the measure of all things, as that being for whom the universe was created, but today he appears, in the theatre of the absurd, as a mere element without clarity of measurement or importance.

A play hailed as *avant-garde* is quickly classified if it remains before the public, and almost before it is able to enjoy the prestige of newness and experimentation, it falls into the category of a standard work. Thus far in the twentieth century, the French theatre has produced two important generations. The first flourished in the 1930's, with such playwrights as Giraudoux and Cocteau, and the second in the 1950's. This latter type of theatre has continued into the 1960's under the designation of "theatre of the absurd." Between these two generations, in the war years and the second half of the 1940's, the existentialist theatre, with the plays of Sartre and Camus, and the work of two independent playwrights, Henry de Montherlant and Jean Anouilh, were predominant. The structure of those plays written and produced in the 1940's was more traditional than experimental. Not until the early 1950's, with the first plays of Ionesco, Beckett, and Jean Genet, is there a marked change in the mode of composition and in the manner of theatrical production that invites such a term as *avant-garde*.

No permanent meaning can be attached to *avant-garde* or its contemporary equivalent *absurd*, save that of "revolt." Revolt usually against some moral or some literary tradition. In recent years "the beat generation" in America, and "the angry young men" in England have unquestionably had their effect on the theatre. The new theatrical art of Albee and Le Roi Jones in America, and Pinter in England is not without parallels with the new Paris plays.

Only in a superficial sense, and in contrast with more traditional forms of theatre, does the new theatre seem characterized by tricks and scandals. Actually it is deeply serious, and it would not be difficult to establish the philosophical debt the new plays owe to surrealism and to existentialism. Ionesco has dispensed with all this problem of definition by claiming that there never has been any such thing as an *avant-garde* theatre, in the sense that all theatre is transitional.

If there is one fairly prevalent trait in the new French plays that caused them to be called "experimental" by most critics and theatregoers, it would be the effort of the playwright to awaken the spectator to a sense of the unusual, to what the surrealists used to call the *insolite*, which is everywhere around us, in the most familiar objects and habits of living. The theatre should reveal to us things we look at without seeing and arouse in us emotions we ordinarily refuse to admit.

The new playwrights of the 1950's and 1960's have not formed a cohesive movement or school. Each one remains a solitary figure, almost fanatically independent. There has been no program uniting them save a determination to create a new kind of theatre. Each has developed his own discipline which is a form of anarchy, a dramaturgy that will not resemble the well-made play or the thesis play, or the more classical play of psychological analysis. The four leading playwrights of the 1950's, Beckett, Ionesco, Adamov, and Genet, are far more isolated one from the other than the playwrights of the 1930's and the existentialists of the 1940's. The solitude in which each one seems to live is an element of their dramaturgy where there is, among the characters, a lack of communication in the ordinary sense.

Les Bonnes of Genet and *Fin de Partie* of Beckett are, for example, isolated works, each complete in the self-destruction it enacts. The early plays of Ionesco also give something of this effect of isolation, of being cut off from other contemporary works. But in his more recent plays, in *Le Rhinocéros*, for example, there is a greater sense of human warmth and human continuity. Bérenger is a character who develops from play to play, in *Tueur sans gages* (1957), and *Le Rhinocéros* (1958), and in the play of 1963, *Le Piéton de l'Air*. The new type of play does not lend itself easily to analysis and avoids a narrative. It is a theatre characterized by a deliberate reduction of psychological discourse. These negative characteristics explain to some degree the startling effect of separate works they give, of plays without antecedents, in which all movement, all action, all character development have been arrested. The characters are often immobilized physically and mentally. They repeat over and over again the same action and the same words without moving ahead, without making any visible progress.

This static trait of the new plays is apparent also in the new French novel. A recognizable subject matter has disappeared from these forms. Robbe-Grillet's hero who looks through the blinds of the window into his wife's room is immobilized in his pose of *voyeur*, and all action has stopped for Genet's criminals, in *Haute Surveillance*. The movements of Genet's characters have been arrested in the physical sense, and they have been arrested in a judicial sense also. In Beckett's *Fin de Partie*, the two principal characters move in opposite directions, Hamm toward death and Clov toward life, but one impulse cancels out the other, and finally no progress is made in the bare room that contains the two men.

The one-act play or short play, which by its limitations emphasizes a lack of motion or development, has been widely used by the new dramatists in France: *La dernière bande* by Beckett, *Oraison* of Arrabal, *La Leçon* of Ionesco, *Le Professeur Taranne* of Adamov. As the significance of the contemporary play turns from psychology to metaphysics, from an analysis of predictable actions to a questioning of reality and first principles, a fundamental pessimism about man has become more evident, and in order to focus more and more attention on this pessimism, the playwrights have diminished the value of the stage set, of the number of characters, of plot, of costume and history. The plays are often suitable for the smallest of stages. They bear affinities with a sketch performed in a night club before an intimate audience, members of an audience who have been drinking and who are beginning to think in terms of big generalities and philosophical truths. The plays often have the brevity and the terrifying concentration of a circus act or a vaudeville stunt. Because the work is cut down to its essentials, it has to be performed with virtuosity.

The plays appear difficult because they do not correspond to our traditional conception of the theatre. *Ubu Roi*, in the presurrealist days, was an attack on the conventions and habits of the theatre-going public, and Alfred Jarry, when questioned about his mystifications, used to reply that comprehensible matters would only dull the minds of the spectators, that what was absurd (Jarry was one of the first to use this now overused word) would train the faculties and memory of the audience. Ionesco, in his play of 1952, *Victimes du Devoir*, outlines this principle when he has his character Nicolas d'Eu explain that there is no longer any such thing as a character who is unified and identifiable. A personality as such does not exist on the stage. All we can hope to see is a man possessing contradictory forces and noncontradictory forces.

The new French theatre has appropriated a philosophical attitude of long standing in the history of philosophy, and one which in recent times was believed in by the surrealists. It is the belief that our vision of reality is an illusion.

Whereas the classical French theatre, where major importance was placed on psychological problems, used a minimum of objects in the action of the play, the new theatre has stressed the presence of objects in the play's dramaturgy. Cocteau's play *Orphée*, in the middle 1920's, used in a magical way a horse, a window, a mirror. An almost bare tree in *Godot* attracts considerable attention in Beckett's play. The telephone in *Les Bonnes* and a dress are constant preoccupations in Genet's play. Ionesco, more than any other playwright, has utilized objects: the corpse that grows in size in *Amédée*, the coffee cups in *Victimes du Devoir*, and a bicycle in *Le Piéton de l'Air*.

In this last play, first performed in February, 1963, at Le Théâtre de France, by J.-L. Barrault and Madeleine Renaud, the character Bérenger and his wife and daughter are living in a small cottage in England where he is interviewed by a journalist. It is obvious in many of his speeches that Bérenger is Ionesco, and is speaking directly in the first person about literature and the art of the theatre. He doubts whether literature and the theatre can comprehend the huge complexity of reality. Man today is living through a terrifying nightmare. These are familiar convictions in the writings of Ionesco, but they are expressed more forcibly in *Le Piéton de l'Air*, where Bérenger claims that literature has never had the tenseness and the power of life. He recapitulates a thought associated with the dramatic theories of Antonin Artaud (in *Le Théâtre et son double*) when he insists that in order to equal life, literature will have to be a thousand times more cruel and more terrifying. With Jarry, Apollinaire, and Artaud, Eugène Ionesco is beyond doubt one of those contemporary writers who have reflected deeply on the state of the theatre today and on the meaning of the theatre. If the theatre is able to change, these men would believe that it might incite the spectators to abdicate their usual state of hypnosis or half-somnolence.

The ambition of many of the new creative artists, novelists and painters as well as dramatists, is to exalt a chaos or a labyrinth where they may live through, and be seen living through, a form of metaphysical anguish which is the mark of the twentieth century. The scene in Sartre's *La Nausée*, where Roquentin rubs a pebble that is smooth on one side and muddy on the other, is one of the earliest where the protagonist experiences a metaphysical anguish he is unable to explain. Between that scene, written in the late 1930's, and the antidramas of Ionesco in the early 1950's, and the films of Alain Resnais in the 1960's, the artists, and especially the dramatists, show us man in situations where his intelligence is unable to cope with his anguish, where he feels surrounded and besieged by an inhuman element. He lives quite literally the drama of the absurd, which is at the same time a drama of mystery and one of solitude where he is conscious of the presence of familiar things that have no meaning for him.

Somewhat earlier in the century than the moment of the outstanding plays of the theatre of the absurd, Ionesco's *La Cantatrice chauve*, Genet's *Les Nègres*, Arrabal's *Cimetière des voitures*, for example, there was apparent in the novels of Malraux and Camus, and in the plays of Jean Anouilh, the theme of man's failure to reach an understanding of himself and his world. The tramps of Beckett's *Godot*, who are unreal phantoms unable to find a place in the world for themselves, had already appeared in the works of Kafka and Henri Michaux. The character Plume of Michaux and the protagonist in *The Trial* are beings without a history, weightless and full of fear and anxiety. They are antithetical to the characters of Balzac, each of whom incarnates a system of behavior and recognizable psychological traits. Already in Stephen Dedalus of Joyce, in Michel of Gide's *L'Immoraliste*, and in Mathieu of Sartre's *Age de Raison*, the European protagonist was a conscience feeling itself drawn into a bottomless abyss of freedom.

The drama of this endless freedom, defined by the existentialists as a psychological fact, is now, in the new French theatre, incarnated by characters who no longer look upon language as the means of communication between human beings. There are usually few characters in the new plays, and often only two at once on the stage, but each one realizes there is no one to whom he can speak. The one who speaks does not expect an answer. The words heard on the stage form a noise that fills the duration in time of the play's action and serves as a distraction from the boredom of speaking only to oneself.

Beckett's tramp (*clochard*) is a choreographic representation of the *outsider*, the everyman of the *avant-garde* theatre. *L'Étranger*, the title used by Albert Camus for his novel, is merely one name designating the nonconformist. He is a type of amnesiac who has lost contact with the past. Alienation is the fundamental theme, although it is sometimes disguised, of the new plays, and the spectacle of this alienation which we watch on the stage, is fully calculated to turn the spectator into himself, to force him to an examination of the human condition. The characters of Arrabal, Vauthier, Beckett, and Ionesco are, in this sense, our own consciences which have reached a superior degree of sincerity. In their most successful instances, the plays are testimonials of sincerity, in which the playwright is more concerned with depicting the condition of man's fate than in demonstrating the tragedy of any one individual hero.

In the space of a very few years, dramatic works that are strange and paradoxical and even subversive have been adopted by an important segment of the theatre-going public in Paris. And the adoption of these plays has been widespread in other countries, in translation. For five years, without interruption, at the Théâtre de la Huchette, the director-actor Nicolas Bataille maintained his production of *La Cantatrice chauve* and *La Leçon* of Ionesco. No such success accompanied the early experimental plays of Jean Cocteau in the 1920's. As the experimental plays of the 1950's establish themselves with some degree of permanence, the once popular melodramatic play in Paris, called the *théâtre de boulevard*, has been gradually losing out. The wit and the sentimentality associated with that form of theatre belonged to the 1930's, and have no connection with the present decade.

The type of violence found in the plays of Ionesco and Genet did exist in certain surrealist writings. The freedom the surrealists wanted to give words endowed them with such power that they became imperious and overwhelming. But the surrealist texts where this phenomenon does occur never became popular. This kind of art reached a wide audience for the first time in the theatre of the 1950's. The other arts participated in this same mode of shock and dissonance: in the music, for example, of Alban Berg (*Wozzeck*) and in the new concrete music (*la musique concrète*), and in such a work as *Déserts* of Edgar Varèse. It is in the perforated bronze statues of Germaine Richier, in the thin sculptured figures of Giacometti, in the paintings of Pollock. These paintings often resemble a labyrinth, an image which has been used to describe the new type of play. One of the French painters of this school, Georges Mathieu, used to appear on the stage of a theatre, in the presence of an audience, and to the accompaniment of a jazz orchestra, entered a kind of trance when, with tubes of paint and long-handled brushes, he rushed at the canvas and covered it as he gesticulated, shouted, leaped back and forth.

These are deliberately evoked examples of extreme freedom in the creation of art, where chance seems to preside, where the art form preserves primitive traits. Such artists do not allow any time to intervene between the impulse to create and the gestures of the creator. The "happenings" of the 1960's, instigated in New York by the composer John Cage, and developed in Paris and Nice, are further examples of this instinct. Alain Resnais' *L'année dernière à Marienbad* is an example of a form that might be called labyrinthine, a work in which the cinematographer has tried to catch something of man's dream world. To reach this oneiric world would be an escape from the mechanized order of our existence, from the development of technology that surrounds us.

The seeming formlessness of modern art (either in the nature studies of Pollock or in the plays of Ionesco) may be interpreted as a compensation for the dazzling omnipresent logic of technology. The works have little formal beginning or end. Their subject matter proliferates without a center and often induces in us that *malaise* which comes from too much space and too little constriction, an uneasiness which sometimes psychologists call agoraphobia.

More than any other, the theatre is a social art and offers to the men and women of a given generation their own portrait. Ionesco is very much concerned, in a philosophical sense, with man's freedom of spirit, and in order to make his public feel the necessity for this freedom, he shows us in his plays the various forms of serfdom in which man habitually lives. We are bound like slaves to slogans, ideologies, verbal mannerisms, and manners. The beginning of *La Cantatrice chauve* is a typical pointless evening conversation between an English husband and wife. The scene is one of boredom and emptiness in which no sense of reality is assimilated.

The method of this writing is an exposure on the stage of our anguish. By seeing our own obsessions on the stage, we are probably liberated from them for at least the time it takes to perform the play. This theory of the purification of our passions was the mission of the theatre for Aristotle. Ionesco chooses for each play an obsession or a mania, and leads the public to laughter over it. In *Le Nouveau Locataire* furniture is accumulated on the stage until there is no space left for the protagonist. This could be man's mania for collecting things, the material encumbrances that stifle our lives. In *Amédée*, the corpse that continues to grow throughout the action could designate the dead weight, the heaviness of reality. Lives can easily become littered with dead things. In the farcical play with a gruesome ending, *La Leçon*, a young woman is overcome by the uselessness of pedantry. The old man in *Les Chaises* incarnates man's dream of greatness and the vanity of this dream.

In many of these instances, Ionesco seems interested in giving a new meaning for a type character very close to the clown. Traditionally the clown is the actor exaggerating our gestures, and traditionally clowns combine sadness with farce. He is a prototype of the modern hero who is humiliated and ridiculous. Ionesco believes that each one of us is less himself than someone else. Man's daily speech, for this playwright, is either empty or hermetic. Comedy can easily rise out of pointlessness of speech or obscurity of speech.

Antitheatre is clearly the opposite of a theatre of ideology, or a theatre of commitment (*engagement*) such as Jean-Paul Sartre has written. Antitheatre is a combination of spontaneity in the dialogue we hear and the rigid mechanistic formulas we ourselves use when we speak. The new theatre is therefore a means of penetrating into the vanity of many of the habits that fill our lives. The Danish philosopher Kierkegaard in his hierarchy of values placed the humorist just before the religious. Both of these types, humorist and religious, are men who, one by means of comedy and the other by means of spirituality, are concerned with eradicating all false values. The new theatre is a serious enterprise. Even if the tone of many of the plays seems a scoffing or a mockery, there is concealed behind the scoffing a deep anguish.

The seriousness, and sometimes the religious seriousness of the new plays, despite their farcical elements, cannot be doubted. The two tramps of Beckett in *Godot* may be Everyman and his conscience. The play is reminiscent of the medieval debate between the body and the soul, between the intellect and the nonrational in man. Certain of their speeches about Christ might substantiate the theory that they are the two crucified thieves. The fundamental imagery of the play is Christian. The tree recalls the Tree of Knowledge and the Cross. The life of the tramps at many points in the text seems synonymous with the fallen state of man. The typical hero of the Arrabal plays is the little man, comparable to Beckett's tramps, reminiscent of Chaplin and the solitary heroes of Kafka. At the dénouement of *Le Cimetière des Voitures,* the spectator realizes he has been watching a transposition of Christ's passion.

The parable in Ionesco's *Le Rhinocéros* is on the sacred individuality of man. As the inhabitants of a small provincial town are transformed into rhinoceroses, the protagonist Bérenger alone remains faithful to his vocation of man. He remains alone, the last soul in the town to resist the epidemic. He refuses to comply with the collective mania, the standardization of his world.

Bérenger, the archetype of average man, grows into the stature of protagonist because throughout the play's action, he is not influenced by words and speeches. In an almost pitiful way he struggles against the exaltation of all the other characters, against an overwhelming force that isolates him. Slowly at first, and then more and more swiftly, Bérenger is compelled to engage upon an experience of solitude. At the end of the play he is totally alone, after observing, without always fully understanding it, a clinical study of conformity and contamination. This solitude of man is at the center of all of Ionesco's plays, and it is always manifested in the same way, with the same admixture of irony and burlesque and humor.

The familiar mannerisms are all in *Le Rhinocéros:* the ritual of commonplaces, the sudden eruption of the fantastic in the most drily banal scene, the meaningless lists of words, the repetitions. But Ionesco added a parable, and for the first time in his career, he conquered a large public quickly and easily. He lost thereby some of the theatrical purity he had demonstrated in *Les Chaises* and *La Leçon,* where no didactic element blurred the simple functioning of the infernal machine, of the antilogic of our world.

M. Ionesco has often disclaimed any ownership of his dreams and obsessions. He sees them as part of the collective unconscious, part of an ancestral heritage, a legacy of all the ages. On several occasions, in articles and reviews, he has spoken of a feeling of human anguish he has been aware of since childhood and which he believes comes not only from his life but from the life of man. It is a sense of isolation, of being encircled by a void, and of being unable to communicate with others. The kind of banal conversation in his plays for which he has become famous is precisely the symptom of man's inability to communicate. Ionesco's speech is often the very kind of speech we hear around us almost every day. His skill is his use of this kind of speech, the forcefulness with which he makes us feel man's incapacity to express his fundamental thought. His plays often give the impression of being autopsies of our unacknowledged, invisible manias. They are in fact the exorcisms of his anxiety. As a writer he has acknowledged his debt to the surrealists. His art reminds us constantly of the anguish of Kafka and the antics of Chaplin.

The dramaturgy of Ionesco makes of his plays an art that is autonomous, existing by itself without the usual reliance on an ideology. The play itself, as it was being written, made its own discovery of realities that had not been defined before the rest was composed. Ionesco has testified to this experience of playwriting. During the very process of writing, the dramatist will come upon unexpected realities and these will become the richest elements of the play. This is in keeping with surrealist doctrine that has always stressed the revelatory power of the imagination. That part of a play, or of any work of art, which is ideology, is by definition total and self-contained at the very beginning. It cannot possibly bring out what Ionesco calls unexpected realities.

The creation, the writing of a play is therefore the discovery of the play. It is based upon elements of surprise, elements that first surprise the playwright himself. It would be significant to compare the explanation which Ionesco has given of his first play, *La Cantatrice chauve*, with the various explanations of his critics and interpreters. Whereas Ionesco has called his play the expression of the unexpected, of the unusual (*insolite*) as it rises up gratuitously from banal language and action, the critics of the playwright have devised many ingenious and contradictory definitions. They have called it an attack on the English bourgeoisie, or an effort to destroy the art of the theatre. They have defined it as abstract theatre or pure theatre or *avant-garde* theatre.

If M. Ionesco has no specific intention or plan when he begins to write a play, he agrees that he has multiple semiconscious or ill-articulated plans in his mind. These become precise as the writing continues. This is a strong stand against playwrights who would reform the world by educating it. Ionesco places himself among those artists hostile to all forms of "truth" or "ideology" which by their very nature seem destined to become forces of oppression. He has referred to two forces of oppression which he considers the most dangerous for the artist: the sclerosis of the bourgeois mentality and the tyranny of political power.

Roger Blin's production of *Les Nègres* by Jean Genet was the outstanding success of the 1959-60 season. The success came from many sources: from the text itself, one of the strongest Genet has written for the stage; from the *mise-en-scène* of Blin who showed himself highly sensitive to the poetry and the dramatic intention of a very difficult text; from the performance of the thirteen Negroes who played at being actors with the seriousness and frenzy of children convinced that their game was real.

Once again, in the history of the theatre, a poet has created a play that is totally outside of existing trends and theories of contemporary theatre. The sumptuous prose of Genet, interspersed with argot and scatological language, is indeed the art of a poet controlling the action of the play, which is the parody of a ritualistic crime. A clue to the dramaturgy of *Les Nègres* is in a letter of Genet published in the 1958 edition of *Les Bonnes* (L'Arbalète) where in six succinct pages, he discusses his total dissatisfaction with the formulas of the contemporary theatre. He denounces the stupidity and triviality of actors and directors who seem to base their art on exhibitionism, on characterizations that come from their obsessions and dreams. The western play has become a masquerade for Genet. He advocates a theatre of ceremony, a return to the conception of the mass, of a theatre for initiates, where the high dramatic moment would be comparable to the Elevation in the Catholic mass. In becoming a diversion, an entertainment, the modern theatre has adulterated the significance of theatre. Genet suggests that what is needed is a clandestine theatre which the "faithful" would attend in secret.

Les Nègres is a nightly ritual, a kind of mass celebrated before a catafalque. If during the performance, one thinks of African ceremonies, of black masses and of certain esoteric-erotic *boîtes-de-nuit* in Paris, one is constantly pulled back to the specific play of Jean Genet, to the poet's creation which transcends all the histrionic types it evokes.

The play, called a *clownerie*, opens with a dance, a Mozart minuet, performed by four Negroes and four Negresses. As they whistle and hum, they dance in front of a casket. Five members of the court enter, the queen, her valet, the governor, the judge, and the missionary. These are Negroes wearing white masks. The intricate relationships between the two groups of actors and between actors and spectators are quickly established. The masked members of the court are whites as Negroes see them when the whites are in power. The eight black dancers are Negroes as they imagine they are seen and judged by whites. They are assembled to enact an imaginary crime (the slaying of a white woman), committed by real Negroes in the presence of false whites. The spectators sense, even before the catafalque turns out to be two chairs covered with a cloth, that this is a ritualistic crime on the nature of love which the man in power feels for the one in his power. The one in power is a queen who demands the love of her black subjects. The subjects are the group of Negroes who are uncontrollable, who are constantly moving about, uttering shouts of laughter, parodying themselves and others, expressing anguish and mirth as if they lived in a world both fictitious and real.

In the original performance, Roger Blin created at the very beginning and maintained until the end, the dramatic ambiguity which is the central situation of the play; namely, the conflicting relationships between actors and public on the stage, and the public in the audience. He did not neglect a more subtle relationship existing between the desire of the actors to amuse themselves as they act, and their desire to amuse us in the audience at the same time. Roger Blin was the master of ceremonies, the master of the strange liturgy which unfolded with alternating spasms of humiliation and fury.

Les Nègres is not a satire on colonialism. The revolt of hatred which the play depicts is much deeper and more universal. The Negroes who speak the opulent language of Jean Genet give expression to a rage that goes far beyond the rage of their race. The oppression from which they suffer is so hostile, so incomprehensible, as to be easily the oppression of mankind. The nightly disappearance of a white woman by a process of magic is one way of exorcism. The play is an incantation, an hallucination.

The parody of the whites (in the characters of the court) is in juxtaposition with the parody of the blacks by themselves. In the earlier play of *Les Bonnes*, Genet studied the curious bond of duplicity between the mistress of the house (Madame) and her two maids. In Sartre's long study of the psychology and art of Genet (*Saint Genet, comédien et martyr*), he analyzes the persistence of this theme in all the writings of Genet. A strangely distorted love joins the saint and the criminal, the guard and the prisoner, the policeman and the thief, the master and the slave, the white and the black. In one sense, *Les Nègres* testifies to Genet's understanding of Sartre's study of Genet. In another sense, the play is about the meaning of theatre, about the distinction between a role to be played and a human existence, about the relationship between a ceremony and life.

The violence enacted in this play is not real. The ritual is a symbolic ceremony. No corpse is in the coffin. There is actually no coffin. At the end of the play, Archibald, the corypheus, affirms some of his opening speeches: *Nous sommes des comédiens, et nous avons organisé une soirée pour vous divertir.* In *Les Nègres,* the Negroes play the personal drama of Jean Genet, according to Sartre, which is the agon between the actor and the martyr. It is a play of philosophical implications: the drama of a man who must play the part of a criminal in the very society that has ostracized him because of his crime.

The concept of sovereignty has always obsessed the imagination of Genet. Sartre believes that he chose evil because that was the realm in which he could hope to reach a status of sovereignty. And Sartre makes clear his conviction that evil is a myth created by the respectable members of society. They tend to call Genet wicked and to use him as a scapegoat who committed the acts which they have been tempted to commit and which they may or may not have committed.

The theme of alienation is prevalent in contemporary literature, but it has never been orchestrated so richly, with such tragic and sensual poignancy, as in Genet's novels and plays. The existences evoked in these works cannot find their realization. These characters fully understand how estranged, how alienated they are, and they are both obsessed and fascinated by this state. The anomalies Genet sings of as if they were the noblest themes for a poet are all present in *Les Nègres* and *Les Paravents.* In *Les Nègres* the characters are conscious that they are actors, as the characters in Genet's novels are conscious that they are alienated from the normal world. Mme Simone de Beauvoir is justified in seeing Genet as a descendent of the *poètes maudits,* and in placing him at the end of a lineage of blasphemers: Lautréamont, Nietzsche, Jarry. But Jean Genet is not a philosopher, and he is not a blasphemer in the real sense. He is the artist who feels guilty by simply being.

15. The Christian Critic and Mauriac

B Y ITS PERSISTENCE and its vitality, the religious problem has shown an ascendency over all other problems throughout the history of French letters. The greatest writers either reflect some aspect of the problem or appear tormented by it. It is manifested in *Polyeucte*, Corneille's tragedy on sainthood, as well as in *Tartuffe*, Molière's comedy on religious hypocrisy. If French literature appears essentially one of psychological analysis, of painstaking investigation on the human heart and sentiments, a tradition extending from the twelfth century romances of Chrétien de Troyes to Marcel Proust in the twentieth century, this preoccupation seems rarely to exist without some reference—and it is often a dominant reference—to religious turmoil and inquiry. Most French writers can be defined by their adherence to religion or by their attack on it. Calvin, at the time of the Renaissance, protested against Rabelais for his "Pagan" naturalism. Pascal, in the seventeenth century, attacked the *Essais* of Montaigne as the writings of a dangerous sceptic. Later in the century, and within the Church itself, Bossuet rose up against Fénelon and his doctrine of quietism. In the eighteenth century. Voltaire sought the ruin of both Bossuet and Pascal, and in the nineteenth century Chateaubriand, in his *Génie du Christianisme*, attempted to rehabilitate Bossuet and Pascal, and undermine Voltaire. It is quite possible to interpret the history of French literature as an almost uninterrupted controversy carried on between those who believe and those who do not believe.

The critical spirit, even in its more limited expression of literary criticism, has never been absent from French thought and literature. Criticism in its specific technical sense, seeks to explain and evaluate a literary achievement. In the case of Pascal, for example, it would try to explain how he was led to write the *Pensées*. It would study the external circumstances of Pascal's life and period, as well as the more secretive spiritual struggles and resources of the man, that led to the writing of the *Pensées*. It would analyze his philosophical arguments, his imagination, his sensibility in order to invest the *Pensées* with some contemporary meaning. And yet it would state, if it were criticism in the best sense, that there is no such thing as the final word or the final judgment about a literary work. The mystery of a literary work that criticism seeks to explain is impenetrable. Literature is concerned with the oldest and deepest dreams and experiences of man. Literary forms, in trying to retain some aspects of these experiences, and literary criticism, in trying to explain literary forms, are fated by their very nature to be fragmentary.

Contemporary French literature is largely oriented toward criticism. It tends to be, even in its creative aspects, an elaborate accusation of the social order, of institutions and ideas. Both Catholic and non-Catholic critics are less concerned today with the study of the beautiful than with their efforts to make out of criticism a form of meditation. In their distrust of a method, of a discursive system, they have appropriated the freer more independent form of the essay.

In a fundamental sense, literary criticism is an explanation of the experience of reading. The analysis of this experience, in the works of the eminent new critics in France—Poulet, Blanchot, Richard, Barthes, Picon—has become so subtle and profound that criticism today is a record of man's knowledge about man. Literary criticism is, more and more, the application of all the sciences: anthropology, psychology, political science. The new

French criticism prefers the work to the author. Sainte-Beuve's method, with its emphasis on biography, belongs to another age. Charles Du Bos was the first, in the twentieth century, to demonstrate an almost exclusive interest in the text. Albert Béguin, another Catholic critic, continued the work of Du Bos, and explored depths in a given literary text of which the author might not have been aware. This subconscious intention of a literary work is at the basis of Sartre's studies of Baudelaire and Genet, and of Charles Mauron's study of Mallarmé.

The Jesuit critic André Blanchet, in his articles on Gide, Malraux, Camus, and Sartre, is actually writing a psychoanalysis of contemporary atheism, a spiritual diagnosis of our times. At almost every point in his articles in *Études,* his attention is focused on the texts themselves. As a critic, he is a judge of the works and not of the writers. In this sound, and, on the whole, prevalent tradition, Jean Onimus, a professor in Nice, occupies today one of the strongest positions. His book *Face au monde actuel* is a Catholic's observation of the important literary works related to Baudelaire's spleen and Sartre's nausea and Ionesco's clowns. Onimus' work of criticism follows in many ways the aesthetic theories analyzed a generation ago by Jacques Maritain in *Art et scolastique* and *Frontières de la poésie,* where the Thomist philosopher saw criticism to be the discernment of values imminent in literary works and where he brilliantly defended the autonomy of art.

The essay is the least pretentious form of literary criticism. The very modesty of its name indicates its method. One tries or tests a book, or an author, or a subject. And one ends always by testing oneself. It is the supplest form of criticism, and it may well be the most efficacious, the most enduring. It is the form of criticism the most likely to outlive contemporaneousness. Midway between the extreme forms of journalism and the heavy volumes of tireless, and at times tiresome, specialists, the essay is that form of criticism revealing the intellectual and sensitive powers of the critic. It is remarkably native to the particular genius of the French mind. In its most personal approach to the various problems of criticism, it comes closest to being an artistic creation.

The essay of the twentieth century, in its multiple forms, has often been one of the vital manifestations of the Christian spirit in France. Charles Péguy, many of whose books are long essays, measured by the lyric intensity and duration of his religious views, was a spiritual guide for the first decade of the century. Jacques Rivière, whose essays are brief and brilliant, became a guide for the second decade, for readers whose attention he held by his example of incessant responsibility toward life and art. Charles Du Bos continued this role of critic in the following decade or two.

The work of Du Bos, known by its title of *Approximations,* so apt a synonym for the essay, is characterized by an unusual scrupulosity in this critic's will to understand the work of art he is considering. He approaches a work or a writer by every means open to him. He lays siege to the life or the book he is studying. He rarely discusses a work he does not admire, and this attitude brings out in him a humility and a friendliness that are rare in critics. He remains always a Christian writer believing that a work of art bears a testimonial to some spiritual reality of which the author himself may not always have been conscious. Deep within a work he tries to find an intention which the artist may not have realized he was obeying. Even in works of an obviously nonreligious character, he is attentive to the slightest echo of the Divine Word.

The writing of Du Bos is characterized by a certain tone of grandeur and nobility deriving in some degree from the very subjects he most willingly chooses, subjects of considerable magnitude: Goethe, Nietzsche, Baudelaire, Claudel, Proust. In the presence of such writers as these, his powers of receptivity were limitless. His thought decides and multiplies in a plethora of long heavily weighted sentences whose form recalls Proust. He carries on a dialogue with himself in the fashion of an intimate journal. Gide once said to Du Bos that both of them were the type of critic characterized by a love of dialogue and by a dislike for affirmation.

The seven volumes of *Approximations* and the two books on Gide and Mauriac, represent a continuous investigation in the combined realms of aesthetics, literature, and spirituality. These realms are never completely separated for Du Bos. He was hostile to any false demarcation between literature and life. To oppose literature to life is blatant absurdity, according to his essay *Vie et littérature* (*Approximations VII*). Each needs the other. Without literature, life would be a river deprived of any meaning. Literature acts as a system of hydraulics capturing and directing the water. Life owes to literature its survival, its earthly immortality.

The focus of his work is the study of what he calls the traces of the spiritual in the world of letters. The essential problem he is most concerned with is the spiritual condition of the writer. In company with such critics as Thibaudet, Massis, and Rousseaux, Charles Du Bos revived and revitalized the problem of the relationship between art and morality. In his early essay on Baudelaire (*Approximations I*), where he analyzed the poet's humiliation and redemptive suffering, and in the later essay on Claudel (*Approximations VI*), which is the study of the mechanics of conversion, Du Bos gave a form of criticism completely independent of traditional academic patterns. Far more contemporary than Péguy, Du Bos continued to study, until his death in 1939, the spiritual life of his generation. The works of both Péguy and Du Bos, in the final analysis, are personal journals where writers are discussed—Corneille and Bergson, in the case of Péguy; and Joubert and Pascal, in the case of Du Bos—as if they were motifs in the spiritual life of modern man.

During the past one hundred years, the religious problem in French literature has been more profoundly reflected in poetry than in prose, although it has often been poetry not rigorously, not doctrinally Christian. During this period, when the Catholic spirit has not been universally persuasive in France, when it has been put to many tests and undergone many attacks, its particular expression, found in the poetry and critical writings of the poets, is the most valid because it is at once bound up with the eternal spirit of Catholicism and with the specific drama and dilemma of man today.

Charles Baudelaire is the source of modern poetry and the poet in whom the spiritual problem appears both in its most agonized and most transcedent form. It is also apparent now that Baudelaire—and not Sainte-Beuve—is the major critic of the nineteenth century. The creation of beauty for Baudelaire contains the promise of a spiritual deliverance. He was haunted all his life by a sense of tragic dualism, and a need to discover a way to effect a unity and harmony between the two opposing forces of good and

evil. The genesis of Baudelaire's aesthetics as well as the genesis of
his personal moral problem is stated in his *Journaux intimes* when
he says that as a child he felt two contradictory sentiments: the
horror and the ecstasy of life. Honest with himself, Baudelaire
never claimed to have known a mystical form of ecstasy. His
ecstasy was more sensational, more voluptuary—at the end of
which he sought, not love, not truth, but some revelation of
beauty as the source of the unknown. His way is mystical in only
the very broadest sense. It might be named a poetical mysticism.
He calls the principle of poetry: human aspiration toward a superior beauty. Its manifestation is in an enthusiasm, a rapture of the
soul.

Les *Fleurs du Mal* reveals a constant search, impeded by vel-
leity or impotence, to get out from himself, from his obsessions,
and master his fate. He believed that artistic creation contains the
possibility of salvation for a man. He was always skillful at forming resolutions and incapable of carrying them out. His destiny
was that of a seeker, a voyager moving toward the unknown, the
different. But his destiny combined greatness and tragedy. His
was the ambition of the poet-artist, capable of changing the
world, of recreating the world by the word. His system was one
of analogies and correspondences, where the poet appears as de-
cipherer of hieroglyphics, as reader of the book of creation. All
the elements of Baudelaire's great ambition that guided subsequent poets were felt and practiced by him as means of uniting
his life with the world, of discovering behind the individual and
the ephemeral, the universal and the eternal. Baudelaire's is the
myth of a lost Paradise, of an Orpheus no longer able to enchant
the animals and bewitch all nature. His personal journal is a form
of critical writing. It is not only indispensable for a study of his
poetry, but it also constitutes one of the key documents on the
problem of spirituality.

More mysterious than Baudelaire's is Rimbaud's case history in
modern French poetry. His brief period of four or five years as a
poet has been examined by countless critics and historians, each
anxious to arrive at a solution, an explanation of the adolescent
destiny. There are as many solutions as there are critics, but all
agree on the essential mystery of Rimbaud's life. He has been
defined by all the opposites: Catholic and Pagan, visionary and
rascal (*voyant* and *voyou*), surrealist and marxist. He has been

compared to Julien Sorel, Villon, Faust, Prometheus, Icarus. But he might simply be called the modern poet, the almost purely intuitive poet who repudiated the logic of philosophers and doctrinaires. He was the visual poet, aggressive and revolutionary by temperament who had alienated the conventional approaches to God and to love. He willed to make himself into a magus, a magician, a voyant. And the magic he learned to control was poetry.

For Rimbaud, the true poet has not yet arisen. We do not yet know what a poet is. But he tells us in his *Lettre du 15 mai*, his major critical piece, that the first study of man is to know himself, the true self, to cultivate himself. The creation of poetry depends on the discovery of the hidden self that we are. *Je est un autre*, wrote Rimbaud, and no sentence of modern times has elicited so much commentary. In his work of a poet man finally reaches the unknown, according to Rimbaud's formula, which is reminiscent of Baudelaire's.

Rimbaud's experience of a poet was always close to the mystical. The poet is defined as the recreator of the world. Before engaging upon such a destiny, his life was characterized by a denial of everything, by insults, insolences, vagabond voyages. From today's perspective it is possible to see this violent period as a *chasse spirituelle*, the title given by Rimbaud to a manuscript that has been lost.

The spiritual significance of Rimbaud's work was first discussed by Paul Claudel. The precise way in which Rimbaud helped Claudel, in revealing to him his mission as religious poet, will doubtless remain a mystery. Within a poetic work that seems to be largely composed of revolt and blasphemy, Claudel discovered traces of a religious drama that spoke directly to him and to which he owed his return to the Catholic faith. In his preface to an edition of Rimbaud's collected writings, one of the important statements about poetry by a poet, he tries to analyze systematically the phases of Rimbaud's drama that had taken on such significance for him. Rimbaud's violent period Claudel interprets as the necessary mutation of genius, the sentimental reaction to his world. The visionary phase, the *voyance*, Claudel calls the way of the spirit. The magnificent images of the *Illuminations* were preparations to seeing truth. The final phase Claudel calls that of belief where, as in the last pages of *Une Saison en Enfer*,

Claudel believes that Rimbaud accomplished a mission in the world, that of a violent reaction against positivism.

From Mallarmé, Claudel learned his lesson on the metaphor, the essential element of his poetics. He learned that a metaphor is a relationship between two objects. The poet's role is to apprehend, to seize the metaphors that exist in the world. This means naming each object and restoring it to its rightful place in a new ordering of the universe, in a new lexicon of the world. When Claudel states that with each new breath of a man, the world should appear new to him, as fresh and as virginal as it appeared to the first man with his first breath, he reiterates Mallarmé's belief about the endless metaphorical richness of the world. By naming an object, the poet gives it its meaning, as God had originally done when He created the world by naming it. The total word, or the total poem, is therefore the universe. Each poet bears in himself a picture of the universe, a subjective maze of images that have relationships with one another. Mallarmé follows an instinctive quest in naming various objects and seeking to understand their metaphorical meaning. Claudel goes farther in willing this quest as if it were a religious obligation. Symbolism, under the initial guidance of Mallarmé, was a spiritual way of understanding and celebrating the universe. It became later, in the art of Claudel, a more frankly religious way of discovering in the midst of endless variety a secret unity. In his *Art Poétique* of 1903, Claudel states that the metaphor is the logic of the new poetry, comparable to the syllogism of the older logic. Things in the world are not only objects to be known, they are means by which man is being constantly reborn. He had not altered his basic belief when, in 1925, he commented on Mallarmé's *Igitur*, in one of his most penetrating critical essays, and called the world not a sorcerer's handbook, a *grimoire*, but the Word (Logos) engendering all things.

Literary criticism has not failed to point out that the lesson of the Incarnation has become a pivotal theme of contemporary Christian literature. This dogma teaches that the supernatural destiny of the Christian is to a large degree ordered and governed by the particular condition of human life he knows. Time itself is a kind of determinant for eternity. Péguy has written in one of his most moving passages that we lead a life temporally eternal. *Nous menons une vie temporellement éternelle.* The tree of grace is deeply rooted. *L'arbre de la grâce est raciné profond.* This is why the Christian believes he has chosen everything by joining the two kingdoms of God and the world. To a Christian, the Marxian solution that states that materialism will lead to a society without class distinctions and where the exploitation of man by man will be abolished, seems oversimplified, unwarrantedly optimistic. History is made by men, and like them it is a complex of good and evil. In it there are forces of disintegration and selfishness that lead to its ruin, and also forces of generosity and love that transform the world and are constantly saving it. The same kind of struggle is going on in the heart of each man. History is as ambivalent as man. The artist, who works more in darkness than in light, will be more prone to depict the man unaware of the forces of good working in him.

During the twenty-year period between the two wars, French literature was given over to a serious self-examination and self-criticism. Catholic critics especially seemed severe in their analyses and reproaches. Henri Massis, as late as 1941, in his book *Les idées restent,* bitterly attacked Gide, Proust, and Valéry for having alienated French intelligence from its real goal, for having undermined the moral precepts of the nation. Claudel called the contemporary atmosphere "morbid and depressing." Today such criticism, especially that of Massis, seems unwarranted and severe. During the same years a strong renascence of Catholic literature and a rehabilitation of Catholic thought were taking place. The study of medieval philosophy, especially St. Thomas Aquinas, received a new impetus from the lectures of Etienne Gilson at the Collège de France, and from Jacques Maritain at the Institut Catholique in Paris. In the art form of the novel, Catholic thought and sensibility were to play an important part after 1930. Two novelists of this period have published critical writings of considerable significance.

Georges Bernanos died in 1948 and was at that time claimed by the astute critic André Rousseaux as the sole contemporary writer upholding the Catholic tradition in France. His books are warnings, especially on the loss of modern man's freedom—freedom of many kinds: political, economic, humanistic.

Among the living writers of the generation of Bernanos, the one who, for thirty years, has been representing the Catholic tradition, has of recent years partially lost his high position of literary eminence. To the younger French reader today, M. François Mauriac is better known as a journalist, as an *académicien,* and even as a polemicist than as a novelist. Even in 1952, when he was awarded the Nobel Prize for literature, Mauriac was looked upon as a weekly adviser to the French, as a chronicler and critic of social and political and religious problems in his journalistic writings.

In the twenty-odd novels he has published—the first appeared in 1909—he is the writer deeply interested in the metaphysics of sin and drawn to the secret unconfessed dramas of his characters. He has given to French literature the most complete and stark picture of provincial pharisaism that exists. He wrote, as early as 1926, *la province est pharisienne,* and continued to study this theme in each of his successive books. He has been called too glibly a Catholic novelist, although in the strictest sense there is no such type of writer as a Catholic novelist. A novel is not a demonstration of a religious belief. It would be more accurate to say that Mauriac is a Catholic and a novelist.

The weekly articles that have been appearing for several years have been collected in book form from time to time under the titles of *Journal* or *Bloc-Notes.* In these pages he shows an aspect of his Parisian personality, an often embittered and vituperative Mauriac. He has demonstrated over and over again his greatness in daring to say everything he knows and believes about whatever controversial subject he is discussing. It is a permanent French tradition, illustrated today by a Mauriac as well as by a Sartre, that the writer must sustain the spiritual life of the country so that it will survive the horrors of party strife.

In *Journal 1932–1939,* Mauriac uses the term "journal" to designate a kind of writing that combines a chronicle of events and personal thoughts. Each article is devoted to an event of the day, to a literary problem or to a religious or sociological issue. These reflections, based on experience and wisdom, are those of a novelist, of a brilliant stylist who practices the art of condensation, of swift judgment, of the poetic trait illuminating a formula or a detail. In his *Journal,* Mauriac remains both the novelist who explores and understands the secret motivations of man, and the worried guardian of a moralistic ideal. By 1947, when these articles appeared in their definitive version, their author had entered upon the second part of his career.

His essays cover a wide range of themes. He analyzes some of the fundamental laws according to which he writes his novels. He argues with Gide over Christianity, at a moment when Gide was close to Russia. He states that the novel of Proust is the only contemporary work whose survival is certain. He describes the art of Greta Garbo in one essay and in another castigates most Christians who "renounce only what has already been wrenched from their hands."

Ce que je crois, published in 1962, when Mauriac was seventy-seven-years old, is a religious essay, one of several written in the fervor of self-examination, composed in order to discern more clearly the meaning of his religious life. Some of the earlier essays, *Souffrances et bonheur du chrétien, Dieu et Mammon, Le jeudi saint*, analyze some of the spiritual problems of our age. *Ce que je crois* is a view looking back over a long life. It is personal in the sense that Mauriac is primarily concerned with telling his reader how he has remained a Christian, although at every point in the analysis of his own spirituality, he sees a relationship with the spiritual problems of his age.

At the very beginning, M. Mauriac announces that he wants the tone of his discourse to be direct and honest and naïvely simple. But the conflicts that arise from the holding of such a faith, the existence of nonbelievers, of strong spiritual forces in the world that are hostile to such a faith, add difficulties of a philosophical and psychological nature. Mauriac avoids a didactic approach to what turns out to be drama in a man's life. For he interprets his being born into the Catholic faith as a drama rather than as a chance occurrence. He narrates, with a feeling compounded of awe and humility, the vicissitudes of his faith and its slow conquest of his life and the permanent victory it represents today for him.

His first communion, in May, 1896, was followed by a very special kind of Catholic training in childhood and adolescence. Women and priests dominated his early life. The piety of Mauriac's mother stressed all the ritual observances of religion, and instilled in her children an almost abnormal terror of carnal impurity. When the young Mauriac began observing the provincial society around him in Bordeaux, he was struck by the discrepancies between the teaching of the Gospels and the behavior of the members of his social class. By the time he reached Paris as a young man, he was moving toward a liberal view of society. He refers to *Le Sillon*, a liberal Catholic organization, and describes how he was upset by its condemnation in Rome and by Pius X's encyclical *Pascendi* (1907), condemning aspects of modern thought already sympathetic to him. He realized that the literary and philosophical masters of his day, Maurice Barrès and Charles Maurras, were not Catholic in any sense familiar or congenial to him. His childhood faith was not merely one element of his life. It was an unattachable part of his sensibility and it has guided him throughout his life in his search for the real meaning of justice and freedom and love. His faith has been his life. It has been the dominant force in his actions, in the achievements of his intelligence and in the impulses of his heart.

The chapter on purity in this small book raises questions that are central to Mauriac's novels. He alludes to the problem of purity as he evokes moments of his childhood and certain moments of crisis, when, as a young man, he wandered in a state of despair through the streets of Paris. Mauriac tries to resolve this problem as he understands it. Sexual desire in man may become one of his chief glories, and it may become one of his chief catastrophes. Impurity is not, for Mauriac, in any sexual act as such, but rather in the spiritual deception and the lie with which a man is able to deceive himself with regard to sexuality.

It is clear from this treatise that Mauriac's faith imposed upon him a militant life in his social role of a Christian. He does not attempt to expound a system, yet there is a thesis uniting all the chapters: the equation he wants to establish between faith and love. The thought on such subjects as love, freedom, purity, and justice are doubtless more acceptable to the majority of Mauriac's readers than the words expressing his faith in the manger once visited in Bethlehem by the Wise Men, and his faith in the empty tomb visited by the women on the first Easter Sunday. Mauriac is proud of his faith, and he does little to conceal it. This pride is so instinctively joined with feeling and tenderness that one listens to his voice as that of a Frenchman, whom many look upon as the foremost writer today, impatient to testify to truth as he understands it.

It is perhaps clearer in this recent book that Mauriac's theology is very basic and even elementary. He is insensitive to the hope of modern man of matching his intelligence with the cosmos and conquering it. The sole conquest that holds him is that of individual salvation. His religious faith as well as his political commitments are related to this personal drama of each soul. He has been an indifferent parishioner, unattached to the group as a whole. He has even been impatient with the elaborate exterior structure of the Church. And yet the ending of the book is one of peaceful submission to the Church in all its aspects. His voice may well be the last of two generations of Catholic writers in France whose work has centered about a religious trust and inheritance. Claudel and Péguy were the giants of the first generation. The second generation, writers born in the 1880's, includes Jacques Maritain (1882), Charles Du Bos (1882), Mauriac (1885), Bernanos (1880), and Gabriel Marcel (1889). By his novels and his extensive critical writing, Mauriac has reached the widest audience of all of his contemporaries.

In his *Journal*, Mauriac writes that "a single novel is proposed to the Christian, his own; a single debate taking place between him and his Creator." His novels are problems posed by his faith. There is still much to be studied in Mauriac's metaphysical turn of mind which is completely instinctive, preoccupied with a very dark, very carnal vision of truth, one which grants little power to man's intelligence and man's will. As a novelist, he is always drawn toward the most secret and most blameworthy parts of his creatures' minds. His characters do not incarnate an ethical system. We see them living in a very particular atmosphere that may well be Mauriac's major literary creation. The summer heat in the region around Bordeaux, the sudden storms, fires in the pine forests, bird hunts, obsessions with the land and with money—these are the elements of most of his novels.

In *Ce que je crois*, believers and nonbelievers can find a common ground. The great Christian writers before Mauriac who have written on the problems of faith in the same mode of question and answer, are St. Augustine, Pascal, Kierkegaard, and Dostoievsky. Mauriac's position is unequivocably stated. He believes that Christ is God and that the Church is the guardian of the words of Christ. He believes in the words used by a priest when he forgives sins and when he changes the bread and the wine into the body and the blood of Christ. This faith, defined in these very few articles of belief, has never been shaken, not even when as a student he was deeply disappointed by the encyclical

Pascendi. His humanism is rooted in a Christology that he himself defines as Pascalian. God is felt in man's impulses to charity.

Mauriac's personal drama is the contradiction he feels between his successful career as a writer—during which he has received honors and glory, and lived largely in terms of the pleasures of art and the intellect—and Christian faith which is, according to the words of Christ, a religion of poverty and charity.

In his combativeness—Mauriac often refers to this trait in his character—he has interpreted literally what Catholicism has taught him concerning the great human problems of equality and freedom. In the major and minor causes of his time, Mauriac in his public role of spokesman has always defended the side of justice. He has kept his eyes on the decisive world problems and considered them from a temporal viewpoint and from the viewpoint of eternity.

What I believe, of 1962, a book of modest proportions, was followed, in 1965, by a much longer book entitled *Nouveaux Mémoires intérieurs* and which might easily be called "What I am." It is a meditation on death (Mauriac was celebrating, at the time of its publication, his eightieth birthday) as well as a meditation on a man's love for life. It is a book written by a man who believes that very soon he will be questioned on what he was rather than on what he has accomplished.

Conclusion: The New Writers
and Critics

THE PRINCIPAL LEGACY of romanticism has been the belief that
the work of the genius will be a revelation, the unique story
and experience of one personality. Romanticism proposed a new
kind of redemption for the writer, to be granted in terms of what
degree of truth is attained in self-revelation. In keeping with this
romantic concept, the new writer has been concerned with relating his most peculiarly personal experience rather than that part
of his experience that is universal and communal. He has moved
away from the classical-humanist concept of the seventeenth-cen-
tury writer, in order to resemble today a type of prophet. Traits
of the prophet or teacher are in Camus, Montherlant, Malraux,
Sartre. The writer stands alone in the revelation of a unique
"message." This message may be upsetting, as in the cases of
Simone de Beauvoir and D. H. Lawrence, and even terrifying, as
it was earlier in Lautréamont, and is today in Jean Genet. But it is
understood in some degree or other by those men who refuse to

analyze themselves or observe the fantasies that move about in their own subconscious states.

Despite this significant legacy of romanticism, the word "individualism" has been used in our century with a different meaning from the one it received at the beginning of the nineteenth century. Its contemporary synonyms seem to be "spontaneous living" or "immediate life." The writer tends to look upon each action of man as having its own significance, its own truth, quite separate from action in its traditional meaning. Each life, therefore, is separate from all other lives, and governed by its own fate, its own discipline, its own individuality. This belief, abundantly illustrated in the early books of Gide, in *Les Nourritures Terrestres* and *L'Immoraliste,* is explored philosophically by Sartre during the 1940's. It is sometimes designated by such a term as "intellectualistic humanism," to differentiate it from other forms of humanism today. The role of the intellect is the faculty in man to understand and analyze and criticize. With the example of Gide, and especially the example of Valéry, this orientation has been central in twentieth-century French literature. It is best characterized by the writer's determination to say "no" to those illusions that cannot be accepted by the pure intellect of man.

In this form of humanism, with its strong intellectualized approach to man's problems, the intellect is primarily critical. The more purely creative forces of the mind and the imagination are diminished or weakened. Valéry's character, M. Teste, is the hero of this impotency to construct in the creative literary sense. Valéry himself appears today, twenty years after his death, to represent the critical analytical mind, rather than the creative artist. This is almost a French temptation: to grow critically rather than creatively. It is observable in some French writers who tend to move from the creative to the critical sphere: Malraux, Cocteau, Blanchot, for example. It is obvious in cases of great literary power where the work is exclusively that of criticism: Poulet, Richard, Barthes. The dilemma of choice, between criticism or philosophy, and the more purely creative literary forms, has certainly preoccupied Camus, Sartre, Simone de Beauvoir, and more recently, Butor, Nathalie Sarraute, Robbe-Grillet. The critical works of these writers are largely explanations of their novels and plays, and at times the brilliance of their criticism makes one wonder whether it may one day overshadow the creative works themselves. Time is more ruthless on a novel or a play or a poem than it is on a critical text which by its very nature takes its place immediately within the context of a long history, and does not have the same demands made on it that are made on a novel or a poem.

The vitality today of French literary criticism gives it an eminence that is not always possessed by the best of the new novels and plays and poems. The quarrel over critical methods, which has opposed Raymond Picard representing the traditional scholarly academic method, and Roland Barthes, seconded by Serge Doubrovsky, representing the newer approach of literary analysis illumined by psychoanalysis and the structural study of themes, has helped to focus attention on very important matters in the realm of literature. Barthes, in his *Critique et Vérité* (1966) and Doubrovsky, in his *Pourquoi la nouvelle critique* (1966), ask questions such as: What is a literary work? What is the meaning of a book? These men, with great acumen and honesty, are studying the relationship between man and art, between a man and his own processes of thought. A significant book is, first, for them, something objective made up of signs and symbols. But in the thought of the reader, this book is the meaning that he gives to these signs. It is his power of seeing these signs. As readers we cannot help identifying ourselves with this book, and with whatever we put into our reading of the book.

Such critics as Barthes and Doubrovsky—and they are far from being alone in their particular understanding of criticism—point out the impossibility of purely objective or purely subjective criticism. It has to be a relationship—and it even, in its highest instances, approaches a drama—between the book and its contents (or the objective factor) and the sensibility and the intelligence of the reader (or the subjective factor) which seeks to penetrate and understand the book. Such a conception of criticism opens up an almost limitless number of approaches or possibilities of criticism. It permits, it even encourages extremely bold interpretations, from the viewpoint of historical literary criticism. Barthes' study of Racine, Goldmann's study of Pascal, and Richard's study of Mallarmé, in order to renovate their understanding of these major writers who have suffered from long-standing arbitrary interpretations by academic scholars, have used new knowledge concerning man's motivations and passions that are revealed

in new forms of the human sciences, such as psychoanalysis, marxism, sociology.

In this controversy, which has reached startling proportions
and publicity, the new French critics are rather politely asking to
take their place beside the historical critics. But the historical
critics, or at least some of the most vociferous ones, such as
Picard, are denouncing the new critics as being impostors. Some
critics of these critics have called the controversy the Dreyfus
Affair of the world of letters!

From all the turmoil, the new critic, in his stature of polemicist
as well as thinker, emerges as a writer who feels competent to
explain not only Racine or Pascal or Mallarmé, but to explain
himself—Barthes if he writes on Racine, Goldmann if he writes
on Pascal, Richard if he writes on Mallarmé—and even to explain
what is taking place in the mind of the reader. It is significant
that the *Classiques Larousse*, which for years have been the an-
notated texts used in French schools, are now being renovated in
a new series, *Nouveaux Classiques Larousse*, which incorporate
many of the views and techniques and actual writings of the new
critics. M. Roger Lefèvre, of the faculté des lettres in Caen, has
prepared an admirable edition of poems from *Alcools* of Apollinaire, in which he demonstrates a judicious use of both scholarly
and new criticism.

In the second part of *Critique et Vérité*, Roland Barthes establishes an important equation: "critic" equals "writer." The rank
of literature has to be granted to Proust's pages on Nerval, for
example, Henry James' essay on Balzac, Sartre's essay on Baudelaire. Literary criticism can be and should be a work of art. It is
susceptible of success or failure in the same way that a short story
is or a poem. In defining critical writing, Barthes is actually defining all literature. Literature is not an embellishment, not a mirror.
It is not a means to something. It does not depend on anything
else. It is autonomous. It is always seeking to reach its own im-
peccable, invulnerable status.

What does M. Barthes mean by "truth" in the title of his
essay? By this key word, he seems to mean the truth of the
symbol, which cannot be separated from the nature of language,
and which is inexorably symbolic. A symbol, used by a writer, always implies that there is not just one meaning, but a plurality of
meanings. If symbolism, then, is the basis of a literary work, it

is also the basis of the criticism of the work. And the critical piece about the novel or the play can, in fact, rival the novel or the play, because it too is permeated with symbolism. Many years ago, Oscar Wilde brilliantly sustained this thesis in his essay *The Critic as Artist*. In speaking of a poem, the critic has to speak of the same rich symbols that he finds in the poem. In using these symbols, he appropriates them. In a way, he steals them, and he sets about, although not always consciously, to rival the richness of the original work. The poet is the lover of the words he chooses for his poem and their symbolic meanings. The critic is therefore doubly a lover, first of the language he finds in the poem he reads, and then of his own language which explains both the poet's language and the critic's own language.

Paul Valéry once claimed that there is no one meaning of a text. There are many readings of a text. The new critics pay close attention and homage to the readers of a text. They tend to look upon a text as a form of mythical writing, where humanity comes in order to experiment with its meanings, in order to comprehend something concerning its desires, its dreams, its dilemmas, its violence. The concept of beauty changes from age to age, and from country to country, whereas the concept of desire, in its alliance with love and violence, is more permanent in the total history of man. This acknowledgment has turned literary study away from the more limiting precincts of aesthetics and directed it toward the vast resources of anthropology. The understanding of Roland Barthes, and of other critics today who share many of his convictions, is, in its deepest implications, almost revolutionary. It is a return to the mythic sources of literature. These sources exist not only in Sophocles but in Proust. From the viewpoint of historical criticism, we know very little today about Sophocles, very little, indeed, about Shakespeare, by comparison with what is known about Marcel Proust. And yet, the new critics will claim that we know everything, because we have the texts of *Oedipus* and *Antigone* and *Lear*, as well as the text of *A la recherche du temps perdu*.

By combining values, signs, symbols, letters, and languages, James Joyce, in *Finnegans Wake*, created an intricate personal scheme of values, a language purely his own, albeit quite decipherable. It illustrates more movingly than most of the major works of fiction—Melville or Proust, for example—the intellectual and sentimental solitude of the modern writer as well as a theory of modern literature conceived of as a hyperbolic spiritual and symbolic adventure. The intellectual, moral, and spiritual principles, which are the foundation of Dante's *Divina Commedia*, are not scorned by Joyce. But they are not looked upon as truth by him. They constitute, rather, the risk of adventure, the mystique of some blind equivocal action, not unrelated to the action in the writings of two adolescent French writers, Rimbaud and Lautréamont.

The goal of these multiple personal quests, represented by such different writers as Gide and Claudel, Rimbaud and Apollinaire, is exaltation in some form or other—headiness, intoxication, enthusiasm, joy. Only the period of the Renaissance can compare with our own, in terms of artistic ambition and confidence and exuberance. Wisdom was looked upon as a new discovery in the sixteenth century by the writers of that age, and today many of the writers of the twentieth century give the impression of being discoverers of what is central in their work. Proust wrote about the dark potency of the subconscious as if he were its discoverer. D. H. Lawrence wrote about the strange power of sexuality as if no one before him had looked upon it in that way. The same freshness and originality characterized Gide's conversion to the immediate and the sensuous life when he related his experiences in North Africa. Maurice Barrès looked upon himself as the first prophet of nationalism, of man's attachment to his native soil. Paul Claudel sang of the joy he found in contemplating the creation as if he were opposing all the other voices of his age. The surrealists in the 1920's, André Breton and Philippe Soupault, in particular, believed they had come upon a new approach to art and life. The somewhat deliberate and even histrionic solitude of the romantic artist of the nineteenth century, Lamartine beside his lake, and Vigny in his ivory tower, became in the twentieth century, the solitariness of the writer, the uniqueness of his theme and subject, and of his view of the world. The loneliness of Meursault in *L'Étranger* and of Roquentin in *La Nausée*, is quite different from that of Chateaubriand's René and Musset's Lorenzaccio. Malraux' participation in adventure in the communist uprising in China in the 1920's and in the Spanish Civil War of the 1930's, forms the basis of two of his most important books of fiction. This word "adventure" which applies equally well to Gide's quest for liberation, to the intellectual quest of Valéry and to the spiritual quest of Claudel, becomes in the decade of the 1940's the existentialist "commitment" of Jean-Paul Sartre.

The revolt of the twentieth-century artist, not only the intellectual artist such as Valéry, and the existentialist artist such as Sartre, but the angry young men of today and the poets of the beat generation, is explicable by his fear of the tendency of science to schematize and departmentalize knowledge, and to make men into specialists. It would seem that whenever science comes to be looked upon as an absolute, or as a way of life, a deep unrest or worry is born in the heart of the creative artist. The religious experience of Charles Péguy, the moral experience of Gide, the experience of action and adventure of T. E. Lawrence, are examples in the early part of the century of a search for values which the intellect alone will not reveal. The letters exchanged between Jacques Rivière and Alain-Fournier, a key document for the philosophical attitude of the age, reveal the sense of failure which the regime of science and nationalism had instilled in the minds of the young intellectuals about 1905. At its beginning, the century was ready and determined to institute new forms of mysticism and new expressions of individualism. It has permitted and encouraged a diversity of beliefs, a diversity of ways of understanding the origins of violence in man's exterior and inner life.

The twentieth century was introduced by strong polemical spirits, men like Péguy, Claudel, and Apollinaire in France, and G. K. Chesterton in England, men who were convinced that the explanations of the world and of human existence were to be sought for in domains other than that of science. The anti-intellectualism of Nietzsche, Gide, and Bergson celebrated a new kind of joy in existence itself, a new belief in man liberated from the tyranny of science, or at least from scientific specialization. To almost all of the young writers at the beginning of the century who were destined to become the key literary figures— Gide, Claudel, Proust, Bergson—the power of man's reason alone, the rationalist spirit, seemed unable to embrace the variousness of life, the multiple and often contradictory aspects of human experience.

As opposed to other centuries, when the major literary figure appeared as the specialist in one genre—Montaigne as essayist, Molière as author of comedies, Flaubert as novelist—the twentieth century, for reasons that would be important to analyze, has produced writers in France who move from one genre to another, who are not easily classifiable as poet or novelist because of the vastness of their work and the several literary forms in which they express themselves: Claudel as dramatist, poet, biblical exegete, essayist; Cocteau as poet, playwright, essayist, chronicler, graphic artist, cinematographer; Malraux as novelist and philosopher-historian of art; Sartre as philosopher, novelist, dramatist, polemicist; Gide as autobiographer, novelist, essayist, dramatist, correspondent. When there is one work, as in the case of Proust, it is so vast that it resembles a *summa* and merges many genres within the narrative of the novel: poetry, history, philosophy, literary criticism.

For the past one hundred years, the novel has been, without any close rival, the most widespread and the most popular mode of literary expression. Traditionally it has always answered the reader's need for an imaginative excitement and for a personal indulgence in sentimentality. But the twentieth century has produced a race of novelists who express in their writings far more than the means of exciting a reader's imagination and satisfying his sentimentality. They are writers who, in another age, might easily have been moralists or philosophers, because their novels are the record of metaphysical, psychic, moral, and political preoccupations.

The newest type of French novel has repudiated most of the traditional themes of the psychological-sociological novel of the nineteenth century. Its audience is limited, but the translations of this type of novel are numerous, and it has reached, therefore, an international audience. It has moreover stimulated the writing of innumerable articles and monographs. The interpretations and glosses on the writings of Samuel Beckett far outnumber the books themselves of Beckett. Each of the critics of the Irish writer, now classified with the French, has attempted to define the complexity of the novelist's mind, to analyze the exploration of the self which we read in *L'Innommable* and in the almost unclassifiable *Comment c'est*.

Beckett is quite possibly the most difficult writer of his generation. He has eliminated most of the conventional effects of fiction—descriptions of characters and places, psychological analyses and plots—in order to devote all of his art to the study of the self, to the exploration of the inner self and to the recording of the inner voices of the self. The illogicality in the novels of Beckett and the heroes of *Molloy, Malone meurt, Comment c'est,* who are shapeless and who live a colorless, vague existence, give to these books a marked symbolic and philosophical intention. Here the literary art is not a novel in any strict sense, nor is it a poem. It might perhaps be called a vision, but a vision of great anguish, of great despair. It transcribes not the life and the activity of a hero, but rather the metaphysical dismay torturing him. Beckett has created a new genre, the most extreme form of writing associated with *le nouveau roman.*

This writer gives us the impression of being a scribe, almost a holy scribe, writing in the name of the human species. The book at times resembles a bag from which emerges a voice, a barely human voice, a captive plaintive voice. There is no body left, or no body visible. It is a body reduced to a voice, an anonymous dying voice. What this voice is saying is no subterfuge, no salvation. Rather it is an expiation, an expression of remorse. In each successive work, the characters of Samuel Beckett, whose very names are indicative of their basic almost foetal condition— Worm, Mahood, Nagg, Nell, Hamm, Clov—move closer to the earth, closer to the position of crawling and creeping. Man himself, his body, his dignity, has been broken down and reduced to matter that is good for the ragpicker. Life has become vegetative and impersonal. It is a life of abjection, spent in waiting. Never has man's solitude been more poignantly demonstrated than in Beckett's play, *La dernière bande,* where a solitary figure, with a tape-recorder, is reliving fragments of his past. It is a play showing the slow implacable disintegration of a character, his physical and mental dissolution.

The new novel has become an inventory, an analysis of psychic traits, but without any interpretation, without any judgment. The life and the sentiments of the characters are apprehended bit by bit, with the impact of successive impressions. Kafka and Proust have often been singled out as forerunners of the new novel. Curiously enough, another forerunner has almost never been mentioned in this connection: Georges Bernanos whose novel of 1926, *Sous le soleil de Satan,* in particular, announces traits of the new novel.

An atmosphere of unreality pervades the actions and lives of the priests in the work of Bernanos. They never seem to act in terms of a coherent and rational and social motivation. Their motivations are spiritual and incoherent, in contrast with the ordinary world of men. Bernanos presents his characters as being solicited by an invisible universe that creates in them reflexes which are incongruous, awkward, even comical. Scene after scene in Bernanos is incomprehensible in terms of recognizable psychological laws. The human adventure that is being narrated does not derive its meaning from a world that is purely human. The actions of the Bernanos characters, their speech, their intentions, are bathed in the atmosphere of the supernatural. In their own way, *Monsieur Ouine* and *Le Journal d'un curé de campagne* are as foreign to the traditional form of the novel as the novels of Beckett, Blanchot, and Robbe-Grillet.

André Malraux, also, has played a part in the evolution of the novel. Both his art as novelist and his philosophy still remain difficult to describe. The legends concerning the man and his post of Minister of State in charge of Cultural Affairs in the Fifth Republic, tend to obscure the position of Malraux the novelist. Even a life of action, as portrayed in his novels, has to be justified metaphysically within some system that defines man as a responsible being. The world described by Malraux as the site of man's fate, the title of his most famous novel, *La Condition Humaine*, is never the site of one particular adventure. In his novels we move from a real world, where a recognizable action is taking place, to another world that might be called the world of anguish and suffering. And we realize, thanks to the skill of Malraux the writer, that there is very little transition between the two. One impression follows the other in what is often a swift cinematographic tragedy. And as in the art of films, Malraux often cuts off a scene in order to make way for a different scene. This art also, in a manner unlike that of Kafka and Proust and Bernanos, is in direct contrast with the traditional French novel, in its swiftness and its seeming incongruities or collage effects. The story or the adventure in Malraux is concrete and narrated in the form of brief truncated episodes, but the intention of the work is to translate the meaning of man's metaphysical destiny.

One other important figure must be included in this listing of possible precursors of the new novel in France. Very few professional philosophers have been novelists. By far, Jean-Paul Sartre is the most eminent and the most successful. There is a prevalent tendency today to look upon the short stories, the novels, and the plays of the existentialist writer as mere illustrations of his philosophy, as mere adjuncts to the principal body of his work. Even if it seems today highly probable that the novels belong to a completed phase of his career, and that he does not plan to complete the promised fourth volume of *Les Chemins de la Liberté*, Sartre has produced at least one very important novel, *La Nausée* of 1938.

Stylistically this Frenchman was influenced by the American novel and by American films, in his use of short chopped sentences, of the stream of consciousness, of italicized passages, of the fusion of objective description with a transcription of the inner consciousness of the characters. Some of these practices, which Sartre discusses in his essay on Dos Passos, for example, will be appropriated by the new novelists, by Nathalie Sarraute and Alain Robbe-Grillet. Beckett will go farther than most, in the suppression of punctuation and the juxtaposition of facts or incidents that will give to the reader the impression of living the exact moment which is being transcribed.

The hero of *La Nausée*, Antoine Roquentin, who is to some degree Sartre himself, is a kind of philosopher. Literally he is, in the novel, an historian, but the book is about his becoming aware of his own philosophy. His philosophical temperament and attitudes are amply described. He is a philosopher in his feelings about the strangeness of all objects. In his analysis of social conformity, about the cowardice of most men who suppress their nausea, Roquentin demonstrates a philosophical attitude. He raises a major philosophical problem in his incapacity to feel the reality of time.

For Sartre the professional philosopher, and for the French writers who are close to him in their scorn for fixed literary genres, who in fact no longer believe in the existence of genres, a strange fate, which might be called a curse, has deprived man of his authenticity. Society is seen by them all, by Bernanos as well as by Gide and Malraux and Simone de Beauvoir, as a comedy in which man plays a dishonest role, a part in contradiction with his real self, and which alienates him from his real self. This pharisaism which the French novelist-philosopher sees as a malady of terrifying virulence, is analyzed by Sartre as well as Bernanos, by Camus as well as Mauriac, as the result of nineteenth-century optimism, of the exaggeration of a bourgeois capitalistic civilization, and of a false kind of humanistic Christianity.

A special kind of solitude characterizes the new heroes of these writers. Each of them seems to be totally alone in the discovery and the forging of his own fate. Before they can create this fate, they have to separate themselves from the rules and the values of what they denounce as conventions. The leading difference between the nineteenth-century fictional heroes and those of the twentieth century would seem to be this change in motivation. The new heroes are no longer concerned with the usual kind of adventure, with the usual experience of love, with the familiar urgency to better their social position. The heroes of Malraux and Camus are concerned with a kind of problem (rather than a passion) with which most men are not concerned. Sartre's Roquentin exists in a social and metaphysical solitude, where he refuses to accept the solution of other men around him. This is a Promethean attitude in which the hero refuses to accept the lies of society and the false values by which men live. He is Promethean in the sense that he is alone in his daring to express an attitude of opposition to the tested acceptable formulas for living within a social group.

Such a word as "Promethean" is useful and apt in characterizing the crisis of humanism as expressed in the literary arts. The original meaning of humanism in Europe was fairly simple: it designated the development of culture based upon Antiquity, on the Greek-Roman traditions. When humanism, a program of development of man's potentialities, moves beyond the limitations of classical humanism, it does grow into an enterprise for which such a term as Promethean is applicable. It is the effort of man to reach beyond the tradition of the past, on which our civilization is based, and to attain to a new accomplishment, to a new power owing to his own effort, to his own knowledge. When man becomes impatient with the limitations of his culture, and wills to break them down, and to embark on a new conquest of man by man, and the cosmos by man, he is quite literally undertaking a Promethean enterprise.

Between the sixteenth and the nineteenth century, Western man passed through an extraordinary series of accomplishments and triumphs, especially in the sciences. In the nineteenth century this man still situated himself within the universe. But the artists of the nineteenth century, the writers in particular, began expressing an attitude of melancholy, of sadness, at times difficult to describe and analyze because of its vagueness, and even a disgust with life, with the situation of man within the universe. This has always been the great function of literature, to reflect the deep consciousness of an age, before the age fully realizes it. The great artist is always to some extent the prophet. Before the close of the nineteenth century, one current of its humanism, which might be called atheistic humanism, had defined God as the creation of man. God was merely the being of man in its most perfect state, man as he should be. To be God, therefore, was to be all-powerful, to escape from the limitations of man. Arthur Rimbaud was one of the first French writers to feel and express in his writing this urge to move beyond his human fate into something godlike, into something excessive, angelic, surreal. And the surrealists continued to feel this challenge, or this temptation. At a time in the twentieth century when such an eminent scientist as Jean Rostand was claiming that the human species as we know it will disappear one day—that human life is a passing phase in the history of the cosmos, that whatever can be called human effort is, relatively speaking, a very brief effort transpiring between two voids—the surrealists, guided somewhat by Rimbaud's vision, were attempting to break loose from the traditional bonds of existence. In a book published in 1966 (*Les Mots et les Choses*), Michel Foucault writes that man is not the oldest problem in human knowledge, that he is a brief moment (*un pli*) in knowledge, probably destined to disappear. *L'homme n'est pas le plus vieux problème ni le plus constant qui se soit posé au savoir humain. . . . L'homme un pli dans le savoir, probablement destiné à disparaître.*

The ambition and the courage of the surrealists were offset by another type of artist who has felt keenly the bewilderment of being a man, the impotence of man facing the world, the uselessness of revolt, the acceptance of nonviolence, of passivity as a way of life. Plume of Michaux, the tramps of Beckett's *Godot*, Camus' Meursault who says to the priest in the prison: "I don't want to be helped" (*Je ne veux pas être aidé*), yes, even such a singer, an American singer from New York and Minnesota, Bob Dylan, who sang his poems in Paris, at the Olympia, on May 24, 1966, who offers no message, no plea, and whose attitude corresponds to that of countless young people in 1966—all of these examples represent the theme of failure, of man alienated from himself.

Unable to learn where he is situated, he asks the question, Where am I? He has lost the thread that might lead him out of the labyrinth. And he asks a second question, even more disarming than the first: Who am I? These leading metaphysical questions are asked by a type of contemporary man who refuses to accept appearances, who refuses to accept the usual framework of a culture, precisely that framework whose function is to tell a man where he is and who he is. When this contemporary man, who has read Rimbaud and studied the poems and paintings of the surrealists, opens his eyes and looks around him, the ordinary object is something unusual, something surprising. The world has a medusa face, comparable to the landscapes of Soutine and the apocalyptic compositions of Marc Chagall. He is the man who feels the need to strip himself of lies, as in the opening stanza of canto II in *Chants de Maldoror*. (*Je fais tomber un à un . . . les mensonges sublimes avec lesquels il se trompe lui-même.*)

Meursault, Roquentin, the characters of Anouilh, and behind them, the poets Rimbaud and Max Jacob, had set out on a search for innocence. They all ask the question: Is it possible to inhabit this earth and maintain a sense of dignity? In almost every case, the answer is negative, and literature became the nostalgia of innocence. It has become in many instances, in Beckett, in certain works of Jean Cocteau, a death chant.

The entire concept of man's wisdom is at stake, of what a man is able to know. But such a query is not new in France. It goes back to the sixteenth century itself, to the humanist Montaigne whose laconic question What do I know? (*Que sais-je?*) reappears in various guises in each epoch of French culture, and is, in fact, a recognizable element of the French temperament. In the twentieth century, Gide's revolt is the most massive recapitulation of Montaigne's doubt. Long before Sartre defined *la mauvaise foi*, Gide pointed out the elements of deceit and dishonesty in every imposed system or order. The establishment of a system is destined to offer reassurance to men, but young men in revolt, young men in anger, refuse to be reassured. Classical serenity is under suspicion today, because its exterior serenity appears deceitful. The revolt of the young—it is sometimes called Byronism —occurs in every age, but in our age the moral disorder is paralleled by an aesthetic disorder. Many of the contemporary artists are champions not of disorder in a futile sense, but in the sense of a search for authenticity of feelings and beliefs. In France, since Gide, the leading revolutionists have been Sartre and Simone de Beauvoir, both of whom have never ceased carrying out a self-examination, a self-accusation, as well as an accusation of others. In his earliest writings, living is denounced by Sartre as being synonymous with lying. And the writer's action is to make this evident, to induce man to live differently, to think differently, to make him fully responsible for what he does and for what is done by others. In current existentialism, this point of view which is central in French thought, is identical with the Christian view of a Péguy and a Bernanos. All of these writers, who differ greatly on certain metaphysical assumptions concerning man, agree that natural man tends toward fatuousness and hypocrisy.

This widespread sense of revolt is fundamentally the somewhat melodramatic expression of a deep-seated anger with existence. The sadistic violence of Lautréamont is related to the same kind of anger, the same impulse to deflate love, to exhibit, with an almost childish glee, the perversions of love. The novels of Camus and Sartre, as well as those of Bernanos and Mauriac, almost as if they were medieval allegories illustrating the wheel of fortune, are constructed on the perpetual vicissitudes of success and collapse, on the insane logic of the solid middle-class where speech, prejudices, and masks are forever covering up truth. The conflict between *les intellectuels* and *les bien-pensants* is constantly present in these novels. This conflict is more acute in France than elsewhere, more central in the social consciences of the writers. It is even difficult to find an exact equivalent in the English language for such a word as *les bien-pensants*. If English has *beatle*, and America *beatnik*, the French language has *bien-pensants* and *yé-yé* and *minets*.

Some of these terms are associated with that abstract place in a French city called *un café*. All the existentialist writers have shown a predilection for the café. The clients of a café are aso-

264 The Postwar Climate

cial, at least during the hours they spend in a café (or a bistrot or a bar). They can appear as derelicts, as men and women having no other place to go, or they may be men and women escaping from the conventional poses of their occupations and habits. They are neutral and unattached in a café. There they have a greater chance of freely inventing their lives. And such an invention is their goal, according to Simone de Beauvoir, in *La Force de l'Age: inventer librement sa vie, c'est de quoi nous prétendions.*

In *Le Déluge,* published in 1966, the new writer Jean-Marie Le Clézio, makes an entire city into an abstract place for the unfolding of an experience which is solemnly that of contingency. This philosophic word *la contingence* has been used by all the French novelists since Proust, and it is another of those strangely French words that seem to have no familiar equivalent in English. *La contingence* is man's participation in life, his experience of a relationship with life. But it is a tragic experience because it is participation within what may be or what may not be. A project has to be made, has to be invented by man, but every project is absurd. Man's freedom to invent his project represents the basic value.

Le Déluge is a work luminously of our day: the continuation of Roquentin's adventure and the beatniks'. It is, first, a minute observation of a city, and embodies the technique of the new novel. It emphasizes man's relationship with ordinary reality. At the beginning of the narrative, François Besson sees a girl in the street and has an overwhelming intuition of death. *Depuis ce jour, tout a pourri. Je, François Besson, vois la mort partout.* He undertakes a long walk through the city, which is Nice. Nice is not named, but the rue Paganini is mentioned, and several other details apply specifically to Nice. Besson describes streets, houses, crowds, traffic jams, stores, neon lights, movie houses, traffic lights, cafés with their tables and *flippers* (the new word for pin-ball machines), which appear as oases in the city's desert. As his walk continues through the city, and as his observation becomes obsessional, Besson succeeds in abolishing any demarcation between himself and the things in the city. Every object is used, as in Pop art: an ash tray in the café (always referred to as a *cendrier-réclame,* a publicity object), cartoons, bits of conversation. The writing is epical in its evoking of a city and its civilization, and it is apocryphal also during the long walk without hope, without anger, with the concern over death. During thirteen days, François Besson observes signs of death everywhere and renounces all the usual bonds existing between a man and his city: love, work, money, clothes, food. He learns how to beg, he even commits murder. But these are stages in his descent. Even his attempts to establish a love-relationship with Marthe and live with her and her young son, is subordinate to the major theme of *Le Déluge*, which is anguish and which is never called by that name. It is the adventure of a man's mind, of a man's conscience, during which the entire world seems to freeze over for him, and his mind grows numb. As Besson listens to the flow of his thought, the city turns into a tomb after showing itself a forest of signs. *A travers des forêts de symboles.* The phrase of Baudelaire's sonnet can easily come to the reader's mind, as he watches Besson force himself into an hallucination with everything that is real, and become a prey to the real city. Besson's walk through Nice is not unlike Baudelaire's walk through Paris, in *Les Sept Vieillards*.

An exact date is given when the experience begins for Besson that was to give him the intuition of death: January 13, 1963, at 15:30. Those episodes that are at all developed tend to move beyond their literalness. In a conversation with a blind man selling newspapers, who accepts life and all hardships philosophically, Besson tells him he is Diogenes living in a barrel. He envies the man's immobile life. The physical act of love-making, in the episode with Marthe, is chastely described in a sumptuous metaphor—*seul au milieu de la gigantesque rosace d'hiéroglyphes en expansion, qui tous voulaient dire la même chose*—enough to indicate its significance, its religious significance. On the tenth day, in the church where Besson will make his confession to a priest, he tries to pray and expresses his submission by bowing his neck before God: *il ferma les yeux et offrit sa nuque à Dieu*. At the end of the book, the more violent episodes would seem to be allegorical: the murder, for example, and the willful blinding of his eyes.

Since the book is essentially about the intuition of death, Le Clézio gives his reader this intuition by fusing the inanimate world of objects with Besson's conscience. The dreams, myths, and obsessions of a man's conscience are projected as he continues his walk of disorder and incoherence and frenzy. The order that emerges from all this is the order of a man's conscience. The art of painting obviously interests Le Clézio. A painting gives an idea of the world, and man is condemned to the analysis of the world, of the novel, of himself. We have today our totems, our rites, and our taboos, and they are here in this book: cafés, Coca-Cola bottles, cigarettes.

A generation separates *Le Déluge* of Le Clézio (1966) and the first book of Antoine de Saint-Exupéry, *Courrier-Sud* (1928). Thirty-eight years have intervened between the publication of the two books. Each one is representative of an age and an art, and notably so. In a page of *Courrier-Sud*, where Saint-Exupéry evokes his childhood, he analyzes an attitude toward life, expressed in all of his books, and which is centrally the attitude of French writers during the first quarter of the century: the need to escape from a world, from a society that lacks greatness, a society that has capitulated to routine and trivial habits. The passage is composed around the word "treasure," which he, as a child of ten, with a playmate, was bent on discovering in an old attic. The treasure hunt is the romantic metaphor for a search, for a quest. A quest may be the reason for existence, and it is, in its appropriate metaphor, allied with adventure, with risk, with insecurity, with everything that makes it the opposite of bourgeois security and comfort.

The passage opens with the words: *Fuir, voilà l'important.* (Flight at all cost.) This was Mallarmé's word, in *Brise Marine*, where he evokes a desert island and sailors lost at sea. It is a word dominating the last episode of Gide's *Retour de l'enfant prodigue*, where the younger brother of the returning prodigal leaves home in his turn, to discover the unknown. It is an essential word for Rimbaud, the flight from Charleville, the escape from the world that has been imposed.

The attic (*le grenier*) in *Courrier-Sud*, where birds come to die, and where old trunks burst open with extraordinary clothes, is compared to the backstage of life, the sides of the stage, *les coulisses de la vie.* Down below in the house, the family is established in warmth and comfort, but the children in the attic know that the huge beams constitute a fabulous world, a ship, in fact, by means of which they can discover and possess a treasure. Children first "play at" the existence, enact the existence of risk and adventure which they hope one day to lead.

The metaphor of flight, in Baudelaire's *Le Voyage*, in Rimbaud's *Le Bateau ivre*, in Mallarmé's *Brise Marine*, and finally in one of the first books of aviation, *Courrier-Sud*, of Saint-Exupéry, is, in Le Clézio, the most realistic of walks through the city of Nice where the most familiar of worlds is rediscovered and described in detail, as the hero's conscience moves through several stages of despair and frustration. His mind is locked up within the inevitable and all-encompassing city.

J. M. G. Le Clézio has found a way of writing in 1966. And that is the miracle of literature. Because Saint-Exupéry had found it in 1928. The historical critics today are still exploring what is around a work: the race of the writer, his milieu, and his period, according to Taine (*la race, le milieu, le moment*). In this way they hope to explain the moral outlook of the writer, his moral conditioning. The new critics move in the opposite direction. They begin with the work itself, with the belief that there is no such thing as objectivity in the creation of a work of art. It is impossible to define the meaning of a work of art once and for all. In the composition of his poem or his novel, the writer is not totally lucid. To claim that he is lucid would be equivalent to ignoring the investigations of psychoanalysis. In France, the critic Charles Mauron, in his study of Mallarmé, has stressed the need of psychoanalysis for an understanding of the difficult poems.

Language is susceptible of a multiplicity of meanings. This is the fundamental thesis of the new critics, this polyvalence of meanings which is the insurance of a work against the corrosion of time, which permits a work to be read in successive centuries, and which permits us to read a work written today, *Le Déluge* of Le Clézio, or written yesterday, *Courrier-Sud*, of Saint-Exupéry, and feel something of its mythic patterns which attach it to the past. As he writes, the novelist or the poet creates another being, quite separate from himself, a fictional character who is the writer himself. Marcel Proust analyzed this phenomenon in some of his most inspired pages of *Contre Sainte-Beuve*. Jean-Paul Sartre made a monumental effort to demonstrate the thesis in *Saint Genet, comédien et martyr*. A work of art is the expression of a subjectivity which is addressed to the subjectivity of the reader-critic.

Index

Index